Tough Times, Strong Women

Hundreds of personal
memories and photographs
honoring some of the common
yet *remarkable* women
of the 20th century.

ALL THE LIVE-LONG...NIGHT? Felicitas Pacheco was working on the Southern Pacific Railroad in 1943, washing engine cab windows at a starting wage of 53¢ per hour. Martha Coronado of Citrus Heights, California says her mom took the job when she lost her husband. Felicitas worked the 4 p.m.-to-midnight shift so she could care for her nine children during the day.

Editor: Mike Beno
Contributing Editor: Clancy Strock
Assistant Editors: Deb Mulvey, John Schroeder, Kristine
    Krueger, Mike Martin, Joe Kertzman, Kathy Mangold
Art Director: Maribeth Greinke
Art Associates: Linda Dzik, Gail Engeldahl, Tom Hunt, Nancy
    Krueger, Stephanie Marchese, Jim Sibilski
Photo Coordination: Trudi Bellin
Editorial Assistants: Blanche Comiskey, Joy Bartol-Snyder,
    Daria Mondo, Mary Ann Koebernik
Production Assistants: Ellen Lloyd, Claudia Wardius
Publisher: Roy J. Reiman

© 1997 Reiman Publications, L.P.
5400 S. 60th St., Greendale WI 53129

Reminisce Books
International Standard Book Number: 0-89821-203-0
Library of Congress Catalog Number: 97-65761

For additional copies of this book or information on other books, write: Reminisce Books, P.O. Box 990, Greendale WI 53129. **Credit card orders call toll-free 1-800/558-1013.**

Contents

HOT DIRTY WORK didn't bother Echo Mae Schaffer, who worked as a welder at the Hartzell Fan Company in Piqua, Ohio during World War II. "Mom took a lot of teasing from the men," says daughter Joretta Leen of Dayton, Ohio. "But she was a more dependable worker than many of them."

Prologue

By Clancy Strock, Contributing Editor, Reminisce Magazine

Pick up a novel written before 1940, and you'll likely discover that the heroine is far different from any woman you've ever met.

She's a fragile creature, completely dependent on the protection of the men around her. She's someone to be adored and placed on a pedestal. She's formally trained in the social graces and little else.

It's unthinkable that she have much education beyond high school, unless she plans to become a teacher. She knows little of the nitty-gritty of everyday living, and really, why should she? That's the concern of men.

The women in those novels flirt coyly from behind elegant little fans and frequently resort to a nearby "fainting couch" when life takes a nasty turn. They scream "eek" at the sight of a mouse, gathering their skirts to jump atop a chair.

The perfect model for women of that era was Scarlett O'Hara, from the 1939 movie classic *Gone with the Wind*. She needed little more than her feminine wiles to put the world at her feet.

But the second half of that film took a startling turn. Suddenly this fragile, empty-headed, fluttery young woman was confronted with the need to survive in a world turned cruel.

She Turned Tough

What amazing strength and resourcefulness she suddenly displayed! Here was a woman who defied the stereotype. She discovered an inner toughness that astonished her...and us.

This story reminded us that the old novels had always been wrong. The sheltered, dependent women they portrayed were the stuff of romanticized fiction and far removed from the workworn lives our own mothers, grandmothers and great-grandmothers had faced.

Yes, the "weaker sex" was nothing but bad fiction...and the personal memories in this book certainly confirm it.

The idea for *Tough Times, Strong Women* jelled some years ago, when we editors at *Reminisce* magazine noticed a recurrent theme of heartfelt memories in letters from readers. These readers recalled strong women they admired, and wanted to pay tribute by sending a recollection about them to *Reminisce*, North America's largest nostalgia magazine.

The more of these letters we saw, the more we became convinced that a book-length tribute to strong women was long

---

"A tribute to North America's strong women is long overdue..."

---

overdue. After all, these women were the glue that held our families and country together through good times and bad.

During good times, our mothers and grandmothers cooked, cleaned, sewed and provided the moral compass for children growing up.

When times got tough, these women played the lead role in keeping the family together. *Then* the character of these strong women really showed through. You'll see why when you page through the hundreds of personal memories and family-album photos in this one-of-a-kind book. I, for one, am pleased to have been part of it.

Buried in Mail

When we editors came right out and asked *Reminisce* readers for specific memories about the strong women they best recalled, we were buried in mail. The stories and photos were delivered by the *boxload*. The best of the bunch have been printed here, and I found them not only uplifting, but intriguing.

For a variety of reasons, many of these women were suddenly confronted with the need to both earn a living and raise a family. Sometimes they'd been abandoned by husbands. Often tragedy had left them widowed or with a disabled spouse.

During the 1920s, or '30s or '40s, these women couldn't expect help from welfare, because programs like Aid to Families with Dependent Children didn't exist until later.

In extreme cases, perhaps the church elders might have a ton of coal delivered during a bad cold snap. Or an anonymously donated food basket might appear on the doorstep. Relatives might stop by with hand-me-down clothes for the kids. Mostly, though, a woman alone had to make it on her own.

During World War II, when husbands ♂

CLANCY STROCK is a retired professor of journalism at the University of Nebraska. He is a book author, free-lance magazine writer and Contributing Editor of *Reminisce*, North America's most popular nostalgia magazine.

went into military service, millions of women joined the work force, handling heavy industry's toughest jobs with skill, enthusiasm and aplomb. Others joined the armed forces, where they freed up servicemen for overseas duty.

As you read these stories about strong women, I think you'll be struck by their courage and sheer determination. Tough as things got, they managed to keep the spirit of optimism alive.

"Yes, things are bad," they must have told themselves. "No, there isn't food in the cupboard. But we'll get through this mess as long as we love each other. Better days are bound to be ahead—let's keep our faith in what can and will be."

BEAUTIFUL BRIDE. Gladys Strock posed for this portrait in 1920. Her unsinkable spirit carried her family and friends through many tough times.

These remarkable women had a way of teaching important lessons in an almost off-hand way, including important things like honesty and the Golden Rule. They didn't have much time for shades of gray—either something was right or it was wrong. Problems came in just two kinds: ones you could do something about, and ones best ignored.

What the children of these women seem to remember most of all, though, is that no matter how hard Mom worked, no matter how worried she might have been, no matter how bleak the future seemed, her love was never in doubt.

She always had time for a hug and a kiss. She had time to hear the bedtime prayers and make sure the covers were tucked in before doing more work long

> "*Tough as things got, she kept the spirit of optimism alive...*"

into the night. Many hours later, she'd shuffle off to her own bed.

Those of us who were children during the Depression never quite grasped what a blow our parents had suffered. We couldn't realize how good things had been in the 1920s. The *Roaring '20s*. The era of the flapper, instant millionaires and a chicken in every pot.

Hey, things just couldn't get much better!

Instead, they got a whole lot worse.

Parents Had It Tough

Not until many years later did I appreciate what parents went through—especially mothers, who'd dreamed of the wonderful lives they'd make for their children.

Instead, mothers of the 1930s found themselves patching coveralls, darning socks, stretching a 3-pound roast to last for five meals and trying new ways to make turnips taste good.

How much did it hurt to face the truth that your 11-year-old son was an important family wage-earner, turning over his weekly paper route earnings every Saturday night?

It finally dawned on me when I had children of my own. Mom persisted in showering them with extravagant gifts.

Whenever I protested, her answer was always the same: "We couldn't do many nice things for you and your sister back when you were growing up, but now we can for our grandchildren."

Those old scars and feelings of guilt were still there a quarter of a century later. No matter how many times I assured her I thought my childhood was just about perfect, she couldn't shake the memories of wanting to make our childhoods even better.

Mom's Love Recalled

That's when I finally understood how truly tough those years had been for her. I tried to explain that it wasn't the *things* or lack of them that I remembered. No, it was her unfailing, unstinting *love* I recalled.

That, and how she was tough enough to cope with everything the world could throw at her.

Her inner toughness never left her, either. When she was well into her 80s, it clearly was time for her to move out of her apartment and into a retirement facility. It was a change she dreaded, for reasons that aren't hard to understand. She was a proud woman who didn't want to be dependent upon anyone for anything.

So after hemming and hawing for many months, she bowed to the inevitable and made the move. It was a sad, sad day for her. She sat huddled in

the corner of her new room and sobbed as my wife and I helped her get settled.

But within a few weeks her spirits again were high…higher than anytime in several years. What was going on here?

Well, it seemed that Mom had decided the key to happiness in her new surroundings was to seek out the lonely or depressed and make *them* happy. "I just had to do something about those sad faces," she said.

Yes, that old toughness in the face of adversity once again was alive and well. Like Molly Brown, Mom was unsinkable.

She was always there for others, helping them weather their tough times. Mom was a strong woman who knew how to be strong for others.

May you enjoy reading about hundreds more like her in the pages that follow. ✦

AFTER THE HONEYMOON, Oscar and Gladys Strock gave the hand-wringer a try in their back yard. Unbeknown to them, they'd struggle to raise two children through the Depression, then send their only son off to war in the Philippines. Clancy was there in 1945, when Gladys and Oscar celebrated their 25th anniversary in photo below.

LIFETIME OF SERVICE. Margaret Buckner, seen here when she graduated from nursing school in 1921, always knew she wanted to be a nurse, says her daughter, Aylette Fogarty of Seguin, Texas. She eventually became a nurse anesthetist and assisted her dentist husband, Bill. Margaret spent her life working in the profession she loved.

Chapter One

A Woman Before Her Time

In her later years, my mother lived in a pleasant retirement home in Dixon, Illinois. This was during the 1980s.

Mom was an avid Trivial Pursuit player, and one of her favorite opponents was a lady of 90-something who'd enjoyed a successful career as a doctor.

A little simple arithmetic told me this lively, witty lady had entered medical school sometime before World War I. I pondered the struggle she must have faced to be admitted to, and successfully graduate from, medical training. In those days, doctors were *always* men.

This chapter is about others like her who, driven by desperation or ambition, pursued careers outside of the home long before the "women's liberation" movement was launched.

Supplemented the Income

For some, it was a matter of survival when faced with the job of raising a family without a man in the house. Others had to supplement the meager incomes their husbands could earn during the tough Depression years.

For still others, it was the urge to pursue a special dream. And for a few, it was as simple as having something mentally stimulating to do.

My own mother, I must admit, wasn't a trailblazer. Back in 1914, she chose what was a well-accepted career for women—teaching school. But to her father, even becoming a teacher was unthinkable. When you finished high school, it was time to marry and have babies.

So it became a case of the immovable object (my grandfather) and the irresistible force (my mother). Stubborn father versus stubborn daughter.

To this day, I have no clue as to why Grampa took such a belligerent stand. My best hunch is that he, himself, had been forced to leave school after a very few years.

Nevertheless, he'd worked hard in later life to become self-educated and had a large library of the literary classics of that era, including the complete works of Dickens, Thackeray and Shakespeare. Maybe he just thought formal schooling was a waste of time and money.

Off to Teacher's College

Eventually Mom left home without his blessing and went off to DeKalb Normal School for the necessary 2 years to earn a teaching certificate. Her kid sister faced a similar struggle and, at 18, slammed the door and strode off for nurses' training in Chicago. Grampa didn't raise meek daughters.

Other equally determined women went into politics, ventured off to foreign countries, entered the business world or took jobs where they could help others less fortunate than they.

Then World War II came along and hundreds of thousands of women moved into the defense industry to produce ships, airplanes and ammunition. Rosie the Riveter was also Wanda the Welder and Martha the Mechanic. Others proved that women could have an important role in the military, even ferrying airplanes across the wide, lonely, dangerous Atlantic Ocean.

Why were we surprised? These were the descendants of the incredibly brave women who left comfortable homes and civilized society to accompany their husbands as America moved west.

Their grandmothers and great-grandmothers had driven the Conestoga wagons, loaded rifles for their men as arrows whizzed overhead and kept their babies warm when howling blizzards drove snow through the chinks of their tiny log cabins.

Bold pioneering was in their blood, whether they thought about it or not. And it still is.

—*Clancy Strock*

When Navy Dad Sailed, Mom Took on Sales

By Joan Zekas
Pittsburgh, Pennsylvania

"THE BRAKE! The brake!" Dad yelled. Mom bit her lip and stifled a sob. She had exactly 1 week to learn how to drive our old Ford.

World War II was on, Dad had been drafted into the Navy and was headed for basic training. Mom just *had* to master that old car. There was no choice.

Dad had been a door-to-door salesman for the Rawleigh home products company and had painstakingly developed a route of loyal customers. The business would fall apart if Mom didn't take over. As it turned out, she was just the woman for the job.

She battled that recalcitrant car for a week, then saw Dad off at the train station. Taking the wheel with a mixture of gusto and fear, she coaxed the jerking Ford to customers' homes through the worst winters northeast

DOOR-TO-DOOR WITH MOM. When Peter Zekas went off to war, his wife, Nell, took over his Rawleigh route, says daughter Joan (far left, in 1944). Mom took care of the route, Joan and brother Gerald. She bartered with some customers, once receiving a doll cradle (above).

her step, often carrying home a treat of Dolly Madison ice cream for my little brother and me.

She took her position as a businesswoman seriously. If a customer was light on cash, she bartered for baby chicks, homemade sausage and, once, a doll cradle we continue to cherish to this day.

Working long hours, keeping accounts up-to-date, taking inventory,

> *"She juggled duties as a mother, wife and saleswoman..."*

ordering merchandise and unloading it were all part of Mom's job.

She also became a promoter with a capital "P". At Christmas, she decorated special gift boxes for her customers, tucking in some red cherry lipstick, English Lavender talcum powder and La Jaynees cologne.

Mom juggled her sales career with her job as a housewife and still found time to write letters to Dad detailing the lives of their daughter and active baby son.

When Dad finally returned home from the war, my proud mother turned over to him a thriving business...and a happy healthy family. What a great "welcome home". ✦

Pennsylvania could dish out.

The roads were slick and every day was an adventure. One time, Mom and the Ford slid sideways down Stegmaier Hill. She wasn't much for talking that night.

Mom was the bane of all streetcar conductors because she was afraid of getting stuck and parked the car far away from the curbs.

The trolleys couldn't pass and the furious dinging of the motormen's bells brought Mom running from more than one customer's home yelling, "I'm coming! I'm coming!"

She Walked Taller

In time, Mom conquered her fear of snowdrifts and other on-the-job hurdles and walked with spring in

The Best Woman Won This Election

By Pamela Watson, Manassas, Virginia

THE MEN in the town of Friendly, West Virginia weren't interested in the 1936 local elections. Instead, they spent their time gossiping and playing checkers…until the women in town formed their own ticket.

That got the men's attention, but too late. The all-woman "Community Party" defeated their male opponents in a landslide victory. The new mayor was my great-aunt, Stella Eddy, the first woman mayor in Tyler County.

Mayor Stella appointed an all-female city council, as well as a new chief of police, Josephine Cline, a 6-foot, 200-pound redhead.

News of the small town's election and unique government quickly spread nationwide. Though Stella had made herself unpopular with the men in town, she became more than popular with the news media. And why not? During this era, a female mayor truly was "a woman before her time".

Paramount Pictures made newsreels of Mayor Stella and her councilwomen in action. Newspapers across North America and even in foreign lands carried stories about the "petticoat government". It was written up in *Ripley's Believe It or Not.*

Cleaning up the Town

As one of the first orders of business, Aunt Stella and her councilwomen decided to clean up the Tyler County Jail. They scrubbed it down, painted the walls and even hung curtains.

Weary law-abiding travelers were sometimes invited to spend the night in jail. Stella received many thank-you letters for her hospitality.

Her penchant for cleanliness extended to the outdoors as well. She passed an ordinance prohibiting "filthy conditions" inside the city limits. The law was primarily emplaced to keep hog farming outside the city.

HER HONOR. When the men of Friendly, West Virginia weren't looking, Stella Eddy was elected mayor. She only served one term, but it's never been forgotten.

One stubborn farmer refused to abide by the law. Visiting councilwomen inspected his property and found no pigs. But further investigation uncovered the recalcitrant farmer's swine hidden under a neighbor's building. Stella sent Chief Josephine to arrest and jail the farmer. The pigs were moved and the lawbreaker was eventually fined.

Besides serving as mayor, Stella was a midwife. Once while council was in session, she and the chief of police were summoned to help deliver a baby. The child was named Stella Jo after the two town officials.

In the next election, held June 6, 1938, the "Community Party" went down to defeat. You can bet the men were a lot more interested in local politics this time. They chose "More Pigs and Less Publicity" as their winning campaign slogan. The smug victors even celebrated their triumph with a pig roast.

So Stella's 2-year reign as mayor ended. But she and her "petticoat government" will never be forgotten in Friendly, West Virginia. They remain an unforgettable part of the history of Tyler County. ⤶

BON TON BREAD LADY. "In Jefferson, Wisconsin back in the 1930s, my Aunt Mabel was the first woman to drive a delivery truck for the Bon Ton Bakery," reports Mrs. Hugh Brown of Delavan, Wisconsin. Mabel left the family farm to take the job, and she made her deliveries door-to-door no matter the weather. When she married, though, it was back to the farm.

STRIKE! When Reva Tibbets was paid 4¢ an hour to split peaches in 1941 (third from right), she helped organize a union. She picketed (above) in July 1942 and remained active in unions.

Mom's Union Activism Wasn't Peaches and Cream

By Marceil Skifter, Grand Meadow, Minnesota

MY MOTHER and father married in Nebraska in 1932—not a good time or place for a couple intending to start their life together as farmers.

They tried to eke out a living, but the Depression and dust bowl proved too much to overcome. So Reva and Clifford Tibbets packed up two young sons and followed other Nebraskans toward a better life in the Pacific Northwest. There Mom demonstrated just how strong she was.

Arriving in Oregon, Mom and Dad became migrant fruit pickers, locally called "fruit tramps". Some days the only food they had was the fruit they were allowed to keep. If Mom was lucky, she could trade peaches for salmon.

Dad found a job in Salem as an ironworker, erecting bridges and high-rise buildings. It paid well, but the constant rain in coastal Oregon kept him out of work much of the time. Mom took odd jobs to supplement their income.

In 1941, she went to work at a cannery in Salem, working on a line as a peach splitter. It was hard work. In one shift, she and her co-workers set a record, splitting *200 bushels* of peaches. They made 4¢ per hour.

She Took a Stand

Long hours, low pay and below-standard working conditions grated on Mom and her co-workers. She decided to take a stand and organize a union.

During a strike, she and a woman co-worker sat on the train tracks leading

---

"Give me a woman who believes in a cause any day..."

---

to the cannery. Their goal was to stop a load of sugar from being delivered. No sugar meant no fruit canning. That shut down the line and management agreed to negotiate.

"Give me a woman who believes in a cause any day," Mom said. "She won't back down!"

Sound tough as nails? Yes, Mom could be that way. But she didn't smoke or drink, attended church and tried to raise her five children with strong values.

Through the 1940s, Mom was even more active, becoming the first woman union organizer in Oregon for restaurant workers.

Her first week on the job, a male co-worker threw some salty language at her during a phone conversation.

That Was a Mistake

Mom hung up the phone, stormed to his office and bypassed a protesting secretary. Barging in, she grabbed a steel smoking stand and demanded that he take back his remark or she'd "part his hair right down the middle".

After a lot of sputtering, the man regained his composure and apologized, explaining that he and the other guys talked like that all the time. He never spoke that way to Mother again, and they got along well after their "introduction".

She gained the respect of her male co-workers and thereafter was able to do her job like a lady.

Mom was opinionated, sometimes meddlesome, but always with a purpose of trying to do good.

I loved her feistiness, the sparkle in her eye and the "I'll-take-care-of-everything" comfort she brought our family. Reva Tibbets was indeed a woman before her time. I know I'll never again meet anyone like her. ⬥

Grandma Soled Shoes as Well as Any Man

By Betty Schwab, Cincinnati, Ohio

RUNNING a shoe factory wasn't considered "women's work" around the turn of the century, but no one ever told that to Grandma. She became the first woman shoe manufacturer in the United States!

I have a scrapbook that my grandmother, Edith Harrison South, filled with many articles and pictures published about her accomplishments as a businesswoman. It's a wonderful story.

Grandmother was a go-getter. She graduated from college, married Grandfather in 1884 and raised three children.

She was teaching school when Grandfather lost his eyesight in an accident while working on the interurban railway near their home in Bethel, Ohio. To help provide for their children, she quit teaching and began selling baby shoes.

She'd previously made shoes for her infant son, taking them to be soled at a local factory. Since she had the ability to make shoes, she reasoned, why couldn't she start her own business?

If the Shoe Fits...

Grandmother journeyed to Cincinnati in 1899 with $10 in her pocket. She purchased enough sheepskin to enter the male-dominated shoe manufacturing trade.

She drew up a pattern and made her first baby moccasins and booties for

> "If women believed in themselves, they'd be happier..."

sale to friends and neighbors. The soft-soled baby shoes were lined with satin and were available in pink, blue and white.

The shoes sold as quickly as Grandmother could make them, so she hired help. She taught 20 neighborhood women what she knew about the art of cobbling, then put them to work. Now she was really in business.

By 1907, she'd made enough to finance construction of a two-story shoe

factory behind her home. She equipped it with a gas-powered engine and the latest in shoe-making machinery.

Production soared to 1,000 pairs of moccasins and booties a week, enabling Grandmother South to travel across the country selling her line of "Sunny South" shoes.

The success of Sunny South shoes gained the attention of the U.S. shoe industry and led to feature stories about Grandma in such popular magazines as *Grit* and *Harper's Bazaar*.

Gaining Recognition

A writer for *Shoe Retailer* magazine described her early achievements:

"Even as 'born musicians' without technical knowledge are able to extract sweet strains of music, so an Ohio shoe manufacturer is making exquisite

BABY NEEDED SHOES. So Edith Harrison South (above) decided she could make her own. They were so popular that a business was started, and Edith became the first woman shoe manufacturer in the United States, making 1,000 pairs a week!

soft-soled booties and moccasins for infants...with no practical knowledge of shoe making as based on previous experience."

Grandmother's story is retold in several clippings found in her scrapbook. All marveled at how she could be a woman, working mother and savvy businessperson all wrapped up in one. After all, she ventured into the business world at a time when most women were expected to stay home and rear children.

Grandma often said, "If women only believed in themselves and what they could do, they'd be much happier."

Her strong will and cheerful disposition enabled her to continue making baby shoes for friends until she was well into her 80s.

Soft-soled shoes for infants were eventually replaced by more rigid designs. So Sunny South company focused its efforts on another enterprise. It enjoyed continued success...as a maker of men's work pants. ✦

ALL BUSINESS. Auntie Mary (above, with Sara Riola in 1916) ran a clothing enterprise in her basement.

Teacher-Turned-Seamstress Made Her Own Way in Life

AUNTIE MARY was a Virginia schoolteacher in 1908 when she married Gideon Beale Spencer, a naval engineer. She quit teaching that year, when he took a job in the Brooklyn Navy Yard.

In the early 1900s, women's clothing was made at home. But Auntie was an excellent seamstress and tailor, and word of her abilities soon spread. By 1915, she'd established a profitable business in the basement of her Brooklyn brownstone.

A basement room was converted into a private salon where patrons waited to be fitted. Three seamstresses worked in the "butler's pantry" off the kitchen.

A "pin girl" picked up pins, kept sewing machines threaded and took orders for specially covered buttons.

Auntie's house was always fun to visit, but looking back, I now realize she ran a no-nonsense business—and that her business acumen was a blessing.

When Uncle Gideon died in a car accident in 1930, Auntie was well prepared to make her own way. She kept her business running successfully for 27 years—the rest of her life. She was a woman before her time, and she had a lasting influence on my life.

—*Sara Hewitt Riola*
Lakewood, New Jersey

Her Mom's Barbershop Was a Cut Above the Rest

TODAY it's not uncommon to see a women cutting men's hair. But back in the 1930s, a woman barber with her own shop had to be rare sight. That was my mom, Cecil Ballew Reehling—a real woman before her time.

She was born and raised a farm girl in Cottonwood Falls, Kansas. After chores, she enjoyed cutting hair for friends and family. All of them were sure she'd attend cosmetology school and become a beautician.

But the Depression was on and barber school was cheaper. So what if she'd be the only female student in the barber school in Wichita, Kansas? She lived with friends, spent a nickel each noon for a bowl of soup and soon completed her training.

After serving an apprenticeship in Emporia, Kansas, she returned to Cottonwood Falls and opened her own shop on Main Street. Haircuts were 35¢; a shave cost 15¢.

Business was good for years. Then one day, while shaving one of her regular patrons, she jokingly held the razor to his throat and demanded, "Will you marry me?" He did! —*Jean Reehling*
Tulsa, Oklahoma

Mother Wasn't Angry When "Spittin' Tacks"

MY MOTHER was known as the fastest "tack spitter" at King's Specialty Furniture Factory in Mayfield, Kentucky.

Viola Edwards was a small but strong woman who became a furniture upholsterer during the 1940s. The trade was dominated by men.

She proved to be adept at her craft. She had to hold a mouthful of tacks and manipulate them with her tongue so they popped from her mouth head side first.

This would enable her to pick them out

NOT TOO TACKY. Viola Edwards was a top furniture tacker.

one at a time with a magnetic hammer. That kept one hand free to stretch fabric, and the other to hammer.

At Dad's urging, she went into business for herself and established a successful upholstery shop. —*Joan Stanley Monroe, North Carolina*

Tough-as-Timber Mom Worked in the Wilderness

A SHORTAGE of *man*power during World War II created job openings in the logging industry in Oregon. My mother and father, Bud and Regina Lowell, traveled there from Kansas to find jobs.

Mother was hired by the U.S. Forest Service as the first female log scaler in the Northwest. Dad often spoke proudly of her ability to scale truckloads of logs while truckers were stopped

LOGGED ON. Regina Lowell (above) was the first woman log scaler in the Northwest when World War II caused a shortage of manpower.

briefly to add water to their brakes.

My parents were living and working in a remote Forest Service guard station when their first child was due, in 1941. Mother moved into a tent camp to be closer to the hospital—56 miles.

Shocked by her temporary housing, her father tried in vain to persuade her to move back to Kansas. My folks moved to a less-remote area after their third child was born.

Today, her boys like to joke that the only time they saw this strong woman cry was when the family dog chewed up her scale tickets—preventing her from reporting 2 weeks' worth of log scale volume to the Forest Service.
—*Richard Lowell, Anchorage, Alaska*

Trucker Mom Helped Dad Double the Income

THE FIRST few times my mother, Leta Overby, drove her truck into the grain elevator in Shabbona, Illinois, the men stopped working to watch her make a mistake. She never did, so the novelty soon wore off.

Mom became the first woman trucker in Shabbona during the 1940s, when Dad opened a cartage business.

Mother reasoned that with two trucks instead of just one, they could double their profits. Dad agreed, so she earned her trucker's license.

DOUBLE TIME. Two trucks made more money, so Leta Overby drove.

After setting out breakfast for my sister and me, Mom picked up a load of shelled corn. She'd level the loads, unload the grain and sweep out the truck box. At other times of the year, she hauled coal.

Some of that coal was given to needy families and the elderly to help heat their homes during the tough winter months.

Mom and Dad were able to buy their first house and raise four children thanks to Mom's perseverance and profits made from two trucks instead of one.
—*Anita Rogers, Dixon, Illinois*

She Managed Household And Two Thriving Businesses

MY GRANDMOTHER, Lillian Hobbs, married in 1926 and had four children in 7 years. When Grandfather purchased a grocery store in Thurmont, Maryland in 1941, she took on the added responsibilities of manager and bookkeeper of the store.

During World War II, Grandma and Grandpa invested in a hardware store for their son to manage when he returned from the Navy.

Meantime, Grandmother managed both stores. She worked 6 days a week from 7 a.m. until 6 p.m. in the hardware store. She routinely helped my grandfather in the grocery store until it closed on Saturday at midnight. Somehow she also found time to can fruits, vegetables and her own jellies!

"She's a generation before her time," my uncle once commented while watching his tireless mother running out one store and into another. —*Ann Dowling Wilmington, North Carolina*

Her House Was Always a Homestead

NOT MANY women homesteaded land alone. My mother did in 1911.

She was 22 years old and single when she applied for a homestead in the Sand Hills of Nebraska. She had a small sod house and barn built on the land, and a windmill was erected for her well.

To prove she lived on the land (a requirement of the Homestead Act), a neighbor testified on her behalf, saying he saw her working on the property often.

In 1915, President Woodrow Wilson issued her a patent on 640 acres of land. By then, she had 4 acres broken and planted in alfalfa. She also cultivated a large garden and potato patch.

During long winter nights, she was cozy in her "soddie" while blizzards and coyotes howled outside. Years later, she married a neighbor and fellow homesteader.
—*Frank Mitchell Park Rapids, Minnesota*

SIX-DAY WORKWEEKS were the norm for Lillian Hobbs (in 1962 photo above). She and her husband owned and-operated two stores.

Grandma Marched with The Suffragettes

IN 1917, my grandmother was the wife of a preacher and shoemaker in Webb City, Missouri. As such, she was expected to stay home with her children.

Hearing about a rally in Washington, D.C. to be attended by suffragettes marching for their right to vote, Mary Martin decided she would like to attend. She discussed it with her husband, who said the idea was poppycock and forbid her to go.

So she quietly saved her egg money for the next 8 months, arranged transportation and left home with $8.32 in her pocket to march with

SUFFERING SUFFRAGETTE. Mary Martin stood up for her belief in voting rights.

the suffragettes! She returned home with more than $2 left over.

My grandfather was so mad he preached about her shortcomings from the pulpit and refused to speak to her for a year. The children, on the other hand, were most impressed with their liberated mother. She believed strongly in a cause and stood up to the man of the house.
—*Jean Lakey Kansas City, Missouri*

Mama Was Too Proud to 'Go on Relief'

By Gus Indelicato, Pocono Summit, Pennsylvania

MAMA often spoke of beating the Depression, and she was proud we never went on "home relief" like many of our neighbors in the projects of New York City.

Papa worked long hours to support us, and Mama did whatever she could to make life better. To us five kids, she was the "queen of hearts", with loving arms hugging us tight. She was also the "queen of clubs", with wooden spoon in hand for discipline!

We each thought Mama had a favorite child, but none of us thought we were the one. In her pronounced "Manhattanese", she'd proclaim, "I love youse all alike." Now I know she truly meant it.

Mama often considered going to work but didn't want to leave five children home alone. An incident involving a pair of shoes changed her mind.

"Always buy the best," Mama used to say. "It's cheaper in the long run." But in 1932, times were so tough that Mama was forced to buy me a cheaper pair of shoes than the Buster Browns she really wanted.

It didn't take long for Mama's old adage to prove true. The soles of the cheap shoes came unglued and flapped as I walked. I tied them together with string—they really looked awful.

My teacher noticed and assumed our family needed help. One day, she called me to her desk and handed me a box to take home. Inside I found a new pair of shoes that fit me perfectly.

Mama was mortified. To think someone felt we needed charity! And after all she'd done to keep us off home relief.

Humiliated by the handout, Mama looked at Father with

MAMA NETTIE (left, in 1938) tended a garden through the Depression. She posed with her family in 1945, when her two sons came home on leave (Gus is at right).

tears in her eyes. "Joe, I can't let this happen," she said. "I just hafta get a job."

Grandpa Peppe had moved in with us, so he took care of the kids. Mama, meanwhile, did piecework in a dress factory. Each week she bought a pair of shoes for one of us and caught up on unpaid bills. Eventually, she even bought an old Cadillac limousine from an undertaker. Around the neighborhood, they called her "the lady that drives the funeral car".

Getting Ahead

Mama continued to beat the Depression in her own determined manner…by making our clothes, and canning fruits and vegetables Grandpa grew in our yard.

With her old Caddy, her children dressed in respectable clothes, a roof over our heads and food in our bellies, things were fine. No one would ever take us for poor again. ✦

PRIVATE MOM. The members of Squadron W, posed at Coffeyville, Kansas Army Air Field in 1942. Private Emma Rohde is third from left, center row.

Mom Wanted "Private Life" …In the Army Air Corps!

IN 1942, my mother, Emma Rohde, had been married 28 years and had raised three sons.

She decided to enlist in the military, and the WAVES turned her down. But the WACs didn't. That was how my mother, at age 49, became a buck private in the Army Air Corps.

They put her on a train to Des Moines, Iowa for basic training. There she marched and worked alongside classmates half her age. She was assigned to the Personnel Office as stenographer and typist, then was promoted to corporal and eventually sergeant.

She earned the Army Commendation Ribbon, and after her honorable discharge in 1946, she worked for various government agencies dealing with atomic energy. Later, she was office manager for a private company, even signing the paychecks.

She accomplished all this after her 49th birthday and didn't retire until she was 80 years old. I'd regard her as a "strong woman" even if she weren't my mother!

—D.T. Rohde
Los Osos, California

Mother's Mission Took Her to the Congo

By Elizabeth Claassen
Moses Lake, Washington

GIRLS growing up during the Depression and World War II dreamed of being nurses, teachers or secretaries. Not my mother. Elvina Martens hoped to become a missionary doctor.

Though it was far from a "traditional" role for a woman, Mother's choice isn't surprising. Growing up in a minister's family, she saw service to mankind in action. Her love of science and willingness to work hard only helped her resolve.

She applied to the University of Illinois College of Medicine. In June of 1950, Mother graduated with her MD. During her internship and residency, she met a seminary student who had a strong belief God was calling him to work in the Belgian Congo.

Mama Ngangabuka?

The doctor and the seminarian fell in love, married and journeyed to Belgium in 1953. There, Mother studied French and tropical medicine while coping with a bad case of morning sickness. Soon they set off for the Congo, and Mother's childhood dream was fulfilled.

There her days and nights were spent caring for the sick. Many nights she crawled from bed to perform a cesarean section so a mother and baby could live. She even managed to have three babies of her own. The Africans gave her the title *Mama Ngangabuka*, or "Mrs. Medicine Woman".

Political unrest developed in the Congo in 1960, so our family packed a few suitcases and left. We went back to the United States, ending up in the beautiful forests of Michigan, where Father pastored a church.

Made House Calls

Mother soon found Africa didn't have a corner on the market for sick and suffering people, for tucked into those lovely forests were tar-paper shacks where life was hard.

She braved icy winter roads on long drives to make house calls. A large suitcase, packed with everything needed for delivering babies, stood at the ready in

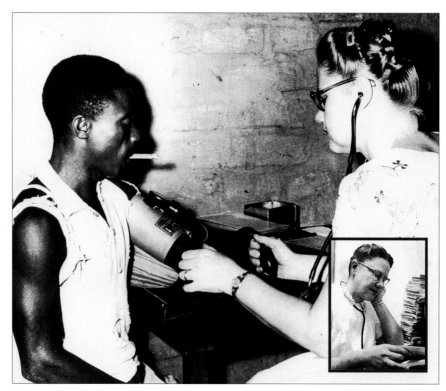

MRS. MEDICINE WOMAN. That's what Dr. Elvina Martens was called by the Africans she treated while a missionary doctor in the 1950s. From Africa, she took her skills to northern Michigan where life was also hard, and a lot colder.

our doorway. Payment for doctoring was unexpected, but eggs and cheese frequently found their way onto our table.

Throughout Mother's career, our family moved often, constantly challenging her to prove herself in new communities.

As she was leaving one town, a patient confided that it had been hard to go to a woman doctor at first, but now she didn't know how she would go back to a man.

Rather than accepting one of the traditional roles for women, Mother fulfilled her dreams of helping others by becoming a doctor.

Officially retired today, she still works a few hours per week supervising a clinic for low-income patients. Her dream of working hard and caring for people is still alive. ✦

NO STOPPING HER. In spite of contracting polio at age 2, Hazel Brown of Pompano Beach, Florida became a pilot, among many accomplishments. She played records for workers at a defense plant during World War II, a plant she later managed. Hazel's neighbor, Alvin Morland, shared the photos.

Mother Felt at Home on the Range

IT WAS A PLEASURE seeing my mother, Bernice Atkinson, astride a horse on our Texas cattle ranch. She became a skilled range rider after marrying in 1934.

Daddy was a very hard worker, but his vision was poor. Soon Daddy's vision was so bad he couldn't tell one cow from another. That was why Mother became a range rider.

Working alongside Daddy, Mother checked the cattle, vaccinated calves, strung miles of fence and helped to market the cattle.

She helped select the breeding stock, too. Daddy gave her some advice and she did the rest. Mother became so good in her judgment of livestock that she earned the respect of the cattlemen with whom she did business. Seeing her work taught me not to be afraid of taking on any job—gender is no hindrance.

Mother will always remain in my memory as the "range rider", but Daddy always called her his "cowgirl sweetheart".
—*Willie Atkinson Thorp*
Chireno, Texas

COWGIRL SWEETHEART. *That's* what Bernice Atkinson was called by husband Roy as she rode their range.

She Was One "Beet" Truck Farmer

BACK IN THE 1950s, most sugar beet farmer's wives didn't haul their crop to market, but my mother was an exception.

Every October for 25 years, Mom spent 2 to 3 weeks in a race against weather and time driving dump truck loads of beets to the "beet dump".

Dad couldn't handle the topping and

"BEETS" WALKING. **Her mother drove the beets to the "beet dump" back in the '50s, says Susan Davis.**

hauling himself, so Mom donned field clothes and climbed behind the wheel of our farm truck, awaiting instructions from Dad on how to slip it into gear and release the clutch.

The engine groaned under the weight of 5-1/2 tons of freshly topped beets, and Mom carried an "extra load" with four small children sitting beside her.

I remember the loud noise of beets tumbling off the tilted truck box. Mom would jump out and "manhandle" the truck's "wing", hooking it properly into place. Then she swung her empty truck around and returned to the field for another load.

On an average harvest day, she made 11 trips to the beet dump...as well as milked the cows, cleaned house and cooked supper for our family of six.
—*Susan Davis, Inman, Kansas*

Costume-Designing Mom Worked, Encouraged, Loved

BORN TO an impoverished cotton picker in West Texas in the early 1900s, my mother, Carmen Denman, never shied away from hard work...and never lost her dreams of creating beautiful things and helping those around her live rich, full lives.

She wanted me to enjoy luxuries, like piano and dance lessons, she'd missed as a child. She sewed clothes for music teachers in exchange for lessons during the Depression.

Her sewing skills developed into a job designing dance costumes for people like Alice Lon, Lawrence Welk's first "champagne lady".

She took up photography as a hobby,

and that, too, turned into a profitable business. She developed and printed photos in our kitchen late at night, financing my college education.

Mother's varied career included being an office manager at the Republican Party headquarters in East Texas and a script writer, receptionist and salesperson for a radio station.

But her greatest role was that of mother. She was my personal cheerleader, constantly encouraging me to reach my highest goals.
—*Jeanne Hale, Kilgore, Texas*

DESIGNING WOMAN. Carmen Denman (above, in 1923) hit the big time as a costume designer when Lawrence Welk's "Champagne Lady" Alice Lon wore one in 1942 (below).

Selling Insurance Was Her Policy

By Jane Allen, Wetumpka, Alabama

INSURED OF SUCCESS. Maggie Allen (with her husband, Red, above left) learned how to plow behind "Pet" (above) and later became a successful insurance agent.

MY MOTHER-IN-LAW had an eighth-grade education, but that didn't hinder her from starting a successful career in the insurance business when she was nearly 50 years old.

Maggie Allen was a true country woman, born in rural Goshen, Alabama. She was 7 when she went to work in the pea fields. Soon this feisty redhead was outwrestling the boys at school.

She quit school when she was 15 and married Red Allen, a slender redheaded man who lived down the road from her family's dogtrot house. She didn't kiss him until the day of their wedding. That just wasn't proper.

They began life together in 1930 on a scrubby farm in Goshen. Maggie worked alongside Red, plowing behind their mule, "Pet", digging postholes and stringing fence wire. The Depression passed by in a blur with a new redheaded baby arriving about every other year.

A Working Mother

Maggie tended fussy babies, preserved fruits and vegetables, sewed and washed clothes. In 1940, she began working at a sewing factory to supplement the family income.

By 1950, she'd had eight children, so she earned even more by driving a school bus part-time and making graduation dresses for high school girls in the community.

In 1962, the manager of American Life Assurance Company in Columbus, Georgia approached Maggie about a job selling insurance. After passing the licensing exam, she plunged into a strange new field.

On her first day, she sold three policies—an encouraging start. Country folks trusted this woman who would sit down, chew snuff and explain insurance to them in simple terms.

A Top Saleswoman

If her clients ever missed a payment, "Miss Maggie" loaned them money to help out. Within a year, she was top salesperson in her district and awarded a trip to Pine Mountain, Georgia.

Maggie's career was going well when she suffered a brain hemorrhage in 1966. She pulled through that crisis and was back at work only months later, energetic as ever.

She became district manager in 1967, and hired, trained and supervised 10 agents. That year, her superiors asked her to start an office in Japan. Maggie would have risen to that challenge, too, but Red had fallen ill and she refused to leave him.

In 1969, Maggie showed a new salesman the art of ap-proaching people and making sales. The gentleman took her advice and eventually became president of the company. He never forgot Maggie.

This "woman before her time" blazed her way into a business world dominated by men. She loved people, had the gift of gab and never met a stranger. The Lord and her family always came first...more than anything, that was the key to her success. ←

MISS SURE SHOT. Jewel Klauberg pioneered her way West as a young wife. Seen here with her child in Colorado in 1922, she could shoot a coyote between the eyes at 100 yards, says daughter Bernice Brown of Wimberley, Texas.

Lively Aunt Ella Was Amazing and Amusing

By LaVerne Halverson, Minneapolis, Minnesota

EVERY KID should be lucky enough to have an Aunt Ella—I'm glad I did!

My Aunt Ella Ohna added sparkle and fun to my young life as I grew up on a Minnesota farm during the 1930s. She was casual, eccentric, self-sufficient, opinionated, articulate and whimsical with a tendency to exaggerate.

My first memories of her are set in the small grocery store she owned in South Moorhead, Minnesota.

Today, the building and health inspectors would likely shut it down. But this humble store with three-room attached living quarters provided a living for Aunt Ella and her young son.

Mom and Dad often dropped me off at the store and left me in Aunt Ella's care while they did their town business.

Enjoyed a Sweet Job

She entrusted me with filling orders at the candy counter. I'd clean the candy case and rearrange the three glass shelves with penny candy, lollipops, jawbreakers and licorice twists. To me, it was a big deal.

Aunt Ella was a born talker, and her conversations with customers extended long beyond their grocery transactions. She'd expound most vigorously on politics (she was anti-Roosevelt) and health issues.

One intriguing trait of Ella's was her housekeeping standards…they sure didn't measure up to Mother's!

Books, newspapers and plants were scattered about her living quarters, and a canary, named "Tweety", perched wherever he pleased.

On Sundays, Ella would close up her store and hitchhike to the nearby town of Glyndon to visit Grandma and Grandpa. Whenever she did, she'd carry all the money from her store on her in case robbers broke in. Often, it was hundreds of dollars.

Ella's wanderlust didn't end with hitchhiking to see her folks. For years, she talked of "moving out West", but no one took her seriously…until the summer day we stopped at her place and found it filled with boxes!

Westward, Ho!

She'd sold the store and was, indeed, moving west. Only she didn't know where. She finally ended up in Bellingham, Washington.

There, she worked in a cannery during the salmon runs. She also grew flowers and fired ceramics in a kiln she acquired along the way.

Years later, I was delighted and surprised when she showed up in Minnesota to attend my high school graduation. Since she'd never learned to drive, Mom and Dad were equally surprised.

Turned out she'd bought a new automobile from a salesman in Detroit and took a train there to pick up the car. The salesman helped her get it started and shifted into gear.

She drove to a motel, read the owner's manual and journeyed through three states in time for my graduation ceremony.

Aunt Ella headed back to Washington alone. From there, she frequently wrote descriptive letters to us in her distinctive script.

One day, a letter arrived with the return address reading "Ella Ohna Field". She'd married Roy Field, a large handsome widower who indulged her whims and idiosyncrasies.

When I eventually married, my new husband and I visited Ella and Roy while on our honeymoon. On the day my new husband and I were headed home, we walked with Aunt Ella to a local wharf.

She made a beeline for a boat and bargained with a fisherman for a salmon. She stuffed, seasoned and baked the fish, serving our last meal together on Lenox china.

Aunt Ella gave me so many memories and inspired me to achieve my goals. Just knowing her erased any thoughts of limitations to what a woman can accomplish, if she wants to. Her memory continues to inspire me. ✧

INSPIRATIONAL AUNT. Aunt Ella (right, and below right in her Bellingham, Washington garden) was an inspiration to LaVerne Halverson (below at age 5).

SERVICE WITH A SMILE was the watchword at the Horicon, Wisconsin post office in 1930. That's Postmistress Margaret Mann standing in back.

Postmistress Served The Community

MY MOTHER, Margaret Mann, was postmistress in Horicon, Wisconsin during the 1930s.

Farmers commonly ordered baby chicks for delivery by mail. I recall Mom receiving many an anxious phone call from a farmer worried about his new arrivals. The post office closed at 6 p.m., but what if the chicks came in on the 7:30 flyer?

Mom would calm any fears with her standard "not to worry" speech, then walk down to the post office to meet the late train. Invariably, she'd ask me to tag along. I never refused.

If one of the familiar peeping cartons with vent holes had arrived, she called the farmer with the news. Meanwhile, I'd lift the lid and enjoy holding the fluffy fuzz balls until the farmer arrived to claim his hatch.

Mom's willingness to go the extra mile for those farmers not only made her special, it was a trait of her generation. Those folks lived by an unwritten rule: Love and help one another.

—James Mann
Lake Mills, Wisconsin

Michigan Mayor Millie Brought Honesty to Office

"I WISH more women would get active in politics. They have a stake to protect—the community in which their children are being raised."

So said my mother-in-law, Millie Stark, in a newspaper interview in 1964.

She was reflecting on a remarkable political career that made her the first woman mayor in Michigan.

Back in 1948, Millie received a call from a city councilman where she lived in East Detroit. "Take off your apron, Millie, and come on down to City Hall," he said.

He explained that the mayor and two councilmen had just resigned over a fight to clean up illegal gambling at a local amusement park. Millie had been a strong citizen supporter of the opposition to gambling.

"I told them I might accept the job for a couple of weeks—until they could find an honest man," Millie said.

Mayor Millie acted fast, ordering gambling raids that resulted in the arrest of 92. Then she rescinded the amusement park's license and ordered the place closed.

Thankful voters elected Millie to a 2-year term in 1949, and another in 1951.

After she served those terms, she willingly gave up her "hobby" of politics. She was more than happy to return to her "profession"—being the most loving mother and best homemaker a family could ever have.

—Gloria Stark
Sterling Heights, Michigan

Mother's Trumpeting Was Center-Stage

IN A FASCINATING PICTURE I have of my mother (below), she held a trumpet on stage at Seattle's Giant Piano Theater during the 1909 Alaskan-Yukon Pacific Exposition.

During her musical days in Seattle, Arena Altenbough Meyer was the only female member of the musician's union, playing trumpet with such bands as Bab's Ladies Orchestra, The Rhythmetts, and Jean Delany and the Night Owles.

As a young girl, Mother was a tomboy and drove a Red Devil automobile and an Excelsior motorcycle on Seattle's unpaved streets.

She and her sister-in-law, Julia, led the Seattle motorcycle parades from 1909 to 1912. Julia also became instrumental in Mother's musical career by accompanying her on the piano.

Retiring from music, Mother organized a children's band and taught piano and trumpet lessons. Our family benefited from her musical knowledge, forming an orchestra of our own.

My sister, Yvonne, and I played in The Rhythm Girls band until our own retirement. We still play for family, friends and fun. —Jobyna Carpenter
Poulsbo, Washington

LOOK FOR THE UNION LABEL. Arena Altenbough (second from right on stage) played trumpet in 1909 and was the only woman in the local musician's union.

Grandma Was a Pro Photographer

By Debby Butts, Topeka, Kansas

MY GRANDMOTHER, Tressa Spore, was born on the Kansas prairie in 1882. Her early years were hard, beginning with the death of her mother when Tressa was only 9.

In 1913, Tressa's aunt encouraged her to follow her dreams and move to the city to study photography. She did so, becoming an assistant to a photographer with studios in Wichita and Conway Springs.

Tressa assited for a year, learning all she could about photography. She saved her money, too, and purchased the Conway Springs studio in 1914.

It was an exciting day when she ran an ad in the *Conway Springs Star*, announcing that "Miss T. Spore" had purchased the studio and was open for business.

Eventually, she moved her studio and living quarters to a new location with a large window to let in more sunlight. The people in Conway Springs were pleased with the up-to-date studio in town.

Although Grandmother wasn't the first woman to work as a professional photogra-

pher, she was certainly among the first. She gained respect from the community with her successful business.

Grandmother sold her studio in 1917, when she married my grandfather. Two sons and a busy role as wife and mother caused her to box up the photo equipment and tuck it away—along with wonderful memories of being an independent woman who'd truly made it on her own.

PICTURE PERFECT. To show her abilities as a photographer, Tressa Spore took these portraits of herself. Tressa worked as a photographer's assistant for a year and in 1914 was able to buy one of his studios (top photo). Tressa ran a successful business for 3 years, until she married. During that time, she was one of the few female photographers.

NOT ALL the strong women of this century were mothers and grandmothers. Sr. Mary Antona Ebo is a shining example of strength—and I'm proud to know her.

In 1946, Sr. Antona entered the convent, becoming one of the first black nuns in the Franciscan Sisters of Mary, in St. Louis.

In the 50 years since, this trained nurse became the first black nun to head a hospital. More remarkably, she was part of history in 1965, standing at the forefront of the civil rights march in Selma, Alabama.

As racial tension mounted in Alabama, an archbishop in St. Louis allowed Catholic delegates to join an interfaith group in the civil rights marches. That group included 48 priests, rabbis, Protestant clergy and six nuns. Sr. Antona was one of them.

On March 10, 1965, she boarded a flight to Selma. The rabbis carried kosher food in bags, she recalls, because they didn't think they'd find kosher food in Selma.

She Was an Unusual Sight

After landing, the contingent was bused to the church where marchers convened. The people there had never seen a black nun.

"A little black girl was playing outside," recalls Sr. Antona. "She took one look and ran to me with her arms outstretched. I embraced her, and it was the kind of affirmation you can't get anywhere else in the world."

At the church, she met the leader of the march, Rev. Anderson. "For the first time in my life," he told the hushed room, "I am seeing a Negro nun. To see her tells me you don't have to be white to be good, to be holy."

Sr. Antona stepped up to address the group, and another black minister hushed the crowd's applause so she could speak. He was Andrew Young, future mayor of Atlanta and U.S. Ambassador to the United Nations.

Then the march to City Hall began. "It seemed like we walked 1,000 miles, though it was little more than a block," Sr. Antona remembers.

"Everyone began saying, 'Put

Sr. Antona Made Civil Rights History

By Judy Schaper, St. Louis, Missouri

the nuns in front!' I was so scared."

A government agent suggested that the men surround the sisters to protect them. Then someone asked Sr. Antona to take off her glasses.

Would Violence Erupt?

"There were squad cars, policemen in helmets, police dogs and bullies holding clubs," she recalls. Finally, the marchers were face-to-face with Mayor Joe Smitherman.

"Today we have one of our own to speak to you," Rev. Anderson told the mayor. "We have someone who shows you don't have to be white to be good or to be holy."

Sr. Antona couldn't believe what was happening as the microphone was thrust before her.

"I am here because I am a Negro, a nun, a Catholic and because I want to bear witness," she declared. Her words were broadcast around the world.

She knelt with the others and prayed, and the violence everyone feared didn't materialize.

Later, Sr. Antona helped a group feed and house the marchers, even offering kosher food to the rabbis. "Today I am the best-fed rabbi in all of Alabama," a grateful clergyman told Sr. Antona.

Back home in St. Louis, Sr. Antona watched herself on three TVs as she ate her dinner of cold scrambled eggs.

Many years later, Sr. Antona met Mayor Smitherman once again. This time, however, he personally escorted her through City Hall.

"I looked into his eyes and saw that he had changed," she says. "The hate was gone."

But the mayor admitted to Sr. Antona that he had a confession: "I've always wondered what happened to that black woman they dressed up like a nun." ✦

HISTORICAL MOMENTS. Sr. Mary Antona Ebo joined the civil rights march in Selma, Alabama in 1965 (top). Her work earned her the Martin Luther King Award in 1994 (left).

SAFE IN MOM'S ARMS. A mother's love brings smiles during the good times, but in times of crisis, it has the power to conquer all. No matter how big or small a problem this little one might face during the years to come, Mom will see to it that things are set right.

Chapter Two

Mom's Love Got Us Through It

No matter how gentle and tender the mother, deep down inside dwells a ferocious tiger ready to take on the world to protect her offspring and carry them through any kind of crisis, great or small.

She will, if necessary, work 16 hours a day to put food on the table…then sit up late into the night to sew a special dress for a daughter's graduation.

When Dad is serving in the military in some faraway land, or some tragedy takes him away forever, Mom becomes a father, too, even if it means learning to throw batting practice in the backyard.

Moms come in all shapes, sizes and colors, but they share one thing in common: Their capacity for love is infinitely expandable.

Whether they have one child or a dozen, they magically bestow 100% of their love on each and every one and use it to help their little ones weather life's troubles.

My Grandmother Stevens was a tiny woman whose body contained a heart bigger than all outdoors. I won't go into the trials of raising five rambunctious kids in those days before electricity, indoor plumbing, central heat, telephones, washing machines and supermarkets—the stories in this book do it better than I can.

Full of Energy

But where that slim, 5-foot woman got the energy and strength is a marvel of nature. She must have been bone-weary every day for the first 40 years of her life.

Eventually the kids married and left home. Gramma inherited a small amount of money, bought a more comfortable home, probably heaved a deep sigh, and looked forward to a life of peace and quiet with Grampa. At last!

Well, sure. Along came 1929 and all the misery that followed. Soon a married daughter's husband was out of work. They were flat broke and had a young baby to boot.

"We've got plenty of room," Gramma said. "Move in until you're back on your feet."

More Boarders to Come

Before long, her married son was out of work, too. He found a job at Montgomery Ward selling stoves, radios and refrigerators on commission. But no one was buying.

"We've still got an empty bedroom," Gramma offered. So the son, his wife and *their* new baby moved in.

Another son, single, came home for a while. An unmarried daughter joined the household at times, too.

There were squabbles and occasional feuds. There were crying babies. Money was a perpetual problem.

In later years, I asked Gramma how she coped with all the turmoil. After all, she was well into her 60s when circumstances crammed six and sometimes eight people back into her home and her life.

"Well," she smiled, "it certainly taught me patience!"

True enough. I can't recall ever seeing her lose her temper. She could be strict and stern, to be sure, and there was never any question of who was in charge of the household. But she wasn't one to lose her poise.

What I remember most is her inexhaustible supply of love. She gave total love to every one of her children, different as they all were. And there was plenty of affection left for her grandchildren.

She typifies what the stories in this chapter are about—gentle women who used love to help their loved ones cope with any crisis.

—*Clancy Strock*

She Had 14 Kids, 10 Rooms, Lots of Love

By Margaret McNeish
Easthampton, Massachusetts

LITERALLY overnight, my mom's whole life changed.

One day she was a housewife alongside a strong providing husband; the next, she was a widow with a challenge —how to support 14 children.

Mom would take her first full-time job, run a 10-room house and cultivate a gigantic garden to meet the challenge, and she'd do it all alone.

The story starts in 1939, when my parents moved us to Plymouth, Indiana to take care of Father's elderly parents. Within 18 months, Mom would lose both her in-laws and husband.

After the estates were settled, she had enough money left to buy a rundown 10-room house with an extra lot for a garden. We moved into that house in May of 1940 and busied ourselves with spring cleaning.

Soon, some men from the city came by and said that since Mom had no means of support, they'd place her six youngest children in an orphanage.

Mom replied that if those men tried, she wouldn't hesitate to use the family shotgun on them! They told her to call when she changed her mind. She found a job instead.

Mom was 44 when she landed her first job—in a chicken processing plant. She stood all day long on a cold, wet concrete floor, doing the jobs most men wouldn't do, like dressing chickens and candling eggs. She worked 5 to 6 days per week.

For working overtime, she could take home all the chicken feet she wanted. The feet were scrubbed and boiled

"Mom did the jobs most men wouldn't do..."

to make stock for vegetable soup.

During harvest season at our house, she canned 300 2-quart jars of her delicious vegetable soup—enough to last all year.

On Sundays, she made chicken, mashed potatoes with gravy, and corn, peas and beans picked fresh from her garden. People were encouraged to plant victory gardens during World War II, and Mom reaped more from her in-

ROUGH DAYS AHEAD. Not long after this family photo was taken on Christmas Day 1938, Dad Sylvester died and Mom Sylvia tackled the job of raising their brood, says Margaret McNeish (in Dad's lap).

tensively cultivated garden than most local truck farms.

She grew enough vegetables for our family *and* for the neighbors, who were allowed to take what they needed.

The neighbors knew Mom wouldn't accept money for the corn and tomatoes they picked, so they baked bread for us. Mom would only accept the baked goods in trade—that way it wasn't charity.

She encouraged us to work together as a family. Those with jobs contributed what they earned, but none of the children were to quit school to take a job. All 14 of us received our diplomas.

Mom did all the things necessary to survive when Dad died. Her love and hard work held our family together.

Mom never spoke unkindly of anyone and instilled strong moral values in us. I don't recall her ever having enough time to sit down and read the Bible, yet I think she led the most Christian life of anyone I ever met. ✦

Sister Margie's Love Made the Family Whole

By Sharon East
Washington Court House, Ohio

I WAS BORN in 1941, the same year my sister Margie graduated from high school in Reeseville, Ohio.

Margie had won a college scholarship and yearned to go on to school. But Dad said college wasn't necessary for women and Margie's help was needed at home. Mother wasn't well and the new baby (me) would need care.

I slept cuddled in Margie's arms, and she later told me any resentment she may have felt went away the first night we slept close together.

During the early war years, when I was 2, Margie traveled to Dayton to work in the Delco plant. She worked all week at the factory and came home on weekends to cook, clean and help take care of my older brother, Kenny, and me.

Managing the Home

When our mother passed away in 1946, family and friends urged Dad to place Kenny (age 13) and me (5) in a children's home.

Margie said, "There will be no children's home and no farming the kids out to separate homes. We'll manage somehow."

Margie strived to keep us together, working her job all day, then coming home to work some more. We had no washer or dryer, so she washed our clothes in the kitchen sink. Then she wrung them out by hand and hung them on the line to dry. She ironed at night.

As she did so, she told us stories, recited poetry and sang songs. To this day, I marvel at the poems and songs she committed to memory.

I loved to hear her sing tearjerkers like *Hobo Bill*, *Old Shep*, *The Baggage Coach Ahead*, *The Letter Edged in Black* or *There's a New Star in Heaven Tonight*. When she sang those, I begged for more!

It was unheard-of for Margie to miss work, but she took time off for my first day of school. I clearly remember that day when Margie walked me several blocks to the big, imposing McKinley Grade School.

Taking Pride in Me

While other children clung to their mothers and cried, Margie praised me for being a "big girl" and not crying. I felt tears coming when the teacher asked the parents to leave. But knowing Margie was proud of me, I fought them and waved to her dry-eyed.

After several more years of caring for us, Margie married. But she remained a strong "helper" the rest of her life, often sharing her home with needy children or stray animals.

She did without material things and enjoyed the simple pleasures of life …laughing, teasing and giving of herself to those in need.

I feel honored and grateful to have

Your father was my father,
and my mother was yours;

They say we are sisters,
but I know that it's more.

You told me stories,
and you sang me songs,

'Til I scarce even knew,
that our mother was gone.

Childlike, I accepted
these things as my due,

With never a thought
of the hardship to you.

And if I had one wish
that would surely come true,

I'd wish each lonely child
had a sister like you!

had such a kind, loving and caring person for my sister and substitute mother. In gratitude, I wrote this poem (above) for Margie. When she read it, tears glistened in her eyes. ✦

SUBSTITUTE MOTHER. Sharon East (at top left) recalls a giving sister who endured hardships like the woman above. Margie worked hard and kept the family together after her mother died.

Button Box Was a Mystery That Relieved a Widow's Misery

By Lela Landis Yoder
Salisbury, Pennsylvania

MY FAVORITE STORY about my mother is a joy to recall because it illustrates her deep love for her children...and she had plenty to love!

When Father died in a farming accident in 1930, I was 6 years old, the 10th of 11 children. Mother had to move us to a 15-acre farm she rented near Canby, Oregon. Only four of the children were old enough to help by working outside the home.

Mother canned and dried lots of fruits and vegetables to get us through that first winter, but as the months went by, the food supply dwindled.

When she wasn't cooking, she did the laundry for all of us, using an old washer with a faulty hand wringer that cracked the buttons off our clothes.

Poor Mother couldn't afford more buttons. So, twice a week, while we kids were taking our baths in a tin washtub in front of the stove, she cut the buttons off our dirty long underwear and sewed them onto clean pairs!

A Labor of Love

She then brought the clean underwear to our rooms for us to wear the next day. What a tedious task to perform on all those pairs of long johns each week! Mother never said a word about it.

On the cold winter night she put the last of the food on our table, I'm sure Mother felt depressed, but she never let it show. I was unaware the cupboard was empty—perhaps some of the older children knew.

After tucking us into bed, she got down on her knees to pray for help from the only source left. There would be no milk for breakfast...nothing to pack for her children's school lunches. Suddenly, she heard a knock at the door.

Puzzled because we knew no one in town, she answered the door in time to

see four Boy Scouts running down the lane. They'd left a large box.

The box contained potatoes, spaghetti, macaroni, oatmeal, rice, beans, flour, sugar, fruits and vegetables. What fun we had putting it all away!

There was one item left after the food was stored...a small box tied closed.

Mother sat in a chair to open it. Inside were buttons of all shapes, sizes and colors. Through tears, she described constantly sewing and re-sewing buttons on our underwear. 'Til then, we hadn't known.

A Lasting Influence

It was 45 years later that I learned what happened. Our pastor asked me to help deliver Easter lilies to shut-ins. My first stop was the home of an elderly neighbor.

She invited me in for a cup of tea. I looked at my station wagon filled with lilies for delivery but took time to visit anyway.

She said, "I can't think of any person I respected more than your mother. She had all those children to raise alone, but never did we see her complain, cry or feel sorry for herself.

"Years ago, your neighbor Frank Cutsforth visited me in my dry goods store to ask if I'd like to add a donation to a box he planned to send to the poor widow woman with all those children. I didn't know what to give.

"We didn't have much money, so I sat down at my desk to think," she continued. "My knee bumped a small box. It was filled with buttons I'd collected.

"I felt a strong urge to give the buttons to Frank for your family," Mrs. Harshman said. "So I tied the box shut and handed it to him."

After hearing Mrs. Harshman's story, I was thankful I paused for that cup of tea. I finally knew where the button box came from...and just how highly folks thought of my loving mother. ✦

FASTEN-ATING TALE. Lela Yoder didn't learn the story of the gift of the buttons until years later. That's Lela at left in second row below. Mom's in the middle of her kids.

Diane Dietrich Leis

Mom's Love Helped Nine Kids Overcome Polio

By Jill Andres Thelander
Little Falls, Minnesota

HOMECOMING. When all nine of Christine Andres' children got polio, things looked bleak. But they recovered, and it was a happy day when Donald, the last to leave the hospital, returned home to his family (above) in 1946.

MY GRANDMOTHER, Christine Andres, raised 10 children, including my father. I always enjoyed her tales of those years, but the most remarkable story of all was her family's struggle against polio.

Just thinking of what Grandmother endured through 4 months in the fall of 1946 leaves me awestruck.

Grandma and Grandpa were raising nine children in a five-room farmhouse near Little Falls, Minnesota at the time. In September, their toddler, Charles, was gripped by polio.

He had a mild case and was treatable at home. But before Charles recovered, Grandpa Frank drove three children with more serious symptoms to the hospital. Things would get worse.

Grandma was too busy caring for sick children at home to visit her hospitalized kids. Within 2 weeks, *all nine* of her children were stricken with polio.

The hospital instructed Grandma to boil hot packs, wring them 'til nearly dry and lay them over her children. Then she lovingly wrapped her little ones in woolen blankets.

She followed that procedure twice daily for weeks, preparing *thousands* of hot packs. Grandpa, meanwhile, drove children to and from the hospital. In all, he drove 2,500 miles.

On October 21, 1946, three of their four remaining hospitalized children returned home. Their last hospitalized son, Donald, rejoined the family at home in time for Christmas. Remarkably, all nine children had survived the dreaded polio epidemic.

With luck, determination and Grandma's strength, none of her children were left with permanent disabilities.

In an interview with the *St. Cloud Daily Times* in 1983, Grandma recalled she was so busy taking care of her children for so many months that she lost track of the date.

But one date she never forgot was the day in 1954 when Dr. Jonas Salk introduced the polio vaccine. Grandma said the inoculation answered the prayers of mothers worldwide.

SISTERLY LOVE. Ida Kiel (left) and sisters Martha and Laura smiled for the camera in the early 1900s. Judy Myers of Phoenix, Arizona shared this shot of her grandmother, Ida, and beloved step-grandmother, Martha. Judy explains that Ida died in 1914 after having twins. So her single sister, Martha, lovingly raised the twins, then, 17 years later, married their father.

Mom Protected and Cared For Quarantined Kids

THE DREADED WORDS "Beware Diphtheria" were posted on our front door by the county health department in the mid-1920s. Both my sister and I had contracted the disease.

Our postman instructed, "Put a cigar box on your porch for the mail—that's as close as I'll get."

Doc gave me a shot of animal serum, and I became one stiff and pained 10-year-old. An official from the health department suggested that my 8-year-old sister and I be isolated in the "Pest House" with others who had diphtheria.

Mother drew herself up to her full 5 feet 5 inches and said, "Over my dead body will you remove one of these girls."

Her words were heeded. Today, my sister and I are healthy and in our 70s. Yes, Mom's love pulled us through many trials.
—Alice Vandendool
Tulsa, Oklahoma

NURSE MOM. The 1923 portrait above was taken just prior to quarantine. Mom Sophia helped Gladys (left) and Alice through that diphtheria crisis. Alice grew up healthy (top right, in the 1940s) and had her own daughter, Nancy, in 1944.

Mother Carried More Than Her Weight

AT AGE 103, my mother, Dora McGuffin, remains upbeat, full of humor and

MIGHTY STRONG WOMAN. Dora McGuffin posed in 1918 with her husband, John Henry, daughter Burnice and son Buddy. A few years later, she'd save Buddy's life.

fond memories. One memory that will live on forever in our family is the day back in the 1920s when Mom saved her son's life.

My brother, Buddy, was 15 then and driving a two-row disk plow on our farm at Plainview, Oklahoma. The plow was pulled by three horses, including a nervous mare named "Snorter".

The seat broke on the plow, causing Buddy to slip down. To his horror, his leg was slipping between two sharp disks.

Buddy managed to stop the team and started calling for help. But each time he yelled, Snorter would prance and try to lunge forward. Buddy held a tight grip on the reins.

Mother was hanging laundry when she heard her son's cries, looked across the field and saw his awkward position. She ran to help but slowed to a walk when she saw how wild Snorter was acting.

She calmly approached the plow, took one end firmly in her hands and lifted it up. Buddy pulled his leg free and miraculously escaped injury. But that wasn't the only miracle.

You see, that plow was so heavy it commonly took two men just to lift one end. Somehow Mother had lifted it all by herself—with Buddy aboard!

Even many years later, Daddy never tired of telling this story.
—Georgia Dea Holland, Miami, Texas

Mom's Attic Nest Was Safe Haven from Storm

MY SISTER and I huddled together in terror during thunderstorms, but Mom used her vivid imagination to dispel our fear of the fierce noise and blinding flashes.

She'd gather us up, grab a cozy blanket and lead us to the attic, where we snuggled together in a spare bed. With Mom in the middle and my sister and I on either side, she'd conjure up cheerful images for us.

She told us to close our eyes, listen to the rain and imagine a million birds dancing on the roof. When lightning interrupted, she told us it was a big spotlight flashing across the dance floor. If we waited a few seconds, we'd hear the big drums roll.

No matter how long the storm lasted, Mom stayed with us until we fell asleep in the warmth of her loving arms.
—Rita Boehm, Mesa, Arizona

MOM'S A TREASURE. When she had to make it on her own, Kathleen Brady (right, with daughter Maureen) found a way. She studied and became a head librarian in the early '60s (left). After retirement, Kathleen became city treasurer!

Mom's Role Changed, But Not Positive Outlook

By Maureen Mobley
Garden Grove, California

I STILL look back with pride and amazement at my mother's strength following a 1960 car accident in which my father died. I was 16 then and had two 11-year-old brothers, and I recall being deeply worried about what would happen to us.

Father had been head of the household in our Signal Hill, California home. My mother, Kathleen Brady, was happy to be a passively compliant housewife. I don't think she realized life could be so different—until she was left with no choice.

Mother had no college education and hadn't worked a day outside the home since her children were born. She must have been so scared after Dad died, but she kept life as normal as she could for us. We still had Christmas that year, full meals and clothes for school.

Mother took a job as substitute librarian and did well.

Then, when the head librarian decided to retire, Mother studied fervently for a civil servants exam that would qualify her for the position.

Mother finally got the job…and what a job she did!

She scheduled after-school "story time" sessions for youngsters in the library. She could be quite an actress, so as she read, she acted out all the parts of the characters.

Bigger and Better

Three years after she became librarian, the city council approved funds for a larger library. Mother oversaw the daily construction, and when the new library was opened, she was responsible to buy more books.

The book supplier was 30 miles from Signal Hill, and Mother was an inexperienced driver. She didn't drive the freeways or make left-hand turns. I helped

BEDTIME STORIES. Aunt Mae always had time for her family, recalls Marcus Vaught of Tampa, Florida. Here she's enjoying a story with two great-grandchildren. Aunt Mae used this same kind of love to help her family through tough times.

her map out a route that led to her destination and back home again using only right-hand turns.

She departed early in the morning and returned late in the afternoon. Everyone in City Hall, which was upstairs from the library, worried about her while she was gone.

She had a budget for new books, so she made her choices deliberately and carefully, determined to get the most for her money. I realize now the sense of accomplishment she felt after her purchases.

She Did a Fine Job

Another part of Mother's job was to collect fines for overdue books, and she did so seriously. If people owed fines, they paid them! She'd drive to their houses to collect.

Upon her retirement, another bigger and better Signal Hill Library was built. Those in charge of the project eased her transition into retirement by including her as an advisor.

When the project was complete, she surprised everyone by running for city treasurer …and winning. The headline "Brady is a Treasure" accompanied her photo in a Long Beach newspaper.

Despite falling asleep in what she called "those boring council meetings", she was elected twice to the position.

Yes, my mother remains a treasure. This feisty woman's love and willingness to try got our family through some tough times. ←

HEALING HANDS. Mother Marie made Shirley Terlizzi's brother well.

This Determined Mother Helped Her Boy Walk Again

MY 5-year-old brother was stricken with polio in 1938. This was long before the Salk vaccine and there was no cure for the disease. The doctors told my mother her son would never walk again.

The only hope they gave her was to try putting hot packs on his legs. Then she had to move the legs for him, so his muscles wouldn't atrophy. Mother had to do this four times per day.

This therapy was so painful for my little brother that he screamed…and Mother would cry. It was too painful to even listen to, so I'd run from the house.

This went on for months. Yes, Mother continued to cry, but she wouldn't quit. She was determined he would walk.

Finally, the doctor allowed my little brother to try and walk. With helpers on either side, he pushed himself to take that first, halting, miraculous step. Now the tears flowing down Mother's cheeks were tears of joy!

Each day brought new successes, and eventually, my brother recovered. He even went on to play high school football. Yes, Mother's love carried him through this ordeal. —*Shirley Terlizzi West Allis, Wisconsin*

Mom's Heart Was Big Enough for Everyone

DURING World War II, Mom's three sons, ages 18, 25 and 27, joined the service. The mailman became her best friend, delivering V-mail letters from her soldier sons.

One day, Mom received a letter from the War Department, informing her that my 25-year-old brother had been wounded. The tears spilled down her cheeks, but she never stopped knitting. Nor did she quit filling and sending parcels to her sons and other soldiers.

Her love for anyone serving their

HOME FRONT HERO. Frances Kline (with daughter Phyllis in 1937, below, and in '62, above) kept the home fires burning for her sons.

country prompted her to form the local Army Mothers Club, a place where she and other mothers could share their joys and sorrows.

Mom's heart seemed big enough for everyone, and her love helped see us through that difficult time, till all three of my brothers came home.

—*Phyllis Kline Alexander Hagerstown, Maryland*

Her Legacy Lives On in Her Children

MOM AND DAD were married in 1928, at age 19. By 1935, they had four children and moved to a little farm on Possum Creek in Oklahoma.

A hailstorm destroyed our strawberry crop in 1937, and we missed our yearly mortgage payment. We lost the farm then, and Dad never was the same. He was hospitalized with a nervous breakdown.

It fell to Mom to provide for us, and she did it all. We moved in with Grandfather, and Mother worked in the fields and spent cold nights firing furnaces to keep young plants from freezing. We kids took turns staying up with her to keep her awake.

But our life wasn't all work—thanks to Mom. In the evenings, she would make a pan of fudge or a bowl of popcorn to enjoy while we played games, read books or recited poetry by the light of a kerosene lamp.

She also made sure Christmas, Easter and Valentine's Day were special. I still have warm memories of those times.

We eventually moved off the farm, and Mom worked as a hamburger cook by day and a nurse's aide at night. She was determined her children would graduate from high school and attend college. Inspired by her love, we all did.

Thanks to our wonderful loving mother, we lead productive and happy lives with our own families today.

—*Mary Hardaway Placentia, California*

"BUSIA" is Polish for Grandma. Katharine Malinowski spoiled her family with food and love, recalls granddaughter Barbara Griffin of Simpsonville, South Carolina.

Mom Didn't Buckle When Tragedy Struck

By John Cermak
Long Beach, Washington

I REMEMBER Mom as a rock. She was stubborn, tenacious and hardworking with an undying faith and love for family.

Born Frantiska Kanda in 1884 to a Czech family in Austria-Hungary, she dreamed of immigrating to America, a land where all things were possible.

Scrimping and saving, she made her dream came true in 1903 when she booked passage on the *SS Bremen* bound for America. Mom was 19.

Her goal was to live on a farm, plant a garden and raise chickens. She joined a sister in Chicago, then read an advertisement in a Czech newspaper. A young Czech farmer out west was searching for a girl to help prove-up on a homestead.

She corresponded with the man, and in 1909, she married him and moved to his homestead on the Nez Perce Indian Reservation in Idaho.

The homesteaders struggled to make a go of their 80-acre dryland wheat farm, which grew to 180 acres as they bought adjoining land.

As the size of their homestead increased, so did their family. I was the last of three children born between 1910 and 1919.

Mom raised chickens and traded eggs for groceries. Our cows provided milk and excess cream to sell. Mom used two $5 cream checks monthly, produce from her big garden and eggs to provide three great meals a day.

At haying time, Dad cut alfalfa with a mowing machine, and my brother Joe and I put the hay into rows to be dried and shocked.

On a June day in 1925, when I was 6, I was following the mower, fascinated to watch it work. I tripped, fell partway into it and badly cut my hand and forearm.

Dad leaped down, cinched his red bandanna tightly over my arm, unhitched "Darkie" our horse and raced me toward home. Mom was shocking hay across the canyon. She saw there was trouble and ran for home, beating Darkie.

Mom called the doctor, and in her broken English, she told him to hurry to the farm.

I don't think she identified herself, but old Dr. Watts recognized the accent. When he arrived, my parents had a conference. Mom emphatically told the doctor not to amputate my hand but to stitch me up with the guidance of God.

Doc did as Mom bid. But he knew I'd need to go to a hospital and see a specialist if I were to have any hope of regaining the use of my hand. Hospitalization and specialists would cost a lot of money, he warned.

We used less cream at the table that year, and Mom provided our food without using any money from the cream checks. More eggs were sold for cash, and my parents didn't hire extra help on the farm…Mom drove the wheat binder while Dad and my siblings

THANKS TO MOM. Frances Cermak sent turn-of-the-century portrait (top) to future husband prior to their "mail-order marriage", says son John. Frances drove horses on Idaho homestead in 1912, where she later saved John's left hand. In 1945, she proudly posed with him at graduation.

shocked the wheat for harvesting.

That fall, Mom paid cash for my surgery. By all rules of present-day medical knowledge, I should have lost my hand the day of the accident, but Mom's fighting spirit helped me beat the odds.

After my surgery, Mom was given instructions on how to help exercise my hand until I could move my fingers and hold things.

I can never repay Mom for getting me through the ordeal. But I saw a glimmer of pride in her eyes the day I finished graduate school with her standing at my side. ↵

A School for the Deaf? Mom Wouldn't Hear of It

By Elizabeth Elftman
Indianapolis, Indiana

IN 1929, when I was 3 years old, I contracted a severe case of scarlet fever. My mother's love not only carried me through that crisis, it sustained me through some tough times and helped me enjoy a productive career.

When I fell ill, our house was placed under quarantine. Mother took care of me 24 hours a day. After many weeks, my illness was gone, but it left me severely hearing-impaired.

I recall many trips to different "ear doctors". All of them said nothing could be done.

> *"Mom heard about a new device called a 'hearing aid'..."*

But Mother's determination never wavered. Every new treatment or doctor was thoroughly investigated.

I had to learn to talk again, and I recall Mom patiently repeating new words over and over until I could say them correctly. She was never cross or impatient with my mistakes.

When it was time for me to go to school, my parents were advised to send me to the Colorado School for the Deaf, 150 miles away. Mother refused to send me that far from home at so young an age.

Off to School

Instead, I attended the local elementary school. During first grade, Mom went to school with me nearly every day. She made sure I sat in the front row so I could see the teacher. I was developing the ability to lip-read.

The teacher was very helpful. When I didn't understand instructions, I would raise my hand and she'd repeat them.

Mother spoke to each successive teacher as the years went by, explaining my hearing loss and the type of assistance I needed.

Sometime during my fifth year in school, Mom heard about a new device called a "hearing aid". She asked our doctor about it. His advice was, "She's doing all right in school and is learning to lip-read. Why spoil all that?" His answer didn't satisfy her.

In the face of objections from my doctor and father, she insisted on seeing if a hearing aid could help me. It did, and I've worn one ever since.

Because my mother followed her instincts and was determined to give me every assistance she could, I owe her more than I could ever repay. She's the reason I graduated from high school, then earned bachelor's and master's degrees.

Five years ago, I retired from a rewarding career as an audiologist. I used my knowledge and experience to help hearing-impaired adults cope with hearing loss. And I counseled parents of hearing-impaired children.

I'm 70 years old now, and Mom knew I loved her and appreciated all she did for me. But I never told her.

Her strength and love enabled me to live a meaningful and productive life. Thank you, Mom, from the bottom of my heart.

PEAS IN A POD. Dad worked two jobs, so Mom, Bernice Breunig, and her 10 children handled the home chores, says Phyllis Brumm of Cross Plains, Wisconsin. Helping Mom shell peas in this 1946 photo were Phyllis' sister Patricia and brother Clarence.

Young Eyes Watched Mom Breathe Life into Infant

MY MOTHER was a farm wife in southern Minnesota during the 1920s. She was also a registered nurse and provided care for her four daughters, baby boy and any neighbor who needed her.

A day before our baby brother was to be baptized, Mother nursed

SON SAVED. Baby Paul (above, in 1939) was rescued by Mom (center).

little Paul and laid him in his crib. Sometime later, I checked on him and found he wasn't breathing. I was terrified because he'd turned blue!

Mother grabbed the baby, checked his airway and told us to fill a dishpan with cold water and another with warm water from the reservoir behind the wood stove.

She held Paul's feet in one hand and supported his head and neck in her other hand. She "folded" him together as if he were bowing, and submerged him in cold water.

She pulled him out and straightened him, then repeated the process in the hot bath. Back and forth she did this for what seemed an eternity. All we girls could do was cry and pray!

Mother doggedly continued her primitive form of artificial respiration and temperature shock treatment until the baby began breathing on his own, then crying. It was the most beautiful sound we'd ever heard.

—*Lois Utter*
Redlands, California

Aunt's Deep Love Overcame The Difficult Times

MY FATHER came home from the Navy Seabees after World War II, and then spent years in veteran's hospitals around the country.

When Mom became ill with cancer in 1946, she realized she hadn't long to live, so she asked her sister to care for me when she was gone.

At age 7, I went to live with Aunt Madeline and Uncle Owen in Richwood, West Virginia. They had no children of their own, so I was a real challenge.

Looking back now, I realize I was quite spoiled when I arrived. I was also angry at the world because of my situation.

I cried every day, was belligerent and acted like a recluse. All that negative behavior was met with nothing but love from Aunt Madeline.

She enrolled me in Girl Scouts and became a leader herself. She saw to it I went to church. Education was always emphasized—I was surrounded by books and music.

Since my father was a veteran, Aunt Madeline received a government allotment for my living expenses. She

ALL'S WELL...Marilyn Seitz admits she was a handful when she came to live with Aunt Madeline in 1947 (left). But both ladies were all smiles in '91.

and Uncle Owen weren't well off by any means, but they saved every cent of that money for my college education.

I graduated, became a teacher and raised two wonderful children of my own. I have a great life today, thanks to Aunt Madeline.

Simply having the stamina to stay with the tough job of raising me is testament to her strength. Her love sustained me through tough years, and it still does today.

—Marilyn Seitz, McGaheysville, Virginia

A 12-Year-Old's Wisdom Remains Lifelong Gift

By Margaret Carone
Waterford, Pennsylvania

ONE mid-October Saturday in 1951, Anne Louise and I took to the fields in search of milkweed pods about to burst.

I was only 4 then, and my sister was 12. Carefully, we separated the pods from their tough stems and carried them gently home in a basket.

We tiptoed into the parlor, where Dad was dozing in an overstuffed chair near the furnace vent. Quietly, we split open the "wishing pods" and set hundreds of fluffy milkweed seeds afloat over his head with the help of the rising heat.

"Wake up, Daddy," she said softly. "We've brought you a hundred wishes."

To this day, I can't release a milkweed fluff without a wave of incredible joy at remembering his shining, smiling face as the seeds swirled gently around him.

All that winter, Anne Louise would prop the covers on my father's sickbed so the fabric didn't weigh heavily on his painfully arthritic joints.

Enjoyed Story Time

She would supply him with books to read aloud to me while I snuggled in her lap in a chair drawn as near as possible to my father's rich deep voice.

His words filling my head, her arms hugging me warmly, I was so much loved that I failed to realize my father was never well enough to hold me in his own lap during those story times.

One April morning before she left for school, Anne Louise snuck our brother's precious Lincoln Logs canister into the parlor, where Dad lay sleeping on the couch.

Spreading them around me, she calmly gave me instructions: I was to build the biggest corral around the best cabin with the tallest chimney ever built. It was to be so wonderful that Daddy could see it even if his eyes were closed; even if his eyes were as far away as Heaven.

My father had slipped away that

morning—he was 38 years old.

Looking back now, I do not believe that I'd have even one clear loving memory of our father if Anne Louise hadn't arranged opportunities like these.

Sister Took Care of Her

When Dad became ill and Mother had to take a job, my sister just assumed the role of being surrogate mother to me.

Though approaching adolescence and a need for her own independence, Anne Louise never questioned the need to take care of me with exactly the same gentleness she'd received at age 4 from Mom.

Common women, like my mother and Anne Louise, have shaped the character of generations in every culture, in every country, in every decade of history.

I've never asked my sister about her memories of that time in our lives. I only know I have a treasure of memories of my father, and every one of them was designed by, and delivered with love from, Anne Louise. ✦

GREAT SHAKES! Repairing a cedar shake roof was no problem for this hammerin' woman. In the pages that follow, you'll meet women who used ingenuity and skill to save money and solve any number of problems great and small.

Chapter Three

She Was a Genius

Once a week, the trash man comes down our street, emptying our enormous black trash receptacles. My wife and I and our neighbors manage to generate a lot of stuff destined for the local landfill. It's much more than you'd think, considering most of these homes contain only two adults.

When I grew up during the 1920s and '30s, my family didn't have a lot of trash. One or two trips a month to the local dump sufficed. You see, I grew up in an age when stuff was expected to last and last and *last*.

Clothes were mended and patched instead of thrown away. When they finally were too disreputable to wear, Mom saved the buttons and the rest went into the ragbag, someday to serve as dust cloths or become part of a patchwork quilt.

Feed bags and flour sacks were washed, pressed and stored away, later to be made into curtains or dresses or aprons. One evening every week, while listening to the radio, Mom got out the mending basket and darned socks…a lost art, near as I can tell.

Saved Waxed Paper

Bread came wrapped in a double layer of waxed paper. When the bread was gone, she carefully unfolded the wrapper and separated the printed outer wrapper from the pure white inner sheet. The result: a dandy wrap for the sandwiches in our school lunch boxes.

Nor was much leftover food ever thrown out. Odds and ends of bologna, ham or chicken went through the meat grinder, along with pickles and Mom's homemade mayonnaise to create a tasty, moist sandwich spread.

Weary, tacky furniture was reupholstered at home or dolled up with slipcovers that Mom made. Time-scarred furniture didn't go to the dump—it was refinished or painted.

My baby crib cuddled not only me but the children of various relatives and friends, getting fresh paint with every new arrival. By the time I inherited it for my firstborn, the crib was more paint than wood. (We, too, slapped on a fresh coat paint and some new decals.)

Made Inexpensive Lotion

Many women discovered how to make their own skin lotion from glycerin and rose extract for a fraction of what the nearly identical product cost at the drugstore. What a discovery! And they were ecstatic when home permanent kits came along.

Come autumn, we filled a barrel in the basement with our own apples and enjoyed them all winter, along with our homegrown popcorn. There also was a root cellar stocked with potatoes and turnips from the garden. Nearby were hundreds of jars of vegetables, jams and jellies put up during the summer.

Waste not, want not, was the rule. Mom even saved those tall round canisters that Quaker Oats came in, because each one, cut in half, became the foundation for a couple of May baskets when spring arrived. Morton Salt canisters were squirreled away for the same reason.

Those oblong wooden boxes from Velveeta cheese were another treasure, good for storing spools of thread, needles and other small items. Brightly decorated cheese spread jars lived on as fruit juice glasses, and we drank our milk from former peanut butter jars.

No, there wasn't much left over for the trash sack. Frugal and creative women saw to that. You'll learn much more about their genius in the stories that follow.

—*Clancy Strock*

Grandma's Face Cream Smoothed Things Over

By Maril Lee Brubaker, Weldon, California

MY GRANDMOTHER, Margaret Hockenberry, was a lovely little woman—a true pioneer—who once used her resourcefulness to save our family from being stranded without a penny.

In 1918, my family moved from Canton, Ohio to California. We set out in Dad's new Paige touring car packed with everything we owned.

Grandma, my two younger brothers and I sat snugly in the backseat while Mom and Dad tended to the driving up front.

In those days, garages were few and far between. There was only about 25 miles of paved road from Ohio to California, so we followed deep wheel ruts in uncharted fields most of the way.

Our ascent into the mountains on narrow roads was painfully slow. Each time we encountered a car coming toward us, we'd have to back up until we found a spot in the road wide enough for both autos.

Trouble on the Road

Dad had to snap on isinglass windows each time it rained. One stormy day, just outside a remote town in Nebraska, we heard a loud snap from under the Paige. We'd broken an axle. A friendly farmer towed us to town with two powerful horses. There was no hotel, so we found a campground and pitched our tent.

Dad walked to the railroad station to send for help by telegraph. The car dealer wired his response shortly, saying it would take 3 weeks to deliver an axle from Detroit.

We settled in for a long stay at the campground. Grandma had owned and operated hotels for years, so she took the lead in making our meals on the camp stove.

As time went by and the part was late to arrive, our funds dwindled. Dad went to look for work at a nearby farm...and Grandma went to work, too.

Back in Ohio, she had concocted a skin cream that she called "Madam Devon's Skin Food". It was white liquid with a drop of red food coloring to add a rosy hue. She'd even had some special labels made.

We walked to a drugstore, purchased some small jars and the ingredients needed for a batch of her beauty cream. Back at camp, she fired up the stove and began brewing her magic potion.

Just the Solution

Grandma had remembered to pack some labels, so I helped apply them. When a dozen or so jars and bottles were filled, Grandma was ready for business.

She and Mother filled travel cases with Madam Devon's Skin Food and walked to neighboring houses, selling their wares.

Grandma returned at dinnertime flushed and weary, but with a handful of bills and an empty case. Mom wasn't as successful—she hadn't sold any.

Grandma took her aside for a pep talk on how to approach prospective customers. Within a few days, Mom made some sales. Still, Grandma was a superior saleswoman.

By the time the axle finally arrived and we departed for the last leg of our journey, Madam Devon's Skin Food was known throughout that Nebraska neighborhood.

What was Grandma's secret? She told Mother to greet customers by saying, "Hello, dearie. I'd like to show you something that will make you prettier than you already are."

Grandma's favorite saying was, "A wisher's wishbone is where his backbone ought to be."

Her ingenuity put us back on the road to California! ←

COOKING UP A SALE. When the family broke down on their trip to California in 1918, Grandma Hockenberry (left) got out the pot and cooked up a batch of her famous skin cream under primitive conditions, much like the woman above making soap. Grandma was not only a manufacturer, she was a super seller who made money.

Mother Transformed Herself Into a Chef in One Weekend

By William Keim, Huntingdon, Pennsylvania

MY MOTHER firmly believed that anyone could do anything, if they were willing to work hard enough. When I was a boy during the Depression, she proved it to me twice.

One day when I was 13, she came home with several boxes of groceries and announced to my grandmother, "I want to learn to cook."

The two began scrambling around the kitchen, removing pots and pans from the oak cupboard. For the next hour or so, Gram gave her daughter quiet instructions.

QUICK STUDY. There was nothing his mother couldn't do, says Bill Keim (left, with Mom Eila)—from cooking to auto repair.

After stuffing a turkey and adding it to the chicken already in the oven, Mother said, "I bought some steak, too. I want to learn to 'Swiss' it the way you do."

"But we already have chicken and turkey started!" Gram protested. "Who's going to eat all this stuff?"

"Call the neighbors," Mother said.

Gram put her hands on her hips. "Eila," she said, "I've been trying to get you to learn to cook since you were a little girl. Why the sudden interest now? Learning to cook takes a while."

"It better not," Mother said with a smile. "I just took the job as chef at the Cottage Restaurant, and I start Monday morning."

Made Award-Winning Meals

She did learn to cook that weekend. Within a few months, the restaurants where she worked were winning Duncan Hines and Diners Club awards.

When I was 16, I traded my bicycle for an old Model A Ford that wouldn't run. A friend towed it home, where I tore the motor down and became lost in the intricacies of putting it back together.

When Mother saw what I was trying to do, her eyes lit up with pleasure. "Wait, Bill," she said. "I'll get a pair of your uncle's overalls and help you out."

After a half hour, she got impatient with my fumbling and ordered me away. When it got dark, she rigged up some lights and kept on working through the night.

At 6 o'clock the next morning, she woke me. "The car is finished and ready for a trial run," she said.

I stepped on the starter and the motor kicked in immediately. The car ran perfectly and continued to do so until I went into the Army 4 years later, during World War II. I sold the car for four times what I'd paid for it. ✦

TOUCH ACT TO FOLLOW. Elizabeth Begalka of Clear Lake, South Dakota says the greatest compliment she received was back in Slovakia, where relatives told her she was just like her beloved "Baba", Grandmother Anna Wargo (above). Elizabeth says she has a long way to go to measure up to Baba, who came to America alone in 1880. (See a picture of Elizabeth and her mother on page 46.)

A REAL PEARL. Pearl Elmquist was a beauty (left, on her wedding day in 1919) who could also handle a mean wrench (right), says daughter-in-law Carol Backstrom of Russell, Pennsylvania. During World War II, Pearl was a "Rosie the Riveter", working in machine shops. After the war, Pearl went to school and became a nurse.

The Mother of Invention

By Richard Thorpe, Travelers Rest, South Carolina

IN THE post-Depression years, my parents were textile workers, raising four children in a mill village. But Mom's poor health kept her from working most of the time.

Instead, she stayed home and did what she could to cut our cost of living and make our lives as pleasant as possible. She used her ingenuity to make sure her husband and children could have more.

Each day, the factory gave Dad a large piece of cloth to protect his clothes. At the end of his shift, the apron was dirty and greasy. Most workers threw theirs away, but Dad brought his home to Mom.

After bleaching out the stains, Mom used these cloths to make shirts and blouses, saving small scraps to make handkerchiefs. I was embarrassed by my homemade shirts—until the neighbors began to compliment them. They had no idea my shirts had once been Dad's aprons.

Mom never tossed out *any* old clothes until she'd stripped them of buttons, buckles and anything else that could be used later. "You never know when you'll need 'em," she'd say.

Mom knew how to stretch the food budget, too. She canned vegetables from our garden, lining our pantry shelves with butter beans, squash, tomatoes, okra and corn.

Used Flour Power

The chickens could hardly keep up with our demand for eggs, so Mom augmented our scrambled eggs with milk and flour. Served with grits or rice, they were delicious.

Mom's creativity also satisfied our emotional needs. Before Easter, many kids in the neighborhood got elaborate baskets filled with chocolate bunnies, candy eggs and artificial grass. We knew there was no room in our budget for such frivolous things.

Sensing our disappointment, Mom got to work on a substitute. Empty metal soda cartons were available free at the grocery store. Mom covered them with colorful crepe paper, added ornate bows and filled them with homemade goodies.

INVENTIVE MOM. Ella Mae Thorpe posed for a photo on Easter Day 1949.

Those beautiful baskets made us the envy of our peers.

Mom loved children and encouraged our friends to visit. On Halloween, our house was the most popular one in the village. Early in the day, she'd sterilize her big cast-iron wash pot. By night, it became a witch's cauldron.

Shared "Witches' Brew"

As the shadows began to lengthen, Mom filled the pot with cocoa, built a roaring fire around it and stood beside it wearing a black dress, stirring the mix until the neighborhood children got curious.

Finally one would ask, "What's in the pot, Mrs. Thorpe?"

"Witches' brew," she'd answer without cracking a smile.

"What you gonna do with it?"

"I'm gonna give it to young'uns when the sun goes down," she'd say.

"Is it poison?" they'd ask cautiously.

"Of course not. It tastes like hot chocolate. That's because I'm one of the good witches. Why don't you ask your momma if you can come back later and get some. There'll be cookies, too."

By dark, there were usually more than 2 dozen kids waiting to sample Mom's "brew".

Many people would say we were poor, but the

> *"She used ingenuity to make sure her family had more..."*

older I get, the more I realize how rich we were. Mom and Dad taught us there was always someone worse off than we were. We lived on Railroad Street, and I'm sure the hoboes riding the rails marked our house in some way, because we invariably had visitors looking for a meal.

If someone told my parents he was hungry, his motives were never questioned. Whatever we had to eat, the stranger was invited to share.

At times, that probably meant Mom had to add more flour and milk to the scrambled eggs. But I assure you she never had any complaints. ⬅

Late-Night Bakery Saw Family Through Depression

By Art Blair, Akron, Ohio

AFTER the stock market crash of 1929, Dad was laid off from the Firestone plant in South Akron, Ohio.

With a farming background and an elementary-school education, he had few skills to offer in an urban job market with high unemployment. Meanwhile, there were four mouths to feed and no appreciable savings.

Mom went to the corner grocery store and made a deal with the manager. He let her have 25 pounds of flour, some sugar, eggs, shortening and other supplies with the understanding she'd return within a week to pay for them.

Each evening, Dad watched my sister and me while Mom slept. At midnight, she got up and started preparing dough for bread and German coffee cakes.

She finished baking at around 5 or 6 a.m. Dad got up then, loaded the baked goods into big boxes and carried them down the street on his shoulders, yelling, "Get your fresh bread and cakes here!"

People who were still employed would respond, knowing they were helping an unemployed neighbor. It also meant they got to enjoy baked goods still warm from the oven.

Dad Walked a Route

The bread sold for a nickel a loaf, and the coffee cakes were a dime each. Mom paid the store manager each week for the previous week's supplies, and Dad established a route for his door-to-door sales.

With experience, Mom learned how to increase her nightly production quite a bit. No matter how much she made,

BAKER AND BABY. When things were tough in the Depression, Art Blair's mother, Mildred (above with Art in 1929), made some dough.

Dad was always able to hawk it all.

Each morning, Mom called Dad and me when the baking was done. The house smelled so good!

I somehow managed to find myself left alone in the kitchen. So, I inspected all the bread and cake, picking out one of each that looked best. Then I'd stick my finger in them! When my parents "discovered" the damaged items, those were left at home for us.

Many years later, I learned my grinning parents were standing on the other side of the swinging kitchen door every morning, watching me through the window as I decided which baked goods looked best!

In the early 1930s, I was old enough to help. The state had small sales tax stamps, which I tore from a pad and gave to each customer. My parents said that my presence added to our clientele because people enjoyed seeing me take my job so seriously.

In retrospect, it gave me excellent training for the work ethic that served me well throughout my working life.

Mom continued baking, and Dad and I continued making deliveries, until jobs became available again through the WPA around 1934-35. ✦

WINDOW TO HER WORLD. Stella Joseph loved to sit near the window and sew, recalls her daughter, Florence Paul of Santa Ana, California. The window was usually open so she could visit with neighbors.

She Swept Surprises Under the Rug

STRONG WILL and a whole lot of spunk...those words will forever describe my all-Italian mother, Mabel Ida Tira Santucci.

Mother's parents emigrated from Italy to Illinois, where she was born. When she started seventh grade, her

MORTGAGE FREE. Mabel Santucci wasn't floored when the note came due—she rolled up the rug! Mabel poses proudly above in 1942.

father told her she'd have to quit school at the end of the year and go to work. She wanted a diploma so badly, she arranged with the principal to do seventh- and eighth-grade work all in one year—quite a feat for a girl who barely spoke English when she started school.

My parents married in 1929. As I was growing up, Father played violin and taught music for a living. He and Mother also kept a tavern. Whenever there was an extra dollar in the cash register, Ma would "steal" it and tuck it under her bedroom rug.

When the $2,000 mortgage came due, my father worried we couldn't pay the bill. Then ma asked me to help her roll back the rug. Dollar bills were everywhere! (And just a few more than 2,000 of them.) Dad was surprised and happy. Yes, Mom always had something up her sleeve—and under the carpet!

—Eleanor Santucci Flower
Ottawa, Illinois

Thrifty Ladies Saved Cotton Bags from Trash Bin

BOTH my mother and mother-in-law lived through the harsh Depression years and never lost their sense of frugality.

In the early 1960s, I was working for a firm that did labeling. One day I brought home 500 all-cotton 10-pound bags about 12 inches square. The bags had been printed incorrectly in red ink and were headed for the trash bin.

Both women were elated by this windfall. First, they unstrung the thread at each bag's opening, making huge balls of twine that would last the rest of their lives.

Then they bleached the bags until they were snowy white and presented their four sons and numerous grandsons with spanking-new handkerchiefs for Christmas—at least 100 apiece. To this day, some of the "boys" are still using those sturdy handkerchiefs.

From the remaining bags, their four daughters received ever-lasting dishcloths. I still have some of them, more than 30 years later. Those women knew how to save!

—Kay Reikowski
West Allis, Wisconsin

As Girl Grew, So Did Her Favorite Dress

MOTHER made all our clothes, but my sisters and I never had a dress made of new material until we were grown. When we outgrew something, Mother would carefully rip out all the seams and turn the pieces into something new.

Such was the case with a dress Mother created when I was about 8, in Seattle, in 1929. The dress had a white bodice, pleated print skirt and a pieced neckline tie. I loved that dress.

I was growing fast, though. The next year, Mother added 4 inches to the hem of the skirt. The following year, she put a white insert at the waist. The third year, she cut down the necktie and inserted it

between the new waistline and the skirt. Eventually a third piece was set in, too.

Soon it was 1933, I was 12 years old, stood 5-foot-8 and wished I'd never seen that dress!

Today, I recognize the humor, love and frugality it represented. Talking about the "hard times" always makes me smile. They were really the *good* times, for all the lessons we learned.

—Cora Armstrong
Spokane, Washington

Mom's Clever Window Box Made a Handy Fridge

OUR FARM in the Missouri Ozarks had no electricity in the 1930s and '40s, but refrigeration wasn't a problem for Mom. She invented a system of her own.

She and my youngest brother built a 2-foot-square box, open on one side, then removed the screen from a north living room window. They nailed the box over the windowsill and covered it with a piece of galvanized roofing to keep out rain and snow.

Now Mom had a "refrigerator", just by opening the window. In winter, she used it as a freezer to hold cleaned rabbits, squirrels and quail. We also had lots of ice cream made from our own milk and eggs.

When electricity finally got to us and Dad bought Mom a refrigerator, she refused to do away with her little box in the window. When they celebrated their 50th anniversary in 1966, she was still using it to cool her pies.

—Florene Nelson
Lynchburg, Missouri

WINDOW PANTRY. Florene Nelson's folks smiled for this picture on their 50th anniversary in March 1966. Note the box in window behind them.

Resourceful Woman Wouldn't Let Loss of Arm Stop Her

By Mary Ware, Fort Valley, Georgia

MY MOTHER had only one arm, but we never thought of her as handicapped. Emma Rodgers was exceptional, a woman of remarkable talents—and she never complained.

Mother lost her arm after an accident in the sugarcane fields when she was 10. The arm was amputated just below her shoulder, but she continued to do her chores along with her nine siblings. Through the years, she worked hard on farms in Missouri and Arkansas.

As a young mother, she'd place my baby brother on her left shoulder while she did household chores. He never fell off. The doctor asked her to show him how she managed to pin a diaper on Willie with one hand. He was amazed.

In 1923, when Father needed someone to meet him at the train station, my independent mother taught herself to drive our Model T. She cranked it up and met him herself.

To supplement our income, we took in boarders. Mother cooked, washed, ironed and prepared lunches for everyone, in addition to raising chickens, milking our cow, tending a garden and canning fruits and vegetables.

Cooked for Guests

She was known as the best cook in our community, and we had guests for dinner almost every Sunday. Some even asked if they could go into the kitchen to watch her prepare the meal.

Mother was creative, too. She hand-painted tablecloths, did hem-stitching, tatted with a shuttle in her mouth and embroidered clothes, dresser scarves and bedspreads.

She also made all our costumes for school and church plays. I didn't have a store-bought dress until I was 13. There were only four things Mother *couldn't* do—file her nails, crochet, braid her long hair or cut up a chicken.

A devout Christian, Mother made herself available to the sick, needy and bereaved, and to new mothers. When Willie was an infant, she nursed him alongside another woman's sick baby. The doctor had said only "mother's milk" would save him. The child's family was forever grateful.

Although she's been gone many years, people still come to me with great stories of things Mother did—things I never knew about. In my 76 years, she was the strongest, toughest woman I've ever known. ↚

NOT A HANDICAP. Emma Rodgers did most everything with one arm, as these photos from the late '20s and early '30s attest. From her courting days (center left, continuing clockwise) to carrying baby Willie Jr., she was mother (with Juanita and Bernice) and wife (with Willie and Willie Jr.).

TOUGH AND GENTLE. That was Myrtle Roberts Marshall, who could make butter and soap, hatch chicks and turn corncobs into sweet syrup.

Mom Was Like A Magician

By Bobbie Pope, Paris, Texas

EVERYONE who knew my mother loved her. She had a merry spirit and laughed often. As Myrtle Roberts Marshall went about her chores, she sang church hymns or whistled a little tune.

The soft music seemed to drift out from her stiff-starched bonnet, which she wore year-round. Her singing was good for her and may have helped others along the way.

Mother and Father moved into the first home they ever owned in 1925. To my three sisters and me, Mother was a magician.

She could take white milk and make yellow butter; put eggs in a warm box and produce fluffy chicks; take pieces of material without a pattern and sew dresses for us; and turn stale grease, water and lye into hard white soap.

Made Sweet Treat

Once she boiled dry red corncobs in water, strained the water and added sugar, making a thick syrup to pour over our biscuits. Imagine that!

When the Great Depression began, life changed little for Mother. She could make do with whatever we had. There was always food on the table for us

SLOVAKIAN FINERY. In 1934, Elizabeth Junas put her daughter, Elizabeth Louise, on her knee for this photo of their finery. Elizabeth was proud of her heritage and dressed her daughter in this charming little girl's dress from Slovakia. Elizabeth Louise's grandmother, Anna Wargo (see photo on page 41), had emigrated from Slovakia to Pennsylvania in 1880, and the whole family lived near each other. It was tough for the immigrants to make a living in the anthracite coal mines, but Anna's daughter followed her lead in sewing, cooking and holding the family together. Today, Elizabeth Louise Begalka lives in Clear Lake, South Dakota and loves to recall and honor her mother and grandmother, two creative and strong women.

and enough to share with relatives who were out of work or homeless.

When the surrounding cotton fields were ready to harvest, Mother sewed canvas sacks for us. With her help, my sisters and I made enough "cotton-pickin' money" to buy our school shoes and coats and material for dresses.

She reared her children, cared for a bedridden husband for 6 years and through it all never stopped singing her hymns.

My dear mother was tough in character, but gentle in spirit. The memories of her strength will stay in my heart forever. ←

Grandma Recycled Before the Word Was Invented

By Pearl Rainwater
Marysville, Washington

NEARLY ALL my childhood memories and influence center on my strong-minded grandmother. She was the wife of a homesteader on 160 acres of North Dakota prairie, the mother of 13 and the one person willing to raise an orphaned child. That was me.

Annie Kirkpatrick was ahead of her time and was recycling before that was even a word. She found a second use for everything, and taught me that "waste not, want not" was a way of life on her Golva, North Dakota farm in the early 1930s.

Flour, sugar, salt and oatmeal sacks were turned into tablecloths, dish towels and pillowcases, which Grandma brightened with her original embroidery.

Stacks o' Sacks

Mattress covers, sheets, aprons, dresses, baby clothes and bloomers were made from those sacks, too. Life seemed to revolve around cotton sacks bleached white in the North Dakota sun.

Smaller Bull Durham bags were dyed bright colors, cut into strips and hooked into beautiful rugs and wall hangings. The strings from the bags' openings were tied end to end and

"WASTE NOT, WANT NOT" was the motto of Annie Kirkpatrick. And when hail brought disaster, why, she just made ice cream!

wound into a collection the size of a soccer ball.

Grandma used the string to tie packages for mailing…anchor bean, pea and tomato plants…and crochet lace collars, doilies and table covers.

Every autumn, Grandma canned several big boxes of peaches and pears. Each piece of fruit in the boxes was wrapped in a square of pink tissue paper. My job was to flatten each sheet and pile them neatly in the pantry.

When we had company visiting, we would carry a handful of that pink tissue to the outhouse. It was like having designer toilet paper—and much nicer than the usual page from

last year's Sears, Roebuck catalog.

We even recycled cow chips. When the sun dried them to the consistency of cardboard, we gathered them for the cookstove. They were easy to light, made a very hot fire and had no odor at all.

After the corn harvest, the corn roots were pulled up and saved for propping up new tomato and cabbage plants the following spring.

By the time those plants were strong and healthy, the dry corn root could be burned in the stove.

Sometimes, strong hailstorms left us with a ruined garden, beaten-down crops, broken windows and balls of ice piled against the buildings.

No Crying Over Spilt Milk

Instead of sitting down and crying over her losses, Grandma would say, "Come on, let's go make some ice cream."

She'd mix eggs, milk, cream and sugar while I gathered a bucket of hailstones for the ice cream freezer. Ice cream was a real treat in those days before refrigeration.

I suspect the neighbors must have known about Grandma's use for hailstones, because they often seemed to

> *"Grandma could find a second use for everything…"*

drop by to "see how we were doing" right after a storm.

Grandma knew about covered wagons and sod shanties, grasshopper swarms and blizzards, setting hens and baby chicks. She wrote poetry and taught me to polka. She taught me to pray "Now I lay me down to sleep" so well that I still say it today.

She was the first lady in the county to learn how to can fruits and vegetables in glass jars. She made headcheese and sauerkraut. She could trim a wild plum bush into a beautiful Christmas tree, and she taught me my sums on a small chalkboard by lamplight.

To Grandma, there was no such thing as a male job or a female job. If something needed to be done, you just got busy and did it. Grandma was a *real* pioneer woman. ✦

CAN-DO GRANDMA. There were always canned goods around Grandma's house, like these. But what Pearl remembers best is the tissue paper the fruit came in.

SAILOR SUIT. Evelyn Corzine shows off suit Aunt Eva made from Evelyn's husband's Navy uniform.

Aunt's Sewing Skills Kept Whole Family in Finery

MY AUNT EVA grew up in a rural area without gas stoves, electricity or indoor plumbing. Each member of the family had to work together to make farm life run smoothly. In 1895, when Aunt Eva was about 15, she began doing all the family sewing.

As Aunt Eva's older siblings married and started families of their own, she made layettes for each baby, plus most of the clothing for everyone else. This was a tremendous help, especially during the Depression years.

Aunt Eva took pride in her impeccable work, giving attention to the smallest detail. She never had any lessons, only tips from the older generation. She never used commercial patterns, either, but her creations were always elegant.

When Aunt Eva married, sewing became her career. No challenge was too much for her.

When her customers brought in their husbands' worn shiny suits, she carefully ripped them apart, ironed out the creases and reversed the fabric to make beautiful suits for the women. They were so professionally tailored you'd think they came from Fifth Avenue in New York City. —*Evelyn Corzine*
New Port Richey, Florida

Mom's Fried Pies Were a Big Hit with WPA Crew

IN 1937, my dad's WPA crew was installing a sewer pipe down the street from our house. Money was badly needed in those days, and Mom decided she could help.

She had an ample supply of home-canned peaches, apples, blackberries and blueberries. Every night, she'd roll out pastry and make a big batch of fruit filling. The next morning, she'd melt lard in a big iron skillet, drop in some pastry, top it with fruit and fry the pies until they were golden brown.

By the time the lunch whistle blew, the workers would be lined up outside the dining room window while Mom and I passed them fried pies wrapped in pieces of newspaper. We sold them for a dime each. There were never any left over for us—Mom was making too much money!

FRYING GOODIES. Like the woman above, Patsy Warwick's mom made good things in the frying pan.

All over our yard, men would be sitting under the trees, eating their brown-bag lunches and Mom's fruit pies while their bosses relaxed in the rocking chairs on our front porch.
—*Patsy Warwick*
Jacksonville, Florida

Mother Pleaded for Ration Stamps for School Lunches

DURING World War II, my mother, Virginia Hempfling, was president of the PTA, which oversaw the lunch program at our school in Walton, Kentucky. The schools were issued ration stamps for food—but never enough.

Mother would set up a card table in our living room to count stamps and work out 2 weeks' worth of menus.

She'd spend hours, sometimes days, trying to figure out how to feed all those children with the few stamps she had. I sometimes saw her cry because there weren't enough stamps for sugar, flour, eggs and meat.

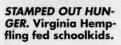

STAMPED OUT HUNGER. Virginia Hempfling fed schoolkids.

We didn't have a phone or car, so Mother would walk around the neighborhood calling on other PTA members, asking for any stamps they could spare.

I can recall only one occasion when she didn't collect enough to serve meat for the students' lunch.
—*Genna Murray*
Augusta, Kentucky

Spring Recitals Were a Bright Spot in Children's Lives

IN THE EARLY '30s, my mother was raising four children alone in a cold-water flat in Worcester, Massachusetts. To support us, she took in sewing from the neighbors and taught piano. She taught us to play the piano, too.

In winter, the parlor and dining room in our flat were closed off. The piano was moved to the back room, where Mother gave her lessons.

At night, after supper, we'd rush into our pajamas and head for the back room. Mother would play pieces like *Let's Face the Music and Dance* while we kids pretended to be Fred Astaire and Ginger Rogers.

In April, excitement filled the air. The parlor and dining room were reopened, and the piano was moved back to the parlor. We polished the furniture, borrowed chairs from the funeral parlor and invited relatives and friends to our annual recital.

We received simple prizes like cards featuring composers, new notebooks and homemade mittens. Then everyone filed into the kitchen for hot chocolate and cookies. Those were wonderful days, because of our wonderfully ingenious mother.
—*Thelma Cline Provost*
West Boylston, Massachusetts

PIANO PUMPERS. The Cline kids (from left, Verona, Florence, Thelma and Robert) had fun learning to play piano, with their mother as the teacher, in the 1930s.

Mom Stretched Hamburger With Eggs and Crackers

IN OUR FAMILY of 11, there was never enough food to go around. But Mother knew how to stretch expensive foods with less-costly ones.

When there were still six of us at home, we sometimes had the privilege of buying a pound of hamburger. To make enough patties to go around, Mother added cracker crumbs and a couple of eggs.

We loved those burgers, and they were probably better for us, too, with more grain and less red meat.

I don't have to scrimp on the food bill now, but I still pull this little trick from my hat now and then for old time's sake—and for our health.
—*Gay Lorenz*
Saratoga, California

Thoughtful Solutions Made Holidays Special

WE LIVED in Syracuse, New York during the Depression. My father was lucky to keep his job, but his pay was slashed by 75%.

Our furniture had seen better days, and Mom patched it to keep the stuffing from coming out.

As Halloween approached, I thought about having a party, but I didn't want my friends to see that furniture. I never said anything about it to Mom, but I'm sure she knew how I felt.

Ever resourceful, she suggested I have a party and drape sheets over the furniture to make it look spooky. It was the best party ever, and my delicate teen ego remained intact.

One winter when times were really tough, some of the families on our block couldn't afford Christmas gifts for their children. So Mom canvassed her friends and collected a bunch of old dolls.

They had dirty faces and wild hair, but Mom carefully scrubbed them, combed the hair, arranged it in curls and made new outfits for each doll, complete with shoes she'd made from an old pocketbook.

Then she delivered them to the parents of little girls to put under their Christmas trees.
—*Janet Trapp*
Hendersonville, North Carolina

Like Yeast, Mom Rose to Every Occasion

By Ruth Gash Taylor, Cedar Rapids, Iowa

SURPRISE! Her mother, Olive, never liked to have her picture taken, says Ruth Taylor. But she was caught this time, emerging from the chicken coop. It was just one of the many jobs that had to be done to keep the family together when Ruth's father died.

SEWING SENSATION. Emja Havlena (right, at 22, and above, in 1970) was born in Czechoslovakia in 1896. She was such a good seamstress, says daughter Gloria Simpson of St. Louis, Missouri, that when she re-made hand-me-downs from an aunt, friends wondered how Gloria and her sister could be so well dressed. After all, their father was working only 1 or 2 days a week. "Mother also planted a large garden and made the most delicious soup from the vegetables she grew. I can still taste it," adds Gloria.

"DAD is dead," I announced tearfully.

Mother never said a word. She snatched the camphor bottle from the shelf and began running down the road through the rain. I stared after her. What good was camphor? Dad was dead!

Dad was driving me back from my piano lesson in a thunderstorm when he suddenly slumped in my lap. I was 7, and at first, I thought Dad was playing a game. Then I looked at him and I knew.

The Velie gently meandered along the road until it bumped into a fence, where the engine died.

We had no close relatives. It was my mother, sister and me against the world.

The Great Depression then settled over Iowa, along with the drought, bitter winters and searing summers. Corn brought 10¢ a bushel; oats, a nickel. But like yeast, Mother rose to every occasion. She worked as hard on the farm as any man.

In Mother's day, a clean fencerow was a status symbol. She battled heat, chiggers, poison ivy and bumblebees to keep hers looking like city lawns.

Cut Lawns for Lessons

She mowed my piano teacher's lawn with a reel-type mower in exchange for my lessons. When the grasshoppers came, she said, "Catch as many as you can for the chickens. It will save feed."

Mother made sheets, pillowcases, underwear and kitchen curtains from flour sacks, after carefully eradicating

> *"Catch grasshoppers for the chickens— it will save feed..."*

the advertising. She laughed about a less-thorough neighbor who made a pair of children's underpants that read "Mother's Best" across the seat.

Laundry was done on a board with homemade soap, and the wash water was always recycled. Mother's flowers, particularly the moss roses, thrived on it.

We had a car, but it never seemed to run, so we walked more than we rode. We walked 5 miles to town for groceries and 5 miles home again. A 24-pound sack of flour gets mighty heavy.

When our financial situation grew critical, Mother became a cook on a Mississippi River dredge, working between Le Claire, Iowa and Cape Girardeau, Missouri. She was able to come home for the weekend when the boat docked in Keokuk, Iowa. Later, she cooked for the Army Corps of Engineers on their office boat.

When my sister and I grew up, she became a teacher, and I went to work for a newspaper. We still own the farm that has been in our family since 1840.

Thanks to Mother's sharp thinking and hard work, our family was able to stay together. In so many ways, she was a genius. ❧

DURING the Depression, we were living in the small mining town of Mascot, Tennessee. After the Crash, my father's job at the American Zinc Company was cut to only 2 days a week.

That wasn't enough to support a family of 12. So Mother, Diana Killian, used her sewing ability and other skills to help us through those years.

Mother never had a sewing lesson in her life, but she could copy a design from the Sears catalog to the last detail. She saved her scraps to piece colorful quilts for our beds, and she cut the good parts from worn overalls to make heavy comforters.

When a coat became faded, Mother would take it apart, press it and turn the material inside out to make a coat that looked brand-new. She bleached 100-pound feed sacks snowy white, then used them to make bed and bath linens and undergarments.

The Bible speaks of a virtuous woman who used fine linens to look after her household. My mother used cot-

FEED SACKS AND ELBOW GREASE. That's what Diana Killian used to make linens and undergarments for her family.

ton prints, bleached feed sacks and elbow grease. As the Bible says, "Her children arise...and call her blessed".

—*Mildred Davis, Knoxville, Tennessee*

Grandmother Worked and Bartered to Help Family

By Lorraine Kincaid
Bolivar, Missouri

IN 1924, when I was about 2 years old, my pregnant mother, little sister and I went to live with our grandparents in Burtonsville, Maryland. My remarkable grandmother made a home for all of us, and we lived there until my siblings and I married.

If my grandmother, Mary Coar, were living today, she should run for President. I guarantee she could balance the federal budget!

We fared well during the Depression, thanks in part to Grandmother's ingenuity. She saved used Christmas wrappings, ironed them and stored them for the next holiday. My sister and I loved to iron the Christmas paper.

She was an expert at bartering, too. She paid for a Singer sewing machine and a beautiful oak china cabinet with eggs and dressed chickens. She also bartered for a beautiful 12-piece place setting of Haviland china.

She Shared Everything

Though we ate a lot of potato soup for supper, our meals were served on matching dinnerware, and the table was set with pretty tablecloths or hand-crocheted place mats. We didn't even know we were poor.

Grandmother knew how to make us feel blessed, and she shared whatever we had with anyone who needed it.

BUDGET BALANCER. When things were tight in the Depression, Mary Coar improvised.

On Sunday mornings, the "tramps" who roamed the country often came in the yard, asking for something to eat. Grandmother never turned them away. She'd seat them at the kitchen table

and serve them pancakes, eggs, sausage and hot coffee. Then she'd send them on their way with sandwiches, fruit and cake or cookies.

Before anyone had heard of "solar energy", Grandmother used it to make strawberry, cherry and plum jams. She'd put the fruit in a big dishpan, sprinkle it with sugar, put the pan on a stool in a sunny spot in the backyard and cover the pan with window glass.

That Was *Slow* Cooking

She'd bring the pan in at night and stir the fruit, then put it back in the sun the next morning. Her jam usually "cooked" in 3 days, and it was the best jam anyone ever ate!

A religious woman, Grandmother was a strong disciplinarian. We weren't allowed to dance or stay out past midnight, even on New Year's Eve. On Sunday, we couldn't read the Sunday paper, play ball or make too much noise. But we did have fun playing Rook, Old Maid and other games.

We learned to make our beds as soon as we got out of them, do our chores without complaint, to pray and be thankful for what we had. Many times we thought Grandmother was too strict, but now we appreciate the values she taught us. She was truly a remarkable woman. ✦

BUSY AS BEES. A quilting bee at the house of Beatrice Stanger (second from left above) was always an occasion, as was this one in Marriott, Utah in 1968.

Grandma Made Quilts for Love, Not Money

By Lois Huston, Kaysville, Utah

I LOVED HELPING my grandma, Beatrice Stanger, make quilts. It was so much fun to watch her prepare the neat stacks of cut fabric shapes and then see the pattern take place as she sewed them together.

During the early 1950s, I was always glad to hear the *click-clack* of her treadle sewing machine when I visited her home in Marriott, Utah.

When the quilt top was pieced, my mother or aunt would help Grandma put the quilt on the frame—straight boards tied together and anchored to kitchen chairs with strips of cloth. They'd spread out the fluffy batting, smooth it with a yardstick and tack on the top.

Now it was time for a quilting bee. Aunts, cousins, friends and neighbors were invited to bring their thimbles, a potluck dish for lunch and perhaps a little gossip.

My cousins and I admired the beautiful patterns, searching for pieces that had come from our favorite dresses. We often sat under the quilt, watching nimble fingers manipulate the stitches. This allowed *us* to hear a little gossip, too.

The most exciting part was the unveiling. When the last stitch was done, all would gather to watch as the quilt was unrolled and the tacks removed.

Then the quilt was turned so we could see the design on the back, and the stitches were carefully examined to make sure they met Grandma's high standards. She was quite particular and was known to take out and redo stitches after some ladies went home.

I don't know how many quilts Grandma made, but they filled her closets. She was offered considerable sums of money for them, but that wasn't her intent. She gave all her quilts away.

Quilts Bequeathed

Each grandchild received one upon marrying. As young girls, we loved picking out which one would be ours, although we changed our minds many times. In the end, Grandma usually made that decision.

Friends and relatives saved all their sewing scraps to give to Grandma. She had boxes and drawers full of them. Even after I married and moved far away, I saved my scraps to take home to her. She was always grateful for them.

I was rewarded with a second quilt, one of the last Grandma made. To my delight, it had been made mostly from the scraps I'd given her. Looking at each piece brings back fond memories of my children...and my sweet grandma. ↩

QUILT OF MANY COLORS. Beatrice displays one of the many quilts she and her friends and relatives made.

She Turned Simple Meals Into Special Treats

MY MOTHER was a very clever and creative person, and that helped our family of five get through the Depression.

Three days a week, she scrubbed floors on her hands for the more affluent people in town. This supplemented Dad's meager income as a tinsmith.

Mom could make the simplest foods a special treat. We loved boiled pinto

BLUE-PLATE SPECIALS. Donald Bouma's mom, Anna (above), always made sure the meals were special.

beans with Blue Karo Syrup simply because she made the meal a special event. We could have them *only* on Wednesday nights. Begging for them on Monday was to no avail. We came to look forward to that special bean dinner.

Then there were Mom's "Interurban Beach sandwiches". For holiday picnics, we'd squeeze into relatives' cars and head for Interurban Beach on Lake Michigan, about 40 miles from our home in Grand Rapids.

We'd have sandwiches of sliced red baloney and fresh liver baloney, which came in casings about the size of a 50-cent piece.

This was exactly what we had for lunch most days, but for the holiday, Mom cut the sandwiches diagonally instead of vertically. It was something special she did only for holidays.

In later years, when Mom's bones ached from arthritis, her one complaint was that she could no longer kneel to pray beside her bed at night.
—*Donald Bouma, Sun City, Arizona*

Selling Home-Cooked Meals Was One Hot Idea

DURING the dust bowl days of 1936, our family of eight moved to a rented farm near Lebanon, Kansas. We had little money except for the small weekly egg and cream checks, but we ate well. We raised chickens, had a huge garden and butchered our own meat.

Mother did all the cooking on a wood-burning stove, which made the kitchen unbearably hot during the blistering summers. She longed for an oil stove, but our finances made that impossible.

In 1939, our landlord sent three carpenters to build a new barn, and Mother offered to cook for them at 25¢ per meal. For 6 weeks, she made them sausage, eggs and hotcakes for breakfast; and roast beef, fried chicken, mashed potatoes and gravy, creamed beans and peas and fruit pies for dinner and supper.

By the time the barn was finished, Mother had saved the $15 she needed to buy her new coal-oil cooking stove and oven.
—*Randall Maydew, Albuquerque, New Mexico*

COOKING WITH OIL. Lelia Maydew (below, in 1969) cooked to finance a new oil stove for herself.

Mom Used Wringer to Speed Bean-Shelling

SHELL BEANS were one of our favorite foods, but removing the soft bean from the shell was a tedious task. Mom came up with an easy method that had the neighbors knocking on her door for instructions.

She'd dump a bushel of beans into the tub of our wringer washing machine, then feed each bean, pointed end down, through the wringer.

The beans would fall back into the tub, and the shells would go through the wringer and fall into a basket. We had to be careful not to get our fingers caught in the wringer, of course.

A bushel of beans was shelled in no time, and we moved on to the canning process. As Mom said, it was "2 hours from vine to jar".   · —*Dottie Carlson, Warwick, Rhode Island*

DRY BEAN. With a wringer like this, Dottie's mom solved the tedium of bean-shelling.

Brown Brothers

She Became Famous for Wartime No-Pumpkin Pie

MY GREAT-GRANDMOTHER, Effie Dean King, became famous during World War I for her contribution to the war effort—a recipe for "pumpkinless pumpkin pie".

She'd made an Indian meal pudding in an effort to help conserve food, especially wheat. When she tasted it, she found it tasted exactly like pumpkin pie.

"I served the pie at dinner and neither my husband nor my daughter noticed that it wasn't pumpkin," she told a newspaper reporter. "They could scarcely believe it when I told them there was not a particle of pumpkin in it."

Her recipe, published in several newspapers, was simple: Scald 1 quart of milk, then add a scant cup of Indian meal and a little salt. When cold, add two eggs, cinnamon and ginger to taste. Sweeten with brown sugar. Put a little cream or milk on top and bake.

In November 1917, Great-Grandmother sent the recipe to the National Emergency Garden Commission, which sent it on to the *USS Grant*.

A baker on that Navy ship served the dessert to "500 pie-hungry men", whose only complaint was that there wasn't enough.

The baker was so impressed that he wrote to Great-Grandmother and asked her to come up with recipes for "gingerless gingerbread" and "meatless mincemeat pie". And she did.
—*Carol Roberts, Afton, New York*

PATRIOTIC PIE. Effie King came up with a pie that helped win WWI.

Brrr-illiant Idea Kept Snow Out of Drafty House

DURING the blizzard of 1949, our little farmhouse in South Dakota was *so* cold. One night when Mom came into our bedroom to tuck us in, she saw snow had sifted in through cracks in the wall and around the windows.

The next morning, Mom took the weed sprayer, filled it with water and sprayed it on the windows and walls outside. The water froze in the subzero temperature, and the ice kept the house sealed up and toasty warm.

Mom's philosophy was, "If it works for the Eskimos in Alaska, why won't it work for a farm family in subzero South Dakota?" And it did. We slept in cozy comfort the rest of that extremely cold winter.
—*Billie Schaible*
Pierre, South Dakota

Mother's Able Hands Were Always Busy

MOM'S TALENTS seldom went unrecognized...I learned that at an early age!

My mother always won recognition for the fabulous costumes she made for me in our elementary school programs during the 1930s. Many of them were made from crepe paper, since the school didn't have enough money for material.

No one had any money in those days, so these school functions were important events in the neighborhood and our only entertainment.

It wasn't until much later that I learned my leading lady-roles were based more on *Mom's* talents than mine!
—*Eva Jacqueline Hughes, Arp, Texas*

SEW TALENTED. Eva Hughes' mom, Thelma, aided Eva's acting. Thelma smiles below in '46, with daughter Gayle.

Quick Thinking Dried Heartbroken Boy's Tears

MOMMA was a bighearted softie, and there's one incident involving her that our family still laughs about.

Cousins from Philadelphia were visiting our Luray, Virginia farm in 1943. We children were jumping off the (clean) pigpen. One of my young cousins, Donnie, landed on a hen and broke her neck. That little boy was absolutely devastated.

He picked up the hen and took it to Momma, begging her through his tears to fix it.

Momma told Donnie to go sit on the front porch and she'd see what she could do. She sent Daddy out the back door for another hen, loosely tied a white rag around its neck and took it to Donnie.

She told him he could take the rag off in a few minutes and turn the hen loose. He was sure Momma had brought it back to life.

After our cousins left the next morning, Momma fixed us a big dinner of chicken and dumplings with the real victim.
—*Mrs. Leo Davis*
Middlebrook, Virginia

One Poor Family's Gift to Another Came from the Heart

By Kay Adler, Gurnee, Illinois

I GREW UP in a small farming community with my parents and five siblings. We never had much money, so Christmas was a struggle for Mom and

> "I'll never forget how proud of Mom I felt..."

Dad. We usually got one toy, a pair of pajamas and sometimes an outfit.

When I was 9 years old, a very poor family with 10 children moved to our community. As Christmas approached, our school prepared for its traditional gift exchange.

The students exchanged names with classmates, bringing a $1 gift to put under the tree. The seven school-age children from the new family were the

only ones who didn't participate.

When we told Mom about this, she called my teacher and asked if there was some way to provide gifts for those children.

Perhaps some other families could buy them, or maybe the school could. The teachers met to discuss it but decided it wouldn't be fair to the other families.

Nevertheless, Mom called three more times with suggestions about how to include those children, and she was flatly told not to get involved.

She Stood up to Them

Mom was a loving, giving person but seldom assertive. I'll never forget the twinkle in her eye when she asked us kids if we'd be willing to give up something special. We were all for it and got

A TRUE GIVER. Her mom, Hazel (second from left), taught the teacher a lesson in giving, says Kay (left), with sisters Wanda and Sue.

busy. My sisters and I washed our dolls and dressed them as prettily as we could. My brothers washed and polished their trucks and tractors so they looked as new as possible. It was a real team effort, and we had *so much fun* wrapping those gifts.

Because Mom wasn't supposed to get involved, this had to be our secret. We couldn't tell anyone the gifts had come from us.

On the day of the gift exchange, we very carefully placed the gifts behind the trees in all six classrooms so the teachers wouldn't discover them.

I'll never forget how proud and happy I felt when my teacher called out the names of the two children who were in my classroom. She stood glaring at me as she handed them their gifts.

But my focus was on the children as they excitedly opened their presents. The girl gently cradled my doll in her arms, and the little boy held my brother's truck so proudly.

While I waited outside for the bus, I saw the other five children playing with their dolls and trucks. They were the happiest kids in the whole world.

As I watched them play, I was so proud of my mom for following her heart and standing up for what she believed in. The teachers had admonished her not to buy gifts for the children, and she hadn't. These gifts came from the heart. ✦

NO HALF-HEARTED EFFORT. Eleanor Millar (left) watched with her brothers as their mother, Eleanor Wenzlaff, showed how she got by on half their income when her husband was inducted into the Army. The local paper did a story in 1944.

WASHDAY BLUES. Monday wasn't the only day a housewife worked hard. As the old saw goes, "Man may work from sun to sun, but a woman's work is never done." That was especially true in the so-called "good old days", with backbreaking washboards, outdoor plumbing and no electricity. But the women did it then and still do today.

Chapter Four

Woman's Work Is Never Done

So here you are, 24 years old, with two small children and suddenly without a husband. Your sole asset is an elderly two-story duplex house.

What to do? That's a real puzzler when you have nary a marketable skill and lack a high school diploma.

Well, there's welfare.

No, never!

So you try to pull a busted world back together as best you can and get to work on the problem. Going back to high school for the two courses you lack to graduate is out of the question. But, they say you can take the courses through an accredited correspondence school. So you enroll, pass with flying colors and get the prized piece of paper.

Now it's time to pound the pavement and check out the job market. You find one, at shamefully low pay, but it's a job.

Ah, the life of a working mother! You get up at 6 in the morning, fix breakfast, get the kids ready for school, dress for work and trot to the bus stop.

More Than 8 Hours

You put in your 8-hour stand-up day as a bank filing clerk and catch the bus home, stopping on the way to pick up all the groceries you can carry. Meanwhile, an elderly angel has been tending the kids since they got home from school.

Howdy, kids. Mom's dog-tired and her feet ache. So give me a hand fixing supper, and we'll talk about your schoolday.

Of course, while all this is going on, there's the house to look after. There's a dripping faucet to fix. A room to repaint. Storms and screens to change. A lawn to mow. Problems, problems. So you learn to be plumber, painter and handyman. Okay, *handywoman*.

And that's just in decent weather. When cold weather kicks in, you have an ancient and balky furnace in the basement to baby along. That means tons of coal to shovel and lots of ashes to haul back to the alley.

It Could Be Easier

One day this ever-weary young woman makes a discovery. She could go on welfare, sign up for Aid for Dependent Children, and be money ahead by just sitting around the house.

No, never!

Instead, she signs up for night school to get new skills that earn her a promotion and more pay.

A few years go by and the son comes home all fired up with his own news. Seems he can get a job as the neighborhood paperboy. "Mom, I can earn enough for the bicycle I want!"

Mom smiles, grits her teeth and says go for it—despite knowing that she'll have a long drive every Sunday morning to pick up his supply of thick newspapers. The appointed hour: 4 a.m. That means early to bed on Saturday night.

What have I left out? Oh, trips to the dentist, sick kids, help with homework, church on Sunday, school events to attend and lots more. Her work was never done.

Somehow she shoehorned in picnics at the park and trips to the zoo for the children and even a smidgen of personal time for herself.

I'm proud to say that Peg now has been my wife for 26 years. What a woman! How lucky I was to find her.   —*Clancy Strock*

Washday with Mom Was A Summer Pleasure

By B.J. Nix, Louisville, Kentucky

JUST the scent of laundry detergent can take me back to washdays when I was a little girl on a summer morning in Georgia.

Our wringer washing machine stood on the back porch, and it was always in motion by the time I got up and wandered back there to find Mom.

After the clothes were agitated, Mom used on old broom handle to fish them out of the tub. She then put the clothes through the wringer—how I wanted to do that task!

But she was forever warning me to be careful, because my fingers, arms—*even my whole body*—could become entangled in the wringer and mashed as flat as those clothes.

And they were *flat*. Our clothes had to be fed into the wringer just so, with the buttons tucked inside. Otherwise, the buttons would pop off and fly across the floor.

Who's Got the Button?

This happened often during my beginning days of helping Mom.

I was probably more of a hindrance than help, and recalling the afternoons Mom spent sewing on buttons confirms this in my memory.

After all the loads were washed, Mom emptied the tub, filled it with clean rinse water and agitated the clothes again. Then she put them through the wringer once more.

By mid-morning, she had three or four big basket loads of damp heavy laundry to carry out to our clothesline. She was particular about wiping that metal line off with a damp rag first.

The clothespins were in a bag that Mom hung on the line. I would hand the clothes to Mom and she'd hang them ever so neatly, in a certain order.

Soon the hot Georgia sun was well up in the sky, and our task seemed never-ending.

Finally, Mom let the water out of the tub, and we used it to scrub off the porch and steps. I loved to swish the broom back and forth and feel the warm soapy water on my bare feet.

Aromas of Bleach and Beans

The back porch and kitchen were filled with the mingled washday aromas of detergent, bleach and the starch that Mom boiled on the kitchen stove.

That stove also held a pot of beans, which would join some corn bread for our simple-yet-satisfying washday dinner. There might be a blackberry cobbler, too and, of course, iced tea.

Mom never had a clothes dryer—she hung the laundry on the line all year

"Mom warned me to be careful near the wringer..."

long. Sometimes the clothes froze to the line.

It's funny, but I don't recall helping Mom at those times. I was probably curled up in a corner, reading, or doing something with my sister and six brothers.

But I do very clearly remember the clean sheets that magically appeared on our beds that night, smelling of the fresh outdoors.

Oh, Mom, how I wish I'd helped you more! Your hard work and love will never be forgotten. ❖

NO BLUE MONDAYS. While her mother, Ollie Follendor (left), probably didn't think washday was much fun, the author (above, in 1945) has fond memories of "helping" with the laundry on sunny summer days in Georgia, and of that unforgettable fragrance of fresh clean sheets.

Hardworking Mom Brought Beauty into Her Family

By Jean O'Dell, Hillsboro, Oregon

SHE STANDS alongside my father in her grease-stained bib overalls as they are headed for their tractors. Both are about to climb onto their Farmalls to get the corn crop in.

I smile as I look at this late-1930s photo of my parents (at right). She's smiling, too—despite having to face the rigors of Nebraska farm life.

Summers were the toughest on Helen Holman, because that was when her garden and trees showered her with bountiful fruit and vegetables.

She had no freezer, so everything had to be canned. That boiling process made hot summer days even stickier.

The same stove that heated the canner was activated on Mondays, as Mom heated wash water for the laundry. It was fired up again on Tuesdays, when the sadirons were heated for pressing.

Used Indoor Clotheslines

How I recall the fragrance of sun-dried laundry off the line. In winter, the clothes often froze stiff on the line. Handling them made Mom's fingers sting. During blizzards, she had to string clotheslines through the house.

Over the years, she cleaned thousands of chickens for our meals and for customers in town. Over 400 hens meant a lot of eggs to clean, weigh and crate. She sold these, along with fresh sweet cream, at the produce store in town on Saturday night. The money she earned paid for our groceries.

Kept Detailed Records

I recall when Mom bought an old typewriter and taught herself to type. She kept detailed financial records of everything: the farm crops, sales, purchases, groceries, clothing. She didn't believe in charging things and never owned a credit card.

Church was important to Mom, and sometimes Dad had to hitch up a team and wagon to take her through the gumbo mud to the highway. There they met another parishioner who drove them to town.

When I was small, she read to me every night. Even today, I can hear

TRACTOR TEAM. Mom was right there working alongside Dad when it came to farming, says Jean O'Dell. That included climbing aboard her own Farmall and also taking care of 400 laying hens.

those pages turning. Sometimes in my mind, I hear her play *The Fascination Waltz* on our old upright piano.

Yes, Mother worked hard, but she also brought beauty into our lives. ✦

LIKE A MOTHER HEN. Hilda Richards had her hands full tending to some 30,000 chickens in the family's poultry business, recalls daughter Frances Kennell. But Hilda always found time for her own brood.

She Ruled the Roost... And the Kitchen Range!

TENDING 30,000 chickens made Mom more busy than a busy mother hen.

She and Dad went into the poultry business during the 1950s, raising baby chicks to the laying stage. Mom fed and medicated the chicks twice a day and gathered eggs three times a day.

She collected the eggs in baskets, machine-washed them, hung them to dry, then graded the eggs and packed them for pickup. Nothing kept her from her duties...not even when an occasional snake sneaked into the coop!

Mom spent a lot of nights caring for the chicks. She had to make sure they weren't huddled and smothering. If there were storms or cold weather, she would keep an eye on the heat lamps to make sure they were keeping the chicks warm.

She never neglected her own roost, however. Mom cooked us marvelous breakfasts before school, and she made sure my sister and I were on the bus before she started taking care of business. Her brood always came first, well before the chicken *or* the egg! —*Frances Kennell Smithfield, Virginia*

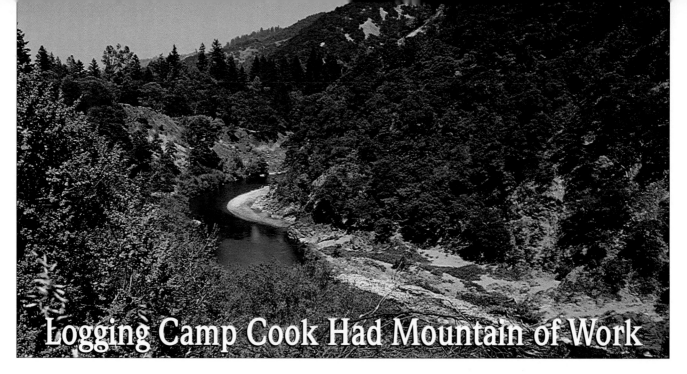

Logging Camp Cook Had Mountain of Work

By Elizabeth Poehlman
Seattle, Washington

EUNICE HAMLIN answered the knock at the cabin door. There stood Rudolph Anderson, co-owner of the logging company that had just hired her husband, Ross.

"We'll be here for supper tonight, Eunice," Rudolph said.

A startled look crossed Eunice's face as she realized 14 hungry loggers were depending on her for dinner.

"Didn't anyone tell you that you'd be cooking for the crew?" Rudolph asked.

No, no one had said a word, but it was too late now. Eunice was hired!

She and Ross had moved into the one-room cabin only the day before. It was part of a remote logging camp at Texas Pond, in the North Cascades of Washington State.

Ross' foreman, Bob Jones, had assured her the next 6 months in the spring and summer of 1942 would be like a "country vacation". Some vacation!

Big Job, Little Cabin

Eunice looked around the cabin. In one corner was a bed and chair. A big iron cookstove sat in another corner. A homemade table sat in the center of the room, with no chairs or benches. There was no running water, no refrigerator and 17 miles of rough steep logging road to the nearest store.

Fortunately, Eunice was no stranger to hard work. The 24-year-old woman had been raised on a family farm in Arkansas and knew how to cook, scrimp and make-do.

The loggers were cutting tall timber necessary for shipbuilding in the war effort. Fortunately, they had plenty of rationing coupons for food and gasoline because of the importance of their work.

Twice a week, Eunice pooled the men's coupons and made the long drive to Tink Wheeler's store in Darrington. From March to autumn of that year, Eunice cooked breakfast, prepared lunches and made dinner for the loggers.

The men made benches to use at Eunice's table. They'd often set the table, help pack lunches and do dishes, too.

A Working "Vacation"

On every day of her "country vacation", Eunice was up by 4 a.m., firing up the cookstove for a big pot of oatmeal, piles of bacon, eggs and hotcakes. And she always had a *big* pot of coffee brewing. She hauled all the water from a nearby stream and still very vividly recalls the day she met a bear on the trail back to the cabin.

Dinners were usually ham or roast beef, fried chicken or Swiss steak with all the trimmings. And always, there was pie for dessert.

The men heartily appreciated Eunice's efforts—Ross' brother, a sign painter, posted a sign near the cabin that read "Eunice's Restaurant".

It was a good joke until the day a carload of sightseers walked into the cabin looking for dinner!

Today, my good friend Eunice laughs as she recalls her days as a camp cook. She says she wished she'd kept that sign as a memento, but she probably used it for firewood.

Her days at Texas Pond turned out to be no vacation, but they left her with fond memories of the days when she was young, strong and the very best cook in the world, in the eyes of 14 hungry men. ↢

FOURTEEN FOR SUPPER! A young bride was told her life in a logging camp would be like a vacation. That was before she learned she'd be the cook for a campful of hungry loggers!

Photos: Barbara Mercurio/RP

Menu

Long Hours, Hard Work Was Grandma's Business

By Rhonda Collier, Chino Valley, Arizona

SERVICE WITH A SMILE. Myrtle Dunsmore cooked, cleaned and waited on tables at the Log Cabin Cafe she and her husband owned in Chino Valley, Arizona, says granddaughter Rhonda Collier.

WHEN GRANDPA purchased a gas station in a small Arizona town, Grandma worked right alongside her husband. She pumped gas, checked oil, washed windows and handled other jobs. Their station was the cleanest in town.

Later, the couple bought another business, the Log Cabin Cafe in Chino Valley, Arizona. When my grandpa died, Grandma worked all alone for the next 18 years to finish paying off their loan. It was far from easy.

Grandma would get up early to sweep, mop and clean every inch of the large cafe and its bathrooms. She opened at 8 a.m. and worked on her feet all through the day, cooking and serving food. Many times it would be after 2 a.m. when Grandma finally got to bed.

When Grandma passed away many years later, she left her business to her three granddaughters. As one of them, I feel blessed to have known this tremendous woman.

By example, she taught us all to work hard and do a good job—vital lessons in life. ✦

Mom's Diner Was a Tasty Place for Kids

By Sandra Ericson, Austin, Texas

HAVING A MOM in the restaurant business meant hard work and late nights for her, but it left me and my two sisters with lots of sweet memories.

At age 18, Mom was left to fend for herself with an eighth-grade education and three children to feed. She tackled the problem with strength, independence and lots of hard work.

She took a job in a busy restaurant in Elmira, New York in 1948. She opened in the morning, cooked all day long and made everything from scratch.

When she couldn't find a sitter for us kids, we'd stay in a little room in back of the restaurant. It had toys, books and a TV. All the workers would drop by with treats like fresh pie and huge platesful of hot French fries. We loved it!

Eventually, we girls would go home, but Mom worked until the restaurant closed. Nevertheless, we had clean starched dresses for school every day.

I remember Mom ironing our dresses at 1 a.m. I don't think sleep was in her schedule.

In the early '50s, Mom opened her own restaurant in Syracuse. At lunchtime, my sisters and I walked to the restaurant for wonderful hot meals of spaghetti or veal and pepper sandwiches. Our friends loved to come along. No peanut butter sandwiches for us!

No matter how late she worked at the restaurant, Mom always had a cake or pie waiting on the kitchen table in the morning for our school parties. For us kids, Mom's hard work was a sweet deal. ✦

LUCKY LUNCHERS. Baby Carol and Sandra (below with their mother, Clara Dengler, in 1946) didn't know it then, but they'd become the envy of their school chums whenever the noon bell sounded.

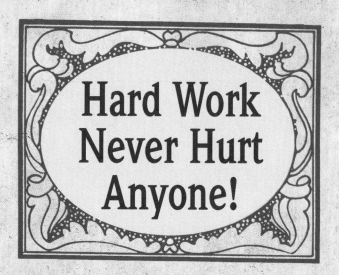

Hard Work Never Hurt Anyone!

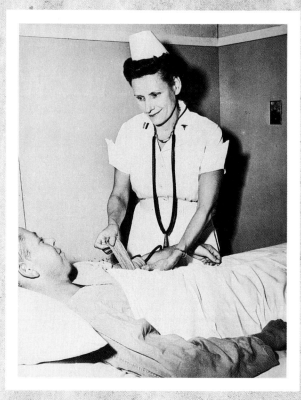

MAJOR AUNT. Viva Buchanan (above) worked as an Army nurse for 20 years, rising to the rank of major, says nephew Bud Hadsall of Southfield, Michigan.

HONESTY. "Any honest work is respectable," was Hazle Crosson's belief, says daughter Mary Colard of Delphos, Kansas. Tending her flock (left) was about as honest as work could be.

SHARED THE BOUNTY. Christina Mogor (left) shares fresh cucumbers with friend Mary Toth in 1938. Christina's daughter, Ida Jancso of West Middlesex, Pennsylvania, says her mom shared all she had.

SCRUB-A-DUB. There wasn't much else you could do when the stoop was dirty in 1918, other than get down on your hands and knees and scrub it.

Brown Brothers

SOLAR POWER. Catherine Richardson dried her clothes on the line in 1931 (right) and was still doing it in 1945 (far right), says daughter Clara Flynn of Sacramento, California. Clara still uses that "dryer" today.

PIE LADY. Vicky Rudd was in California working in a restaurant when this photo (left) was taken in the '40s, says niece Madge Raymer of Sweeden, Kentucky. Madge remembers good times she had with Aunt Vicky when they lived together in a mining camp on the Nolin River in Kyrock, Kentucky. Vicky moved west when her son went into the Navy.

LAUNDRY BUSINESS was booming in 1927 for Tillie Hause. She earned from 10¢ to 25¢ per load, doing loggers' laundry at a sawmill camp. Son Rodney Hause of Ogema, Wisconsin shared the shot.

Work to Be Done? Mom Dug Right in!

NO ONE worked harder than Mother, so no one appreciated modern conveniences more than she did.

During the 1930s in western Iowa, Mother worked hard as a farm wife. Then, when my father gave up farming to become a carpenter, she helped build our house.

While Father was away building other people's homes, she'd work on ours. At age 47, Mother dug the basement to our house by hand. She mixed mortar and laid concrete blocks until she couldn't lift them any higher over her head.

So whenever a work-saving invention came along that made her life a little easier, she was thrilled. Her electric can opener was something she couldn't live without!

Mother always said a lot of hard work makes you appreciate the little things.

—*Leta Wiest Chester, Boise, Idaho*

SHE DUG RIGHT IN. Dorothy Wiest gave the word "housewife" new meaning. She didn't just take care of the family's house, she helped build it in 1959, digging the foundation by hand.

Green-Thumbed Mom Kept Clippin' in Cleveland

WORK WAS the reason Dad wouldn't let Mom have a backyard and garden. She had plenty of work already, raising her family in Cleveland in 1942. Besides, having to tear down the old garage to make room for the yard meant more work for Dad!

Of course, Mom got her way. Dad tore down the garage and put up a white picket fence. Then he and Mom moved about 10 tons of topsoil and peat moss to the yard.

Mom planted flowers, a vegetable garden and a small patch of lawn. All of it grew, much to Dad's surprise. But he shouldn't have been surprised at Mom's next request: a lawn mower.

Dad said we couldn't afford a new one, but he'd look for a cheap used one. Mom finally got her mower in the summer of 1948.

What did she do about lawn cutting all those years in between? She actually got down on her hands and knees with a scissors!

—*Robert Duwe*
Cleveland, Ohio

Ups and Downs of the Harvest Kept Her Going

IT WASN'T EASY for Dad to reap all he'd sown on our farmstead in Fossil, Oregon. Harvesting wheat on that hilly terrain was difficult ...but Mom's help got him through.

My mother, Jewel Stout, worked as "header tender" on the combine that Dad pulled with his Caterpillar tractor. As they bumped around and around that hilly land, she had to stay alert, raising and lowering the blade on the machine to pick all the wheat heads possible. Mom didn't miss many!

My sisters and I later married men who helped Dad with the harvesting chores. But Mom kept her combining job! Dad said that she was the only one he knew who could get every possible head of grain into that combine.

—*June Crafton*
Prineville, Oregon

SHE'S A COMBINATION. Jewel Stout was both mother (at left, with Bonnie, June and Tisha, in 1942) and combine operator (below, on the homestead, in 1950).

Blue-Ribbon Mother Won Family's Hearts

MOM WAS a real winner...and she had the blue ribbons to prove it!

For many years, Pearl Chapman White was a fierce competitor at the Crawford County Fair in Missouri. She'd bring farm produce, garden crops, canned goods, bakery items and sewing projects to be judged.

After she left the farm, she said she had a box of ribbons tucked away. Imagine my surprise when I counted *408* ribbons!

Mom loved the farm and preferred working out in her garden than in the house. Through the 1930s, she held us all together during tough times.

She made dresses, aprons and pajamas for her family out of feed sacks. In fact, I was still wearing feed sack pajamas when I left for college. —*John White San Diego, California*

NO DOUBT ABOUT IT, John White's mother, Pearl, was a real winner. She had 408 county fair ribbons to prove it, but John knew Mom was a winner all along.

DOING FLOORS, as this woman is, was a job Nancy Bearce's mom saved for late at night. See story at right.

Family Worry Made Mom Weary

MOM never slept...at least that was the way it seemed!

She was always the first one up in the morning, fixing a healthy breakfast for my sister and me to stoke up on before school.

Of course, when evening finally came, my sister and I went to bed long before Mom did. She stayed up late to mop and wax our linoleum floors when no one could track the fresh wax around.

One weekend, Mom surprised us by laying down for a little catnap in the middle of the day. It was so unusual we were worried!

"Are you all right?" Dad asked her, stepping into the bedroom. "Feeling okay?"

Sometime later, I walked in and woke Mom with the same questions. Then, my worried sister woke Mom again to check on her well-being. At that, she got up and gave up.

Exasperated, poor Mom sighed, "Trying to rest with all of you around is impossible!"

—*Nancy Chesney Bearce Montrose, California*

"Easy as Pie" Wasn't So Easy for This Baker

MOTHER was a hardworking Kansas farm woman, and I can't recall a time when she didn't seem tired.

When Father died in 1945, leaving her with two children to raise and no outside job skills, she moved to town. There, in Holton, Kansas, she went to work in a cafe, and eventually opened a pie bakery.

She'd be peeling apples and squeezing lemons at 4 a.m. By 9 a.m., her fresh pies were ready for sale at three local restaurants.

A newspaper wrote an article about her in 1978 when she reached a milestone...*100,000 pies*! She doesn't bake pies anymore, but everyone in Holton remembers Mabel Cress, the Holton Pie Baker. —*Joyce Jones, Boise, Idaho*

PILE OF PIES. By 1978, Mabel Cress baked over 100,000 pies in her Holton, Kansas pie shop. Mabel doesn't bake anymore—and who could blame her!

Gramma's Days Were Filled with Love and Labor

By Patricia Gabree, Scotia, New York

MY GRAMMA, Mary Antinore, lived a "simple life"—simply filled with hard work! I've never met anyone who gave so much to her family.

When I was growing up in the '50s, we lived on the same block as Gramma and Gramps in the small village of LeRoy, New York. Gramma's days usually started at 6 a.m., preparing a quick breakfast for Gramps, who worked at the Lapp Insulator plant.

She'd do dishes, make the bed, straighten up the house and hang a load of laundry outside before driving me to elementary school in her cranberry-red Bonneville. She'd sit as tall as her 5-foot frame would allow. She was proud as punch of her car!

Back home, she'd tackle the living room with her trusty Kirby, vacuuming the floral carpet and turquoise-colored cushions on the couch and chair. She'd polish the furniture, mop the red and white kitchen tiles and Ajax the bathroom from top to bottom.

She'd mend or iron until 11 a.m., when she started the noon meal. Roast, potatoes, vegetables and desserts would be ready for Gramps, my parents, my aunt, two uncles and me to share at noon.

Brief Breather

Afterward, as the men had coffee, she'd relax for a rare half hour, watching a portion of *Search for Tomorrow* and *Guiding Light*.

Gardening consumed her early afternoons. Roses of every color bloomed around the perimeter of the backyard. She crossbred roses to produce a shade of coral that local florists hadn't even heard of. Every year I had my

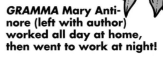

GRAMMA Mary Antinore (left with author) worked all day at home, then went to work at night!

back-to-school picture taken next to a ceramic pot filled with pink and purple petunias.

Inside, she'd snip, water and fuss with her African violets. She'd adjust the venetian blinds to get just the right amount of light for them. She had to stand on a chair to care for her tall vines of English ivy.

Around 2:30, Gramma would begin to bake a little something for Gramps' sweet tooth—apple pie, chocolate cake or "meatball cookies". I got home from school at 3:15 and was the first to sample the warm goodies. My favorites were the meatball cookies, a sugar-glazed ball of chocolate chips and raisins.

Then I'd help Gramma prepare supper, something quick and easy that my aunt could finish preparing later.

Time for Work

Gramma never had supper with us. She'd be at her job at the Jell-O plant, working one of the machines that poured the pudding or gelatin into boxes.

She would hum an Italian song as she got ready for work, ironing her pink uniform, combing her hair and putting on a little rouge. She'd send me out to pick one of her roses, which she'd wear in her lapel.

Leaving the house smelling of Ivory soap and Ponds, she'd blow me a kiss and walk the three blocks to start her workday, just as ours was coming to an end.

I now wear the first wedding band Gramps gave Gramma, and I have one of the African violets from her flower room in my home. I always keep her example of love and strength in my heart. I hope I'm making her proud! ✦

BACK IN 1920, we were living on a small dairy farm in southern New York. Our family consisted of my parents, my sister, a brother and me.

In December of that year, our mama died. The makeup of our family changed dramatically, but not our lives. We were able to stay a family, thanks to years of hard work willingly accepted by Mom's sister, our loving Aunt Anna.

She lived in Sussex, New Jersey with her husband and two sons, one of whom was only 2. Within a week of Mom's death, they left their comfortable city home to move into our big old farmhouse with us. We had no running water, indoor plumbing, central heating, electricity or conveniences of any sort.

Aunt Anna took over the responsibilities of mothering five children and running this new household as if she enjoyed it.

Monday was washday. She used three galvanized washtubs that stood on heavy wooden boxes. She carried water from the well and heated it in a copper-bottomed boiler on the stove. Then she added Babbit's Lye and boiled the white clothes.

Endured Hot Chore

I can still see the sweat trickling down her face as she stood beside that steaming boiler, stirring the clothes with a broken broom handle.

In the first washtub, she rubbed Kirkman Borax or Fels Naptha soap on the soiled clothes. Then she turned the clothes over, soaped side down, and scrubbed them on the washboard with all her might.

When the clothes were finally clean, they were rinsed in the second and third tubs. The last one always had a bit of bluing in the water. She later hung the clothes to dry.

Tuesday was ironing day. Using heavy flatirons with a detachable handle, Aunt Anna heated them on the kitchen stove and pressed the clothes on a padded plank between two chair backs. She even ironed dish towels and our underwear.

Later in the week, she baked—and not only bread and biscuits. She made all kinds of luscious cakes, pies and cookies, all from scratch.

Kept Treats in the Cellar

She treated us to creamy rice pudding, bread pudding and johnnycake. Our cellar shelf was always laden with

What Tasks Aunt Anna Took on

By Bertha Riseley
Summitville, New York

SECOND MOTHER. Aunt Anna (above right, with her sisters, in 1925) became a mother to nieces and nephew in a time of need.

treats, and we were free to help ourselves.

Sewing and mending took up another day of the week, and Aunt Anna was an accomplished seamstress. For example, she made six lovely dresses for my sister and me when we graduated from high school in the same year.

On Class Day, we wore silver-gray crepe trimmed with marabou. For the reception, it was changeable taffeta, and on commencement day, white silk. Our dresses were the envy of all the girls in class.

When Saturday rolled around, it was time to clean our big five-bedroom house. Every room had to be thoroughly tidied. Carpeted floors were swept, linoleum floors were scrubbed and the furniture was dusted. All the bedding was changed, and windows and lamp chimneys were washed. The stove was blacked and polished.

Despite all this constant work, Aunt Anna never said no when we asked her to join us on berry-picking or nut-gathering expeditions. She jumped right in when we went sledding or swimming.

When I was 15, she gave me the complete works of William Shakespeare. Aunt Anna loved good music, and she shared it with her Victrola. Her few records included Enrico Caruso and Galli-Curci. We kids liked the Harry Lauder records better.

I know I'll never be able to pay worthy tribute to this dear woman, this second mother of ours who willingly gave up her comforts and dreams to care for three motherless children and their bereaved father.

She took on the toughest job in the world and handled it lovingly, graciously, capably and unforgettably. ✦

LABOR-SAVING? It might not look like it, but this hulking early-day vacuum cleaner, from around 1915, was a big improvement over what women had before. That, of course, was a broom, dustpan and elbow grease.

Brown Brothers

Immigrant Mom Worked for Family—and Others

By Louie Ricci
Chico, California

ARMED WITH strong will and a third-grade education, my 23-year-old mother sailed from Italy in 1912 to find a better life in America.

Father had arrived the year before and found work as a miner in Illinois. He sent money to book Mother's passage, but she and my 2-year-old sister, Natalie, had to ride on the lower deck with the cattle. Their 3-week journey to Ellis Island seemed like a lifetime.

Mom spoke no English, so she had to have a note pinned to her clothing, giving instructions to train conductors to help her reach Cherry, Illinois.

Opened Boardinghouse

Once reunited with Dad, Mom displayed her will to work hard. Immediately realizing the local miners needed housing, she persuaded Dad to let her open a boardinghouse. Before long, she was cooking, washing clothes, ironing and packing lunches for nine miners.

In 1919, Mom and Dad moved to Decatur, Illinois. They had two more children by then and were able to purchase a good home for the family. Not long after, I arrived on the scene.

Parents Helped Others

The stock market crash was hard on everyone, but it didn't devastate my family since Mom and Dad didn't trust banks and had hidden their savings in our house. They gladly lent money to others less fortunate.

Working in the mines had taken a physical toll on Dad, so in 1930, they decided to go into business for themselves. Mom did laundry for a number of clients, including a restaurant. She washed 80 tablecloths a day at a nickel each and earned a penny for every napkin.

Mom's day started at 4 a.m., when she washed the tablecloths in the wringer washer. If the weather was good, she'd hang them out back; if not, laundry was draped over furniture and hanging from every curtain rod in our house. Dad ironed the laundry, and I folded it after school.

Despite some tragedies our family encountered, Mom always remained strong. My older brother, Primo, died at age 20 of tuberculosis. Only 7 years later, the disease took my sister, Minnie, who had a husband and two children.

Mom took in Minnie's family and often cared for other youngsters. It was

> *"Mom displayed her will to work hard..."*

sometimes quite a madhouse, with Mom caring for five extra children and running a business.

That same inner strength that helped Mom on the boat to America came through time and time again. She proved herself courageous enough to go after her dreams, and she was capable enough to manage money and run a household.

Her feisty spirit, hard work and good nature will never be forgotten. ✦

FIREWOOD FUN. The women joined the men to cut wood back on the farm in the '30s, says Beatrice Barthel of Monticello, Minnesota. Her father, Fred Klucas, and grandfather, Arthur Monrean (third and second from right), were joined by Lillian Hitter (center) and Julia Vitak (right), who look like they weren't bothered by hard work.

Mother Taught Daughters About Preserv-erance

By Irene Zimmerle
Elgin, North Dakota

MOTHER'S GREATEST source of pride were the hundreds of jars of preserves that lined our basement shelves during the 1930s and '40s. Our family never could have survived—or eaten as well—without them.

Canning sweet corn took all day. Armed with gunnysacks, Mother, my sister and I would pick the juiciest ears we could find. Then we'd rip off the outer leaves and pull away the silk.

Using sharp knives, we cut the kernels from the ears and partially cooked the corn. Once the jars were packed and processing in the old copper boiler, we hauled the husks to the hogs.

It was a long tedious day, but our spirits were raised when we saw the golden rows of jars waiting to be opened and enjoyed!

From the time the first vegetable poked its tiny head through the ground to the last piece of fruit we

> "*From the first vegetable to the last piece of fruit, she kept the boiler busy...*"

picked before winter, Mother kept the boiler busy. She started with rhubarb, then peas and beans.

Chore Bored Children

Canning days were long and tedious. It was downright drudgery for us kids to pick and clean chokecherries, wild plums and bull berries. Then we had to cook and strain them and cook the juice into jelly.

For me, gooseberry picking was the worst. Their thorny branches caused me sore arms time and time again! Then, each little berry had to have a sticker removed before it could be made into a sauce. To this day, I don't grow gooseberries...they're too much work!

By autumn, the cellar was an impressive sight. Mom showed her colorful canning warehouse to all our visitors. They'd ooh and aah at the magnificent display.

Mom taught me at an early age how to do a job well, have patience and, most of all, to have pride in a job well done. Even today, I still enjoy canning. Now *there's* proof of Mom's persistence. ✦

STOCKED SHELVES. Audrey Zimmerle is admiring Grandmother Maria Horst's handiwork stored in the basement in 1956 (inset). Maria's daughter Irene now enjoys canning.

SHE CAME A LONG WAY. When Iris Self Lyons came to Colorado, it was in a covered wagon, says daughter Jean Pelley of Cedaredge, Colorado. Iris studied nursing in 1938 (right) and later became a rancher's wife. Along with caring for three children and helping on the ranch, Iris drove 11 miles daily to work at the local hospital, usually at night.

SHE MADE ENOUGH DOUGH. Celia Inserra (below) dreamed daughter Louise would go to college. Her dream came true, thanks to Celia's ravioli.

Lotsa Pasta Paid For College Tuition

MOTHER'S GREATEST DREAM was to see her daughter graduate from college. It was a dream she was willing to work for!

In the late 1940s, Mother made 1,000 ravioli for 4 days a week, every week. She supplied the pasta to a chain of Italian restaurants in Pittsburgh. She also sold ravioli to neighbors and friends for about 90¢ a dozen.

Mother's dream came true; her pasta put me through Penn State. Now *that's* food for thought!

—*Louise Lockwood, Miami, Florida*

Husband's Death, Debt Didn't Defeat Grandma

MY GRANDMOTHER, Saphronia Hummel Miller, was like dynamite—lots of power in a small package.

Grandpa died in 1910, after 28 years of marriage to Grandma. That left her in charge of almost 700 acres of mortgaged farmland. She also had to care for 10 of her 14 children still living at home.

Though Grandpa had written explicit instructions about what to plant, when to sell and how to work together to hold the family and farm together, Grandma wasn't experienced in business and knew it.

Three court-appointed appraisers advised her to sell the farm and apply the proceeds to the debt. But when Grandma learned the law would allow her 3 years to settle the debt, she had other ideas.

"Tend your own business these 3 years and I shall attend strictly to mine," she told the men. "At the end of the 3 years, every cent of this debt will be paid."

They had their doubts, and so did Grandma's children. To them she said, "God gives special care and blessings to widows who trust in Him. With His help, I will show those appraisers it can be done!"

And she did. Not only did Grandma pay the farm debt in full, she also paid off another good-sized debt incurred

FREE AND CLEAR. When Saphronia Miller (above) was left a mortgaged farm, she worked hard for 3 years to pay it off, erasing the doubts of some local land agents as well as those of some of her children.

by two of her sons. Since Grandpa had signed their note before his death, Grandma felt it was her responsibility to make sure it was paid.

Yes, Saphronia Hummel Miller may have been only 5 feet tall, but she was one dynamite lady!

—*Christine Scbeffel, Pryor, Oklahoma*

Hard-Drivin' Mom Used Horsepower

MY MOTHER, Mary Repic, could hitch up our team of horses, Bessie and Charlie, and plow, drag, plant or do whatever else needed to be done on our farm outside North Branch, Michigan.

When Mom and Dad got their first Ford tractor in 1940, Mom immediately learned to drive it.

That came in handy when she had to make the 2-1/2-mile trip into town for groceries. We only had one car, and Dad used it for work.

—*Joann LaValley*
North Branch, Michigan

SPUD BUDS. Ol' Bessie and Charlie pulled when Mary Repic harnessed them to the potato digger.

IN 1977, my mother celebrated her 96th birthday with a very special telephone call...it was the first call she ever made!

Mother didn't want to bother much with "newfangled contraptions", perhaps because her old-fashioned ways worked so well. And working all her life was something that worked for Mother.

Our family lived in Spillville, Iowa, a town so influenced by its Czech heritage that the old language was still spoken in many homes. To this day, I remember the Czech specialties my mother used to make— fruit tarts called *kolachys*, and many kinds of breads.

Mother baked every day of the week. An invoice from the Turkey River Valley Roller Mills showed that in 1918, she purchased 1,000 pounds of "Gold Standard Fancy Patent Flour" and 100 pounds of "Pure Bohemian Rye Flour". The bill for the year, which included a half ton of bran for the chickens, was $96.10.

Happy Harvester

During summer, Mother reaped nature's bounty. Rows of berry preserves lined our basement walls, while wild herbs like chamomile, linden and elderberry blossoms were dried and used for teas. The whole community enjoyed

Hard Work Kept Mother 🍎 Young at Heart 🍎

By Cyril Klimesh, Sebastopol, California

the wild mushrooms that Mother picked and sold.

Mother raised her eight children single-handedly after my father died. Somehow, she managed to keep Dad's Ford garage in the family, with the help of my two older brothers.

Plenty of Food

Because of the business, some considered our family well-off. In actuality, it brought in very little, and Father's illness had wiped out our resources. But we had a car to drive, and Mother's hard work ensured there was plenty of food on the table.

Periodically, Mother attended a feather-stripping, carpet-sewing or quilting bee. She was active in local events and church work.

Despite their busy schedule, she always found time to take us on walks in the woods to pick nuts, gooseberries, elderberries and, of course, mushrooms.

Mother's garden remained a great source of joy. When Mom turned 90, one of my sisters, thinking the garden was getting to be too much work, suggested to the plowman that he make it a little smaller.

Her scheme backfired when Mother complained that he'd done such a poor job she had to spade the edges to bring the garden to its proper size! ←

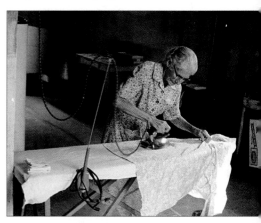

OLD WAYS ARE BEST. Mary Klimesh wasn't one for newfangled work savers. At age 96, she still enjoyed doing the wash and ironing (above). She mended everything herself (top), and to relax, there was reading (left).

Log-Rolling Mom Never Complained

BACK IN 1945, my dad bought a farm in Vermont, and we did a lot of logging there. I was 16 then, and Dad I would work all day in the woods. But we couldn't have survived the winter without Mom.

I'd skid logs a half mile to the skidway, where Mom could see me from the

HOOKED ON LOGGING. If Charles Boothroyd was having trouble with a log, he could be sure his mother, Dorothy (left), would drop what she was doing, pick up a cant hook and help.

house. She would drop her regular work (cooking, baking, hauling water or stove wood) and come to help me. She'd grab a cant hook and start rolling logs onto the skidway.

If she ever wanted to take a trip to the store, she'd climb onto the front of the bobsled pulled by our team. Including the horse harnessing, this round-trip took 3 hours in the cold. That same trip takes 10 minutes today.

Whether working or traveling in the cold, Mom never complained.

—Charles Boothroyd
Tolland, Connecticut

Finding a Tribute for Hard Worker Was Tough

WORDS CAN barely describe the labor and love that filled the life of my mother, Virgie White.

Her day began at 5 each morning, when she baked scratch biscuits for Father and me. After doing the dishes,

WILLING GIVER. Virgie White was generous with her help to her family and others in the community.

she reported for work at a garment company. After her 7:30-to-3:30 shift, she helped Father at his job as custodian at the church, then came home and made dinner. Finally she sat down—at her treadle sewing machine, for she made all our clothes.

She gave of herself willingly—babysitting for young couples to give them a little time alone, and inviting newcomers to our dinner table.

When she died in 1982, I agonized over how to inscribe her tombstone. After many days of prayer, the answer finally came. From the book of Ruth, it reads simply, "Thou hast shown kindness." No better words describe Mom.

—Beulah Knieriem
Middleburg Heights, Ohio

Mom Worked Wonders With Her Trusty Apron

MOTHER HAD hundreds of chores a day that turned our house into a home. She was never without her apron when she tackled her tasks.

I can see her now, coming in from the garden with a mess of green beans, garden peas and maybe an onion. That apron made a good "carryall" for the meal she was preparing.

Minutes later, the apron would be carrying just-hatched chicks needing to be placed in a warm spot, in the sunshine or by the stove.

If the telephone rang while she was baking, the apron served as a duster. She'd wipe her hands, so as "not to track it on the floor", she'd say.

I can't think of another tool that worked as hard in Mom's hands as her trusty apron. *—Theo Smith*
West Plains, Missouri

PIE MAKER. Mildred Welch (left) of Harrington, Delaware has lived a full life, says daughter-in-law Grace, also of Harrington. Mildred is famous for the pies she bakes, which are sold at local fund-raising events.

Hard Work and Generosity Were Willie's Legacy

By Pete Morris, Arlington, Texas

LOOK OUT, WEEDS! When Willie Morris got on the business end of a hoe, her garden had clean rows.

I JUST received my inheritance from my mother's estate, and the memories came flooding back. It all began on an old poor tenant farm near Argyle, Texas.

My mom, Willie Morris, could get up at dawn, fix breakfast, wash the dishes and still nearly beat my father and us three boys to the field.

She'd leave the cotton patch at noon, fix lunch, feed all of us, wash the dishes and return to the field by the time we returned.

Then she'd leave again in the evening, fix supper, feed us and wash the dishes, and be ready to listen to *Fibber McGee and Molly* on the radio by the time we got our outside chores done.

Sometimes on blistering days, she'd leave the cotton field and pick a hot watermelon. She'd carry it a mile to our house and cool it down in our icebox (we had no refrigerator). That melon would make a sweet treat with our garden potatoes and okra in the evening.

Had Little, Gave Lots

Mom was a soft touch for everybody. She didn't have much, but as long as she could write checks, she'd give to anyone who asked.

If the Boy Scouts or Camp Fire Girls came by, she gave them a dollar each. She always gave money to the church.

Mom lived to be 96, and when she was in her 90s, she wanted her hair fixed every single week—not because she wanted to look nice, but because she thought the lady who did it needed the money.

Mom thought the ultimate gift would be to leave a little money for her sons, grandchildren and great-grandkids. How proud she would have been!

After we paid her last expenses, the balance of her estate was divided. My check came to $334.20.

"Well, Willie," I thought, "I can't spend the money on myself. After all, you wouldn't have.

"So, let's see…$50 each to three great-granddaughters for savings bonds for college. And $50 each to a grandson and granddaughter for bonds to go toward their retirement. And $50 to Arlington Charities so a few souls can eat tonight. And $34 to the church.

"How's that, Willie? You like that breakdown? What's that? Oh, my! The 20¢. I forgot.

"That will be for some chocolate kisses. I'll raise them to the heavens and toast you for your sweet life and what it meant to so many people. Here's to you, Mom!" ←

MODERN KITCHEN. This housewife was probably glad for the opportunity to cook with gas in the early '20s. This stove might seem old-fashioned now, but after firing up a wood-burner every morning, a new gas-burner had to be a real labor-saver for the lady of the house. No matter how many labor-savers are invented, there's still plenty to do to make a house a home.

IT WASN'T ALL WORK. Willie Morris and husband, Lavernne, dressed up to step out when this photo was taken in 1941.

NOW IT BEGINS. A lifetime of learning was just starting for these kindergarten pupils in 1910. A dedicated teacher could make all the difference in the world on a young mind, and these children may remember their first teacher for the rest of their lives. Teaching is a profession that takes much skill. But its rewards are often great.

Chapter Five

Terrific Teachers

The awesome task of educating our children has, within my memory, been primarily handled by women. But it wasn't always that way. In the early days of this country, the "schoolmaster" was a college-educated man.

And there was the rub. Females usually had a hard enough time just finishing high school, much less attend college. Then around the turn of this century, things began to change.

Young ladies were welcomed into "normal schools" where, after 2 years, they were awarded certificates that qualified them to teach in elementary schools.

My mom was one of the new breed. Her graduation picture from DeKalb Normal School shows a group of smiling young women, ready to launch careers as educators.

Mom's first job was in a country school in northern Illinois. It's still standing but has been converted into a home. The first year, she hiked more than 3 miles on gravel roads, come rain, sleet, snow or shine, arriving at 7:30 to prepare for the day's work.

Started the Stove

In winter, she started a brisk fire in the stove to take the chill off a building that matched the temperature outdoors. She pumped water for the water bucket, checked the outhouse and ran through her plans for the day. The students ranged from first through eighth grade, so a daunting day lay ahead.

The next year, she "boarded" with farm families in the school district, much nearer to school.

Recently I received a letter I cherish. It was from a lady who wrote, "I clearly remember Miss Stevens (Mom's maiden name), who was my first teacher. She was a kind young lady who took an interest in every student."

All of us remember particular teachers from our past. Usually it's because they had a unique ability to excite and enthuse us. They somehow made us *want* to learn and excel.

They also went beyond the expected. They taught us, but they also *cared* about us. They often dipped into their own meager income to take us on field trips or buy school supplies our parents couldn't afford.

A friend of mine, son of a man who abandoned his family, dropped out of high school to help support the family. He went to work in a Cleveland steel mill.

Two weeks later, his high school English teacher walked into the factory, found the boy and said, "John, do you really want this to be your life? Don't waste a fine mind. Come back to school and we'll find some other way for you to earn money for your mother."

Returned to Learn

John went back to school and then on to college. He eventually retired from an executive job with a large corporation, after a rich and rewarding career.

All thanks to a teacher who cared.

In this chapter, you'll find fond memories of teachers who had the gift of caring. Their students were, in a very real sense, their children and their family.

As Paul Hostetler so aptly puts it in his story on page 77 about his teacher, Miss Mackey, "We're all forever grateful for her investment in our lives."

What a splendid choice of words, "Her *investment* in our lives." She invested her time and talent and passion in young lives… and reaped the dividends in the form of gratitude and love.

—*Clancy Strock*

Power of Silence Taught Him a Lesson

By Jim Luker, Chesapeake, Virginia

IT WAS SPRING, I was a high school senior and spring fever was rampant. Anyway, that's what I'll blame for what happened that day in 1952 in Cayce, South Carolina.

A friend and I were stuffing books into our lockers before lunch. He was telling me about an incident that had happened in his Sociology class just before the noon bell rang.

Mrs. Foster's belt had snapped when she bent over to pick up something she'd dropped. It was an event long overdue, and some students had made predictions and even bets about when it would take place.

Just as I was about to collapse with laughter over the thought of this scene, something appeared in the corner of my eye that caused me to freeze—Miss McCaskill, our English teacher.

My friend continued the story, disregarding my efforts to stop him. Miss M paused for a moment, a moment that seemed like hours, then turned and when back into her classroom.

Trouble Now!

"Oh, no," I said. "She heard us!"

"Well, it happened," my friend replied. "What's wrong with telling the truth?"

That wasn't the problem. It was a matter of being overheard by a person whose standards would never include discussing another's misfortunes.

I felt sick inside thinking Miss McCaskill had seen a side of me I wasn't proud to have exposed. In her class after lunch, I had an uneasy feeling, even though this was my favorite class.

The feeling intensified when I saw what Miss M had written on the blackboard:

There is so much good in the worst of us,
And so much bad in the best of us,
That it ill behooves any of us
To talk about the rest of us.

But as I sat through that hour when I was supposed to be studying *MacBeth*, I began to rationalize the events before lunch. Soon I was guilt-free and even began to feel a little self-pity because of Miss M's finger-pointing verse. By the end of the hour, I was plotting revenge.

He'd Get Even

After school, I lingered until Miss M locked up and went home. I went back inside and persuaded the custodian, Mr. Spigner, to loan me the key to the room so I copy a poem on the board—which was the truth. It read:

There is so much good in the worst of us,
And so much bad in the best of us,
What a wonderful time all of us
Have talking about the rest of us!

The next day, I felt smug and satisfied as my peers asked

"I felt smug and satisfied..."

---

if I was the clever one. I admitted nothing, but they knew.

Miss M said nothing and carried on as usual. My point had been made.

When I came to class the next day, the poem was still there. Still Miss M said nothing, and I found myself sneaking glances at my stroke of genius. By the end of class, though, I wasn't as cocky as the day before.

On the third day, the awful verse still had not been erased. It seemed to loom larger, much larger than my diminishing ego. It had to go.

That day after school, I played the same game with Mr. Spigner. I got into the classroom and restored the poem to its original state.

On the fourth day, Miss M rose from her desk and erased the verse. My heart stopped and I gave a short prayer of thanks.

Miss M turned to the class, flashed the sweetest, most sincere smile I'd ever seen, and said, "Well, I think we've seen enough of that."

I sure had.

In the years that followed, Miss McCaskill supported and encouraged my efforts as I continued my education. But she was never so effective as she was those 3 days in 1952, when she exercised the power of silence. ❦

FUTURE TEACHERS. It was 1912 and Florence Thompson (left) was only 16 and already at teacher's college, says daughter Audrey Wendland of Jasper, Georgia. She taught until she married at age 25.

MOM THE TEACHER. What if your teacher was also your mom? Pat Traxler (fourth in the left row) knew what that was like in 1935. Her mother, Gladys Krause (standing at rear), was her teacher in Herbster, Wisconsin.

Teacher Made Reading A Magical Trip

By Paul Hostetler
Mechanicsburg, Pennsylvania

EVERY DAY when I was in second grade, Miss Mackey would stand in front of her eight grades, open a storybook and invite us to take a long ride on her magic carpet.

It was 1932, and we students at Number 10 School near North Lawrence, Ohio flew to faraway places. In wide-eyed wonder, we discovered *Little Boy Blue, Alice in Wonderland, Oliver Twist, The Arabian Nights, Tom Sawyer* and more.

When I eagerly responded in reading lessons, Miss Mackey got me additional books to read on my own.

I learned only a few years ago from a high school teacher that Miss Mackey would beg, borrow and steal books from all possible sources to keep her students interested in reading.

After I completed third grade, our family moved to another school district. How I missed Miss Mackey!

When I entered sixth grade, the Number 10 School closed, and Miss Mackey came to our school to teach the first three grades.

I didn't know that until I saw her out in the school yard one day. She was surrounded by happy playing children, but when she spotted me, she rushed over and gave me a big hug and kiss.

Not in Front of the Guys!

Her gesture both highly pleased and greatly embarrassed this 11-year-old boy. My buddies snickered and hooted.

I remembered that incident again a few years ago, when I went back to Ohio to visit this remarkable teacher. She had been happily married for many years and was now Mrs. Amstutz.

I told her I was at long last getting around to thanking her for the great influence she'd had on my life. We reminisced together as time stood still.

When I was ready to leave, I reminded her of the time she embarrassed me in the school yard. I told her I was going to "embarrass" her in front of her husband. I gave her a big hug and kissed her soft cheek. She was in tears and I was, too. Her husband smiled in understanding.

A few days later, I received a photo she snapped of me in front of the schoolhouse door 6 decades ago. Only a mother and a devoted teacher could have loved that ragtag lad!

I treasure the photo, along with the greatest gift Miss Mackey could have given her students, the ability to ride on enchanting magic carpets. We're all forever grateful for her investment in our lives. ↩

Catherine the Great Worked Many Miracles

By Elmer Freeman, Spokane, Washington

SHE WAS a farmer and a musician, a taxidermist and a stone mason. She could be as tough as nails or as gentle as a lamb. No wonder I remember her as Sister Catherine the Great!

I remember being awestruck, terrorized, amazed, proud, scared, admiring and puzzled by Sister Catherine—all within the same hour.

She was our principal and Superior to the community of sisters who taught at St. Mary's School in New England, North Dakota. I entered first grade there in 1926.

Sister Catherine had a way of swishing her black habit and veil as she entered our orchestra room that left no doubt about who was in charge.

When she picked up her baton and

> *"There was no doubt about who was in charge..."*

announced what we were to play, we had little more than a wink of an eye to get music on our stands and be ready for the downbeat.

I was always glad I played saxophone and sat in the back row. She was a violinist herself, and the violin section was right in front of her. Every other week or so, she'd break a baton when the violins messed up.

If a farmer was on his way out of town after unloading some wheat, Sister Catherine would flag him down. She'd explain that she needed a load of petrified wood from the Badlands, some 20 miles west of town.

Had a Construction Habit

Then she'd usher three or four sisters into the farm truck, and away they'd go to get enough material for one of her building projects.

One of the few tourist attractions worth seeing in our little town was the magnificent grotto Sister Catherine built from petrified wood on the corner of the school grounds.

She built a shelf around the main hall, where she mounted a collection of snakes, gophers, jackrabbits, pheasants, badgers, skunks and any other form of life that crawled, walked or flew in our part of the country.

Because half of the students were boarders, we needed a considerable quantity of vegetables during the school year. Sister Catherine oversaw the planting and tending of the 1-acre garden that produced a quantity and quality of produce unknown to any other gardener in the county.

There were whispered complaints of "supernatural" help in Sister's gardening efforts. She didn't argue. After all, what better time to pray than when spending hours on the business end of

a hoe, working her way down endless rows of potatoes?

When it started to bother Sister Catherine that her shoes wore out quicker on one side than the other, she started buying shoes a size too large. That way, she could switch her shoes from right to left and thus wear out both sides completely.

Nobody doubts that Sister Catherine went to Heaven when she died. What is less certain is just what the Good Lord did with her once she got there.

Most of us think that if Heaven has enough rocks, critters and violin players, Sister Catherine will take charge and immediately improve things. Even Heaven may be able to use a bit of her supernatural touch. ✦

Schoolboy Crush Rings in His Memory

By Evert Schrotenboer, Allegan, Michigan

I REMEMBER, with great clarity, the day I first fell in love. I was 11 years old and entering sixth grade.

I'd never liked school until that day, but everything changed when I walked into the classroom and found the most beautiful woman I'd ever seen! In a soft sweet voice, she introduced herself as Miss Heller.

She was 19 and a recent graduate of Country Normal School. Her every movement was graceful and her smile ravishing.

My attitude changed. I became diligent in my schoolwork and made my parents proud. For the first time, I experienced the feeling of success, and I *loved* school. Most of all, I wanted to please Miss Heller.

Then one day Miss Heller arrived at school wearing a diamond ring. I noticed immediately because I spent much of my time following her every movement. She glanced at the ring often that morning.

A Visitor Arrived

At the end of the day, there was a knock on the door. Miss Heller ran to the door, opened it and greeted a tall blond man. She brought him into the room, holding his hand. She smiled and announced, "Class, I want you to meet Gary, my fiance. We're going to be married."

Married? *Married?* I couldn't believe what I'd heard! How could this be? *I* was going to marry her. I looked at this man with loathing but soon realized that I was beaten. I knew Miss Heller would never marry me.

I became discouraged and lost interest in my schoolwork. But then I rallied. I wasn't going to give Gary the satisfaction of seeing me fail. I began to work with a vengeance, but without the joy I felt before my heart was broken.

One of my classmates was a boy we called "Weird Billy". He was bigger, older and a bully. He'd been held back several times.

Billy had the irritating habit of stealing. He'd take anything he could get his hands on. The odd thing was, he'd seldom keep the objects. He would just throw them away.

As a precaution before messy art projects, Miss Heller began taking off her ring and putting it in a little decorative box on her desk.

One day when she opened the box, the ring was gone. Miss Heller screamed in shock. She was devastated. She questioned us, but no one had any information. When I glanced over at Billy, I knew this was his work.

During recess, I got some of my friends and we tied Billy to a tree, where we "urged" him to confess. He finally confessed he'd taken the ring, wrapped it in his bubble gum and thrown it in the wastebasket.

When the bell rang, we trooped in. Everyone took their

> "I'd never liked school until that day, but everything changed..."

seats but me. I walked to the wastebasket and began to rummage through it.

"What is going on here?" Miss Heller demanded.

I found the old gum and dug out the ring. I walked over to Miss Heller and triumphantly handed it to her.

She was shocked and bewildered. She took the ring, then glanced around at us disheveled "interrogators", and at Billy, still tearful and wiping his nose on his sleeve.

Miss Heller began to understand what had happened. "I think we'll say no more about this," she said. "Class will begin now."

Miss Heller got married, and I lived through it. I found out that being a good student was pretty nice, and I continued to do my best.

Billy didn't turn out to be a criminal. In fact, he became a respectable, successful businessman.

I don't know what happened to Miss Heller after that year. But for me, she'll always be 19 years old, the most beautiful woman in the world, and my first love. ✦

CRUSHED. Having a crush on your teacher, as schoolboys in class at right might, usually leads to heartache.

Teacher on Horseback Was a Welcome Sight

MY MOTHER, Charlotte Gerlach, was affectionately known as "Miss Lotte" when she became a schoolteacher at 16. Back then, being a strong woman was part of the teaching requirement.

When she arrived at her one-room schoolhouse in Hillside, Colorado, my mother would build a fire in the morning, see that there was wood for the stove, break ice on the water pails, clean the schoolhouse, plus write and direct school plays and programs.

During the flu epidemic of 1917-18, she had another job to add to her duties. The schools were closed, so Mother rode her horse, "Babe", around to all the various ranches—some many miles apart—to deliver medicine and messages and inform the community of impending funerals.

She never got the flu that year. She credits her health to being outdoors all winter. —Dorothy Young
Canon City, Colorado

Her Gift to One Student Helped Generations More

I WAS in kindergarten when I decided I was going to become a teacher, and I never deviated from that goal.

In high school, my encouragement came from Edith Fairchild, a teacher who allowed me to spend free time with her, checking papers and tutoring fellow students.

Miss Fairchild was not only my beloved teacher, she became a trusted friend. She had a unique way of drawing out my problems and helping me find satisfactory solutions to them.

Just how good she was at this was proven at graduation, when my classmates voted to wear evening gowns for the commencement ceremony.

I was devastated and wept in Miss Fairchild's arms. I knew my immigrant parents couldn't afford such luxury. The Great Depression wiped out the meager savings they'd entrusted to a bank that had failed.

Then one day I found a large box on my desk. It contained an exquisite white evening gown and this message:

Dear Elinor:
Work as if the whole world depends on you. Pray as if your success depends on God. Teach as if each child is a personal gift from Him.
Your Friend Always,
Edith Fairchild

That advice, given to me by a teacher who cared, became my "Golden Rule". It enabled me to have a dual career, one as wife and mother of six, and the other as a teacher for 53 years, recently retiring as professor emerita of education. —Elinor Tripato Massoglia
Chapel Hill, North Carolina

Imaginary Journeys Took Children Far

OUR TEACHER, Mrs. Thelma Hird, could transform her one-room schoolhouse into just about anything. She was my grade school teacher in Lewiston, New York in the late 1930s, and I'll never forget her.

She once built a train out of just two benches. We then took turns as engineer, conductor or passenger. We had to collect tickets, make change and let the passengers tell about the cities we traveled to. We learned a lot of geography on those imaginary train trips.

She also built a store in our school to help us better understand business. As sales clerks or the manager, we learned how to write checks and make bank deposits. As shoppers,

Teacher Brought Smiles During Depression Time

THE DEPRESSION seemed to touch everywhere but Marjory Sage's classroom in Caro, Michigan. She never had any children, but she made all of us her own.

When Shirley Temple movies were showing in town, she invited four or five of us girls home with her and took us to the movies. She'd drive us home early the next morning in time for our farm chores.

She was one of the few people we knew who had a car. It was always a "lift" to see her on the road—particularly for those of us who had over 2 miles to walk to school!

If we were sick, she'd bring us our homework, books and a treat, either a sucker or a slice of chocolate cake. Looking back, I realize she was the greatest treat of all! —Maxine Teall
Iron City, Georgia

we learned how to be thrifty.

Mrs. Hird is in her 80s now and is as active as ever in her community. Her special pleasure is to show her former students the replica one-room school she had built in her yard. That schoolroom sure took us places!
—Florence Chandler, Naples, Florida

THE BUSINESS OF TEACHING. To help Florence Chandler and her fellow pupils learn about business, their teacher, Mrs. Hird, built this model store in their classroom in Lewiston, New York in the 1930s.

This Taskmaster Became Boy's Inspiration

By Howard Johnson
Fremont, California

I WAS never a great student—in fact, I failed first grade. When I reached fifth grade, I suffered a severe case of appendicitis that set me back another year.

I returned to school in 1936, 2 years older than a regular sixth grader would have been. Worse yet, I was the *only* sixth grader in our two-room schoolhouse at Mayville, North Dakota.

I was having a hard time with Miss Ugland, my new teacher. She couldn't understand why I didn't want to do my schoolwork. I tried telling her I didn't

---

"For the first time in my life, I really liked school..."

---

know how to do it, but she thought I was lazy and didn't want to put forth the effort.

In trying to take all the stubbornness out of me, she made me stay after school almost every day. Since this did not work, she finally realized I was willing to do the lessons but could only perform on a third- or fourth-grade level.

When she learned that I was so far behind, she understood she'd been expecting me to do work far beyond my ability.

Took Joy in Learning

From then on, she spent extra time with me during class and after school. I took my lessons seriously and tried my best. It was slow going, but I finally discovered the joy of being able to read and do math.

By the end of 3 months, I had mastered addition, subtraction, multiplication and division. I could read as well as any other student in school. For the first time in my life, I really *liked* school.

I always wanted to tell Miss Ugland

J.C. Allen and Son

that she was truly a great teacher, but I didn't see her after I'd left grade school and moved on in my life.

In the summer of 1989, though, my wife and I attended a reunion of Mayville State University's class of 1949. I asked one of my old acquaintances, a local mail carrier, if he recognized the name Irene Ugland.

To my surprise, he knew her many years ago and introduced me to some people who might know her. As her name was mentioned, a lady responded, saying her name was Irene and her maiden name was Ugland.

LESSONS FOR A LIFETIME. A patient teacher like the one above remains in the memory of Howard Johnson.

The moment I saw her, I recognized my sixth-grade teacher! She was the one who set the spark that ignited a complete change of life and attitude for me. I told her that it was because of her I continued my struggle in school and became a teacher myself.

After all these years, I was finally able to give her that big bear hug I had been wanting to give her for so long! This teacher truly changed my life. ✦

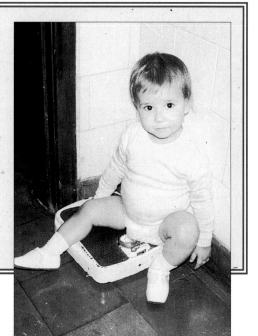

THANKFUL ORPHAN. Heidi Wooten was a 13-month-old Brazilian orphan in 1965 when she was adopted by Ruth Miller Smith, a teacher and missionary. Heidi, of Hanahan, South Carolina, says when they came back to the United States, her mother went back to teaching. When Heidi started first grade, it was at the school where her mother was a teacher. Now a mother, too, Heidi says she has a good example to follow.

Teacher Shared Love and House

I ATTENDED a quaint one-room school in the late 1940s. Wharton Independent School stood on a hill in Fayette County, Pennsylvania. Mrs. Emma K. Wilkey was our teacher.

She was broad-shouldered, firm and always in control of her classroom. She was formal, organized and strict. But we knew Mrs. Wilkey loved us.

During the week, she stayed at her elderly father's house, a quarter mile from school. On weekends, she'd return to her large white farm home near Perryopolis. She often took a couple of students home with her to spend time with her and her husband.

I was thrilled when Mrs. Wilkey took me, because it seemed like a vacation. We had a very large family and there was never enough money to go on a real vacation.

Mrs. Wilkey would always give us a little gift to take back home. One that I especially remember was a package of nice soft undershirts. They sure helped me and my siblings keep warm on cold winter days when we had to walk 4 miles to the schoolhouse.

I will forever be grateful to that wonderful teacher for her kind acts of charity to the poorer children in the community.

—Betty West
Capon Bridge, West Virginia

ONE BIG FAMILY. Betty West (fourth from left, standing) still has warm feeling for her teacher, Mrs. Wilkey.

This Teacher's Lesson Wasn't Found in Textbooks

MY FONDEST MEMORIES of grade school days center around the best teacher I ever had. Vera D. Jefferson was my seventh-grade teacher in 1931.

Many were suffering through the Depression then, and I'm sure Miss Jefferson was one of those victims. She had only two outfits she wore the whole year through.

One was a tailored black suit with shiny lapels and a white blouse. The other outfit was a wool jersey dress, speckled blue and white. Both garments were always spotless and well-pressed.

Most of us students were also victims of the Depression, so it's a wonder we could ever make fun of our teacher's limited wardrobe. In those days, I was wearing hand-me-downs and even some dresses made from Welfare-donated material. But I regret to say at times, I joined in the secret giggling and scoffing.

Rumor had it Miss Jefferson had parents to support, and the money she earned from teaching had to be meager.

Despite our mockery, by the end of the school year, all of us students totally honored Miss Jefferson. She demonstrated dignity in spite of lack. By her example, she taught us that self-respect is superior by far to outward displays of fashion and wealth. —Enid Treffinger
Federal Way, Washington

Surprise! This Teacher Knew How to Have Fun

ON MY 13th birthday, a friend from the farm next door asked me to go play at a pond nearby. We hadn't played very long when she wanted to go home. I thought that was odd.

When we reached my house, there on the porch were my friends and family, all singing *Happy Birthday* to me. They had a cake and gifts for me, too, and I was astounded. Never before had my birthdays been celebrated with anything more than a spoken "Happy Birthday".

The party was arranged by my seventh-grade teacher, Miss Doxtator, who did *so much* for me.

She made sure I read all 296 books in the little library at our one-room school in Jamesville, New York. At the conclusion of seventh grade in 1940, she said she'd done all she could for me, and her inspiration carried me through high school, college and on to my own teaching career.

But I don't think anything she ever did meant as much to me as that little surprise party. What a wonderful, giving person Angeline Doxtator was—and she remains so in my memory.

—Doris Otis, Adams, New York

Afternoon Lessons Put Music In Students' Lives

CELIA SCHUSTER was always busy, having to teach all eight grades by herself. But she found time to be generous with her musical talent.

Mrs. Schuster taught at the one-room schoolhouse I attended in Pine Grove, Wisconsin during the mid-1930s. She offered free after-school piano lessons for anyone willing to practice the scales and pieces diligently.

I started in fourth grade, learned my pieces and soon could play my favorite songs as well.

This musical instruction enabled me to learn bassoon for the high school band and, later, pursue choral singing as a lifetime hobby. Mrs. Schuster's unselfishness and encouragement enriched my life. —Betty Heinrich Antonie
Madison, Wisconsin

FIRST SCHOOL PHOTO. Betty Antonie had graduated when this picture was taken in 1937. It was the first photo of the student body at the one-room school in Pine Grove, Wisconsin.

She Taught the Fine Art of 'Seeing'

By Jo Anne Anderson Crane, Jamestown, California

I RECENTLY retired after 20 fruitful years of teaching art to grade schoolers. Any success I may have had I owe to my high school art teacher, Anita Christiansen.

We met in 1948, when I was a freshman. I loved art but didn't know much about it. Over the next 4 years, Anita and I became close friends. Even though she was about 20 years older than me, we bonded like sisters.

Anita taught me the rules and mathematics of art as well as art history. More importantly, she taught me to use my eyes, to look a little deeper, to notice every little detail.

Then she taught me to look again. The idea was to see

> *"She devoted so much of herself to her students..."*

something more than just the obvious, both in nature and in people. I remember only encouragement, never discouragement; advice, not criticism.

One year some of us entered paintings in a competition. The paintings were sent to San Francisco, some 200 miles north of our small town, for an all-state high school exhibit.

She Paid the Way

Anita drove three of us to San Francisco to see the show and visit some galleries. She paid all the expenses. It was a wonderful experience for a small-town kid.

Anita was a widow. Her husband had been killed in World War II, she had no children and never remarried. She devot-

ed much of herself and her life to her students.

I graduated in 1952, went on to college, then married in 1953. Anita was in Yosemite and couldn't attend the wedding, but she sent me the only telegram I've ever received.

Later, when Anita traveled to Guatemala, she sent me a silver necklace to represent the unbroken chain of marriage, and a pair of earrings called "wedding baskets".

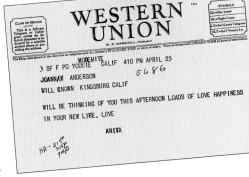

Over the years, we lost track of each other. I had six children, and when my youngest entered school, I became the art teacher there.

I always meant to try to get in touch with Anita again, but I kept putting it off. Then one day I got the news that she had died.

It was too late for me to say, "Look what you did for me!" How I wish I could hug her again and say, "Thank you. You changed my life."

INSPIRED PERFORMERS. Ruth Emick (third from right, standing) of Warren, Pennsylvania says her teacher, Margaret Stoddard (far right), set an example and inspired her to go on and become an ordained minister.

Jack Bryant

Determined Woman Wouldn't Be Left up a Creek

By Harold Bell, Fort Worth, Texas

MY GRANDMOTHER, Elizabeth Dollahite Hale, came from a family of teachers. So this true-blue teacher knew what to do when she learned of an opening at a nearby school.

After the death of my grandfather, Grandmother was left to fend for herself on a hardscrabble farm in Coleman County, Texas.

She was 29 years old, facing large medical bills and had six

> *"Elizabeth wanted so much to make a good impression..."*

hungry children to feed. So she took the necessary classes to reinstate her lapsed teaching certificate.

The next problem was finding a school that needed a teacher. When she heard of an opening at a school 8 miles away, near the little town of Santa Anna, Texas, she made arrangements to meet the school's trustees.

There was a lot at stake—the job paid $40, a good salary just before the turn of the century. Elizabeth wanted so much to make a good impression that she and her 9-year-old son, Claude, washed the family wagon and gave the shabby wheels a new coat of bright red.

The next morning, Elizabeth and Claude set out to meet the trustees. A heavy rain the night before flooded the creek that flowed between the main road and the schoolhouse.

As she drove toward the schoolhouse, Elizabeth could see three men standing on the creek bank, waiting for the water to recede.

When she realized they were also applicants for the teaching job, she snapped her reins and turned the horses directly into the flooded stream!

The trustees waiting at the schoolhouse were so impressed by her courage and determination they hired her on the spot.

One of the trustees yelled across the creek to the three other applicants. He told them to go home, a teacher had been hired.

Elizabeth Dollahite Hale spent the next 30 years as a teacher at that one-room school. During her years, she witnessed plenty of Texas history and told me of it often, until her passing in 1955.

Texas artist Jack Bryant captured the legend of this woman on canvas in 1990. His painting (above) hangs in my home —it's a testament to the determination of a young teacher. ◆

CHALLENGING JOB. When Irene Atkinson began teaching in 1934, her one-room school had a coal stove, no plumbing or electricity and no custodian, says daughter Ilene Steinkruger of Colorado Springs, Colorado.

A Job, a Home, a Diploma

By Ervin Helland, Leesburg, Florida

WHEN I left the Bethesda Orphanage near Willmar, Minnesota in 1925, I was 15 years old, recently confirmed and just graduated from the eighth grade.

I got a farm job near Comfrey, and that fall, I was encouraged by the other kids I'd come to know to start high school. For the next 2 years, I was really busy, working on the farm and going to school.

It only lasted 2 years because I didn't have the money to

>―――←

"I want you to come back to school..."

>―――←

continue. I concluded that was the end of my schooling, and my employer gave me no encouragement to continue.

Then one day I received a note from Mrs. Richard Anderson, the high school teacher and wife of the school superintendent. She asked to see me on my next trip to town.

School had been in session for 3 weeks when I went to see Mrs. Anderson.

"I've been proud of your work in my algebra and geometry classes, she said. "I want you to come back to school."

"It's impossible," I replied. "I don't have the money, the clothes or whatever else is required."

What Could He Do?

"I want you to go to the Comfrey Hotel and talk to Mr. Maloney," she said. "He's in need of a helper. You'll have a place to stay and the opportunity to work for other merchants here in town."

I was thrilled! I walked on a cloud to the hotel on the other end of town where Mr. Maloney, a gentleman of close to 80 years, was sitting on the porch.

I got the job, and within 48 hours, I was happily situated

Teacher Loved Children For Nearly 50 Years

MOTHER started teaching at age 18, in a one-room country schoolhouse during the late 1920s. She remained a full-time teacher for 47 years, proof that she had real love for children.

If one of her students wasn't catching on with the lessons, Mother would work with the child after school, or she'd give up an evening to go to the family's home and help. Often she did so on Saturdays.

Mom adopted me when I was 10 months old, and through the years, I had to share my mom with a lot of other children. I didn't always understand her love back then, and I'd sometimes get mad at her. Today, as an adult, I look up to her for it.

My mother lived to be 78 years old, and when she passed away, I received over 600 cards from her former students. Yes, Mother loved children...and they loved her in return. —*Susan Onion, Biggsville, Illinois*

in my new positions as janitor, desk clerk, waiter, bellhop and doer of whatever duties there were to perform.

I was then happy to walk into Mrs. Anderson's class and be received wholeheartedly by the most wonderful teacher and the greatest kids in the USA.

I graduated in 1929 with my class of 22, parentless, but proud and happy. I had the support of a lot of people, including Mrs. Anderson, in Comfrey, Minnesota, the greatest little town anywhere. ←

COACH. Besides teaching, Strawcy Caudill Vandruff (right) coached the girls' basketball team in Pennington, New Mexico in 1926 (left), says daughter Edith Priest of Clayton, New Mexico.

H. Armstrong Roberts

WHATEVER IT TOOK. Through the years, wives and mothers have had to cope with tough situations not of their making. If things didn't go as Dad planned and the job disappeared, or the wind carried away the topsoil, or Uncle Sam sent him a "greeting", Mom had to cope. She wasn't above getting down on her knees, if that's what it took.

Chapter Six

What Sacrifices She Made

Although we are blissfully unaware of it in our childhood years, our journey through life is full of surprises. Or, to paraphrase Robert Burns, life often leads in odd directions.

It's certainly true of most marriages, where stability is especially prized by wives. Unfortunately, husbands had a way of unsettling things just about the time his wife optimistically thought things were settled.

She'd no sooner get the curtains hung and met the neighbors than her mate would decide they ought to see if Kentucky was as fine a place as Daniel Boone said...or seek gold in California...or join the Oklahoma land rush...or try to get rich in the Texas oil fields.

Not that he was fiddle-footed. He just thought it was the best thing to do for the family.

"Pack up and load the wagon, Amanda, and we'll move out at dawn," he would announce.

Sometimes he'd just head out on his own, never to be seen again. Maybe the Indians were unfriendly or a bear was hungry. Too often in this century, he went to war and met his fate. You just never knew. Then Amanda was left with a bunch of kids to raise and no money in the sugar bowl.

Strong Women Prevailed

Whatever the situation, Amanda did what all the Amandas have done for centuries. She coped. She learned to make do. She developed new skills. She was persistent, untiring and uncommonly ingenious. Countless Amandas are still doing it today.

Several years ago, I met a wonderful couple who ranched in New Mexico, just a hop and a skip from West Texas. It's a land of vast, flat vistas and ranches so far apart you can't see another house on the horizon.

It's no place to live if you enjoy skipping over to the neighbor's for a cup of coffee and a friendly chat. And you want to put a lot of thought into your grocery list, because it's a 40-mile drive to the store.

On my first visit, I immediately thought of an old joke that my farmer father loved to tell. An unfortunate farmer finally had to put his wife into a mental institution. The man, thoroughly puzzled, said, "I can't imagine what caused it. She hasn't been off the farm in 14 years."

Shared Tough Work

But what I found there in New Mexico was a close, loving couple who shared every aspect of ranch life. They had just been honored for winning a corn-growing competition. "That was *my* corn," she boasted. "I was out there every day, moving the irrigation pipes."

If you've never moved irrigation pipes, count your blessings. It's tough work, especially under New Mexico's 100° summer heat. But you have to do it to get a crop.

As a bride, she may have had qualms about ranching in New Mexico, but it was what her husband thought they should do, so she made the best of it.

Some women on the following pages made similar sacrifices, and many others accepted even tougher ones—whatever it took to raise a family and bring joy to those they loved. They went without so that others, often unsuspecting, could enjoy a special bit of sunshine in their lives.

Alas, we rarely realize how much these brave women sacrifice for us and seldom thank them enough. —*Clancy Strock*

Treacherous Alcan Highway Took Mom Home

By Sue Firmin, Flathorn Lake, Alaska

MY CITY-BORN PARENTS heard the call of the wild long before they visited Alaska, the land of their dreams. Jane and Stanley Wilk were married in 1945 and later honeymooned in that state.

They formed such a strong attachment to Alaska that a month after they returned home to Rochester, New York, they packed up their belongings and headed straight back!

I recently found my mother's journals describing her and my father's early days in Alaska. I'm again struck by her dar-

---

"They packed up and headed right back to Alaska!"

---

ing adventuresome spirit and the sacrifices she made to follow her dreams.

Mom and Dad started their journey in July 1947. They jammed all their worldly possessions into a 21-foot house trailer attached to their Jeep. The heavy load included Dad's motorcycle and Mom's electric washer.

Harrowing Journey Ahead

Mom wrote in her journal, "It wasn't easy to bid our parents good-bye, but we weren't reluctant to leave the big industrial city. It held no promise of the outdoor life we both wanted."

The drive from Rochester to Alaska was supposed to take 2 weeks. Little did Mom and Dad know they'd spend 7 long weeks on the road.

The first of countless flats occurred in Michigan. They ended up staying a week in that state, because they exhausted all their spare tires and had to order more. They were back on the road July 30, in the full heat of summer.

The temperature soared to 110° in Montana. The tires became so hot they couldn't be touched with bare hands. At every creek crossing, Mom and Dad stopped to pour cold water over the tires. To lighten the strain, Dad unloaded the motorcycle and followed Mom driving the trailer.

Next Stop, Anchorage

In Canada, they encountered heavy rains that turned the unpaved roads into rivers of mud. For days, traveling was so slow they didn't top 5 mph. Hours were spent getting themselves or other travelers unstuck. When the mud became so

ALASKA BOUND. After their wedding on May 5, 1945, Jane and Stanley Wilk (above) honeymooned in Alaska. They stayed a month, then returned. But not for long. Soon they headed back (below left) with Jeep, trailer and motorcycle.

thick that the motorcycle wheels no longer turned, they put the bike back in the trailer.

On August 18, it snowed in Ft. St. John, Canada, making the roads and mountain passes even more treacherous. But they inched along. Finally, on August 28, they pulled into Anchorage. Mom said she suddenly felt at home, which was funny, since she and Dad were 5,000 miles from the only home they'd known!

They built a lean-to against the trailer and lived there until they found land for their home. Mom had to do laundry by heating water on the trailer stove—she still couldn't use the washer they'd lugged from New York.

In 1948, they bought a small parcel of land south of Anchorage. They built a small log cabin and dug a deep well. Mom worked right alongside Dad, clearing brush, putting in footings and peeling logs. There they lived among the moose, fox, coyotes, porcupines, black bears and lynx. During the next decade, as they raised a growing family of three children, they saw a need for an even bigger house.

Chain Saw for Mother's Day

They built two more homes in the following years. One Mother's Day, Dad bought Mom a chain saw...she was delighted. Now there was no limit to the land she could clear!

In the midst of all her work, Mom still found time to paint and capture the wilderness of Alaska on canvas. It seemed as though living in Alaska satisfied her soul.

She often called Alaska her "chosen country". She made a good choice—today the whole family shares her love of the land. ✦

She Went from Comfy Living to Adobe Dwelling

By Winifred Ross, Lenore, Idaho

FRANCES ROSS was a schoolteacher in Illinois, intelligent and truly refined. In 1915, she gave up her comfortable urban life for a cowboy. That year, she became a frontier wife in a one-room adobe shack in the high desert of California.

Living in isolation was something young Frances had to learn. The shack she shared with husband Lee was the only dwelling at the Twentynine Palms oasis when they moved there.

They went to town but twice a year for supplies. It took 2 days of bumpy travel by horse-drawn wagon just to get there.

Soon there were two baby boys in the family. Imagine saddling up horses, packing supplies and herding the cattle up to the mountains for the summer, with two toddlers to look after. They camped out there with their little boys until fall.

Remained a Lady

Despite the rugged conditions, Frances always dressed in lady-like skirts and high-button shoes. She rode sidesaddle with a baby in front of her. The photos taken in those days showed the children clean and bright in freshly washed and ironed clothes. Every hair in Frances' lovely coiffure was always neatly in place. Her many letters home to her family reported she was happy and enjoyed life with her cowboy, Lee.

Frances and Lee moved to a series of ranches, then a dairy farm, and added two more boys to their tribe. I married one of their four boys, and Frances influenced my life when I was an 18-year-old bride.

She taught me to knit, crochet, cook, can and "make do" with resources at hand. She didn't learn all that in the comfy urban setting she once enjoyed.

Sacrificing that easy life for the love of her cowboy made her a happy person all her life, and in so many ways, she passed her happiness on to me. ⟵

ADORABLE ADOBE. This one-room adobe shack (left) in Twentynine Palms, California was home for Frances Ross after she married cowboy Lee Ross in 1915. But she lived a good life and raised four fine boys. The family photo at far left was taken in 1918 and shows sons Cliff at 2 and Fred at 3 months. Two more sons came along later.

Mother May Have Been Small, But Her Determination Was Huge

I WAS 16 years old at the height of the Depression, when Mother and I found ourselves alone and homeless.

Only 5 feet tall and 98 pounds, Mother was small but determined. She found work in an old hotel in a poor part of town. There, for payment of 50¢ a day and a room for us to sleep in, she made up 50 beds a day.

Her small delicate hands wrestled heavy mattresses and blankets, tucking and folding, until her arms hung limply at day's end. But that wasn't her only job. She worked 4 hours each day at a sewing machine making work pants. The job paid $4 a week under Roosevelt's NRA program.

The second job wouldn't have been necessary, but Mother went the extra mile to provide for my education. She paid my tuition to beauty college so I could work at a trade.

Mother's indomitable spirit would not allow her to be defeated or feel sorry for herself, which would have been easy. She'd been deaf since childhood.

—*Helen Gleason, San Francisco, California*

Mom Gave up Long-Awaited Perm to Buy Tricycle

IN THE MID-1930s, Dad was working for the WPA, making very little. There were four children in our family, so Mom supplemented our income by making artificial flowers and plants, which I sold door-to-door.

Mom had long dreamed of getting a permanent, which cost 50¢. She started setting aside one penny a week. After a year, she finally had enough and set off on foot for the 2-mile walk to the beauty parlor.

Just as she arrived, the store next door was setting out some used items for sale, including a small red tricycle priced at 50¢. Dad told me later that as much as Mom had wanted that permanent, her decision was an easy one.

We'd never had a tricycle. I can still remember seeing her pushing it down the block. It was one of the biggest thrills of my childhood.

Mom did bargain for it, getting the shop owner down to 40¢. With the dime she had left over, she bought a bottle of green sticky stuff women used to curl their hair.

Mother love —there's nothing like it!

—Art Blair
Akron, Ohio

Daughter's Formal Request Wasn't Likely to Be Granted

I WAS so excited to be invited to a formal dance during my high school years in Omaha, Nebraska.

I had a formal dress to wear, but no warm wrap that would be appropriate. It was winter, so I was in a quandary.

Mom knew my anxiety was mounting as the dance date approached. She kept encouraging me to believe something good would happen.

But the Depression was upon us, and I knew there was no money to buy a wrap.

The night before the big dance, I went to bed thinking I'd have to call my date and tell him I couldn't go after all.

COST CUTTER. When Pat Lux needed a coat, her mom, Hazel Halsey (right), found a shortcut solution.

Morning came, and when I rose to get dressed, there on my bedroom chair was the most beautiful black plush formal jacket I'd ever seen!

My dear mother, who was a wonderful seamstress, had stayed up all night to make the jacket her daughter had been praying for. Mom cut up her only winter coat for the material.

Tears flowed as I thanked my mother for making this dream come true.

—Pat Halsey Lux
Walla Walla, Washington

Grandma Loved to Hoard For the Horde She Loved

OUR FRUGAL GRANDMA lived for years on only $40 a month, never treating herself to anything. For years, the whole family gave her cash as gifts.

We felt satisfied, knowing the money would make it easier to treat herself to the niceties she deserved. We should have known better.

When we found out she was saving the money and giving it right back to us kids as gifts, we had to come up with another plan to help her. We started giving her groceries, which she had to use. That way, we knew she'd keep the gift for herself.

To this day, I have an envelope with $3 from Grandma. I'd never spent a

cent…Grandma's pennies saved have earned me millions of memories!

—Millie Karow
Pardeeville, Wisconsin

GIFT OF LOVE. Grandma Herreman (above) gave granddaughter Millie Karow millions in memories.

Mother Made Sure Her Child Came First

MY MOTHER made all of our family's clothing, so you can imagine how much she relied on her treadle sewing machine.

In 1939, I had the opportunity to take music lessons at school…provided I had my own instrument. So my parents made a big sacrifice and bought me a clarinet on credit.

During an especially lean month, bills were due and my parents had to choose—the sewing machine or my clarinet.

Mother didn't hesitate. She gave up her sewing machine and sewed by hand from then on.

What a wonderful sacrifice for her little daughter.

—Betti Swenson
San Diego, California

Mother Dressed Them in Her Finest Fashions

MY MOTHER, Louisa Schuetzle, looked so elegant in the "coming-to-America" dress she sewed at her home in Odessa, Russia. It was one of few cherished possessions that came with her from the homeland, where she'd left her parents, sisters and brothers.

One Christmas was particularly lean, so she ripped apart her beloved dress

so she could sew dresses for me and my sister and an outfit for my little brother. She stitched pretty designs on the buttons of the dresses and little baby ducks on my brother's outfit.

She was a great lady who always dressed us as neatly as she was. This was only one of a lifetime of sacrifices she made for her children.

—*Lilly Klos, Baker, Montana*

Would Mother Be There For Child's Proudest Day?

LEARNING TO READ was my greatest accomplishment in 1944, when I was in first grade. One day, my teacher announced we could invite our mothers to school to hear us read.

What excitement! It was my fondest wish that Mother could be there, but I knew it couldn't happen. She had to care for my two younger brothers, and besides, there was no way for her to get to school.

The big day finally arrived. Giggles and whispers filled the air as we lined up to go inside after recess. Everyone—except for me—knew their mothers were there, ready for our special presentation.

As we entered the room, I looked up, and there was Mother. She was wearing a special

AMERICA DRESS. Louisa Schuetzle (left) was proud of her dress. But when her daughters needed clothes, it became one of the many sacrifices she made for them.

dress I'd never seen before...to me, she looked like an angel! There were other mothers in the room that day, but I only saw mine.

Even now, my heart fills with gladness at the memory, for I know she made a special effort to be there.

—*Nancy Taylor, Tampa, Florida*

Mom Started Her Own Hot Lunch Program

WHEN I was in first grade, I walked each day to a one-room schoolhouse in rural Kentucky. One of my fondest memories of my mother dates to that year of 1928.

Noon was approaching, and I was surprised to see Mother appear at school. She wanted me to have a hot lunch, so she brought me some spaghetti—the first I'd ever eaten! Mother walked nearly a mile to school in the rain just so I could have it hot.

Some 70 years later, I can't eat spaghetti without thinking of Mother. I'm sure my lunch back then only came from a can, but in my memory, that spaghetti remains the best ever.

—*Irene Fahey, Decatur, Georgia*

MOTHER WAS A WORKER. When Erma Britton went back to work at the Weinberg Shoe factory in the 1960s, there were still women there she worked with during the Depression. Daughter Scharleen Brownell of Waukesha, Wisconsin says her mother could sew anything and fix anything. Erma proved it by repairing things around the house, including the car. Mom's homemade fudge was the best, adds Scharleen, who thinks her mother would have made a great pioneer.

Gardening Mother Kept Her Family Together

By Elma Riccio, Mt. Iron, Minnesota

TOUGH TIMES taught my mother-in-law the importance of family. Because of the sacrifices she made, I learned that lesson well!

When Lena Riccio's mother died around the turn of the century, she and her three siblings were placed in an orphanage in Chicago.

Lena, the oldest of the four, watched over her two sisters and brother in the orphanage until their father found work in the mines at Mt. Iron, Minnesota and sent for the children.

She was 16 when she married William Riccio, an immigrant from Italy looking to work in the mines. They had five children and a small home.

But when the big flu epidemic struck during World War I, William took ill and died, leaving Lena to raise the family alone.

She then found out that she was 1 month pregnant and would soon have a sixth child to care for. Her experience in the orphanage strengthened her resolve to keep her own family together.

She convinced her neighbors to plow a patch of land for her to raise a garden. She cleaned houses for people in town, along with the railroad depot. She sewed clothing for neighbors and raised chickens.

Meager Salary Paid Tuition

She only had a third-grade education but returned to school—to work hard. She took a job at the local school cooking and doing janitorial work. She even washed football uniforms by hand until the school got a washing machine!

On her meager salary of $40 a month, Lena put her oldest son through college. She worked at the school 42 years before retiring.

The tough times never hardened Lena. I married her son Daniel in 1948 and enjoyed learning the wisdom of this world-wise woman.

SPLENDID SPUDS. Lena Riccio with a mountain of Minnesota potatoes to feed her six hungry children.

She taught me how to make all sorts of wonderful Italian dishes—ravioli, homemade noodles and special holiday treats. We sat together many evenings, Lena with her crocheting and me with my embroidery.

Lena lived to a ripe old age...she died a week before her 103rd birthday! Her plucky spirit lives on, through her family and the sacrifices she made for them. ✦

Laundry Gave Mama an Extra Load to Handle

By Billie Chesney
Kingsport, Tennessee

YOU HAVEN'T LIVED until you've felt a half-frozen sheet slap against your face in a fierce Kansas wind.

Oh, how my mama used to live!

As a way to earn extra money while caring for my father and us three kids, Mama took in laundry during the late '30s and early '40s. It was backbreaking labor that kept her going from dawn until well after dark.

First, she heated water in a large boiler on the kerosene cookstove and carried it to the wringer washing machine. She filled two galvanized tubs with water for rinsing and made starch in an enamel pot on the stove. She had to stir it constantly so it wouldn't get lumpy.

Several of Mama's customers were employed at the veteran's hospital nearby. Some weeks, she washed and ironed 60 white shirts!

It was my job to starch and sprinkle the clothing, handkerchiefs and pillowcases. I had to roll everything up tightly to "set".

Late-Night Ironing

Daddy would doze in his rocking chair, long after his farm chores were over. Mama, meanwhile, would stand at the ironing board in the living room as my sisters and I played Chinese checkers or did our homework.

When she finally reached the bottom of the ironing basket, Mama would sing out: "That's the piece I've been looking for all week! The *last* one!"

Sometimes she'd swing that last piece around her head in celebration. But most of the time she didn't reach the last piece until we were fast asleep in our beds.

We never knew if Mama slept at all ...after a long night ironing, she was always the first one up. We'd hear her in the kitchen, stirring oatmeal and coaxing us out of bed. "Get a move on... you'll be late for school!"

Eventually, my family moved away from the farm when I was a freshman in college. Mama quit the laundry business and took a retail job in town.

Finally she was able to send out her laundry and have somebody else do her ironing. Now *that's* living! ✦

FAMILY. Billie, Mama (Martha), Daddy (Bill) and sister Shirley in 1946.

Gold Rush Brought Grandmother West

By Julie Larsen, Oakhurst, California

DREAMS OF GOLD brought my grandfather to Goldfield, Nevada in 1904. Sheer determination prompted Grandmother to follow a few months later.

Because she was expecting a baby, Georgianna Wilson was unable to accompany her husband when he left Harrisburg, Pennsylvania. Once the baby was old enough to travel, plucky Georgianna took the train as far as Tonopah, Nevada. Because the mining camp was still 25 miles south, she'd have to take a stagecoach the next day.

She rented a room at the Mizpah Hotel, a wood-frame, one-story structure. The rooms were cold and drafty...she could peek through the cracks of the board siding and watch the goings-on in the little mining town that never slept.

The next morning, she bundled the baby in a heavy wool blanket and set off for the stage stop. She was anxious to show her husband the daughter he hadn't yet seen. She looked forward to a well-cooked meal, a hot bath and a warm bed, comforts she hadn't seen since home.

Not What She Expected

The stage journey was difficult. It took all day and part of the night, due to a blinding snowstorm that hampered travel. Finally, the coach arrived in Goldfield.

It wasn't at all what she expected! Shacks and tents lined the muddy bog that was called Main Street. Georgianna was happy to see her husband, but not this town.

Holding a lantern high to light their way, he escorted his young wife and infant daughter past the shacks and into the open desert. In front of a board-sided tent, he proudly told Georgianna this was her new home.

The floor was dirt, and a bed in one corner sagged almost

ADVENTUROUS GRANDMOTHER. From the goldfields of Nevada to a cattle ranch in California, Georgianna Wilson (left, around 1900) was ready for any adventure life held.

to the ground. The fumes from the kerosene stove burned her eyes.

The conditions were primitive, but Georgianna proved to be a woman of incredible resources. Before long, she set up a large wood-burning stove for cooking and a sewing machine.

She Was Soon in Business

She had three new tents freighted to her. She used one as a kitchen and started cooking for miners. She rented sleeping space to miners in another.

Since there were no banks, she kept her hard-earned money and gold nuggets buried in the corner of the chicken pen.

She was one of few white women in Goldfield. The majority of the town's inhabitants were miners and Paiute Indians.

Once, she heard a baby's cry and looked out to see a stout Indian woman running across the desert with her daughter under one arm and her sewing machine under the other. Georgianna caught up with the woman and saved my mother. She never saw her sewing machine again!

New Adventures to Come

The mines had played out by the time she and Grandfather left Goldfield in 1911. They moved to the next boom town, Los Angeles, California.

Grandmother went on to raise three children and become one of the first female building contractors in southern California. By the time she reached her 60s, she was running her own cattle ranch in the San Joaquin Valley. Life in the Wild West was nothing but adventure for this girl from Pennsylvania! ✦

HOME, SWEET HOMESTEAD. At home in the mountains of north Idaho (below), Florence Matson piled brush in 1921. She had come a long way from the big city of Chicago (left, in 1916) and found living pretty primitive. But she made the best of it, says daughter June Pomerinke of St. Maries, Idaho, and made it a home.

Mom's Small Sacrifices Made Her Girls Smile

By Becky Janes
Bridgeport, Washington

MY MOM made so many sacrifices for my sister and me as we were growing up in the late '30s. But we didn't know about them at the time because Mom never complained about anything.

For instance, we kids were always hungry, but Mother never seemed to be. We couldn't understand it then, but looking back on our economic situation, I'm not surprised now.

Yes, stretching dollars was the name of the game for Mother, and she was truly a winner!

She could come up with all sorts of tricks to make things inexpensive. An apple crate became a spare chair, an old barrel with a pretty cloth over it became a table.

Early in life, we realized you don't have to be rich to be happy!

There were times, though, that temptation got the best of me. Even though I knew we couldn't afford toys from a fancy department store, I couldn't help but show Mom the most wonderful stuffed panda sitting high on a shelf.

He was out of our reach...in more ways than one. Mom gasped when she saw the $5 price tag. She patted my hand, smiled and told me a story that took my mind off that beautiful bear. She knew how to keep our spirits high.

Mom almost always met us at the

door with an after-school surprise. Like the afternoon she greeted my sister and me with the words, "Eenie, Meenie, Minie and Oscar."

She laughed at our puzzled faces and told us to look around. We finally discovered Eeenie, Meenie, Minie...three goldfish! And Oscar? He was a little green plant!

Gifts Brought Giggles

Another time we came home to find Mom standing in the middle of the room, a smile lighting up her face. When we asked what was so funny, she shrugged and said "go look in the kitchen".

We ran to the kitchen and found a box on the floor. When we opened it,

SMILE MAKER. When Becky Janes and sister Donna were 5 and 4 in 1938 (far left), their mother, Mary (above), found ways to make them happy, even during the tough times of the Depression. No wonder they're smiling.

out bounced a fat butterball of a puppy!

Most of these after-school joys came at little cost. But one day she splurged and bought me my heart's desire, that huggable, lovable stuffed panda bear I thought was out of reach.

In the end, Mom was able to give me my panda bear by working hard, sacrificing and saving money. It was a tough road, but along the way, she taught me a valuable lesson: Keep a smile in your heart, and *nothing's* out of reach! ↤

Mother's Roadster Taught A Lesson of Sacrifice

By Betty Hoose, Cadillac, Michigan

MARIE CLUTCHED the precious paycheck she'd just received from the country school. She got into her old Model T Ford, carefully deposited the check in her purse and snapped it tightly shut.

The check was for $105. And to think she'd collect eight more checks like this before the school year was finished!

As she drove toward home, Marie was suddenly inspired. She decided to stop in town to look at the new cars and pulled into Butcher's Chevrolet Sales. The salesman led her to the new 1928 roadsters.

He told her it was the new sports car, the first convertible in the low-priced field. He spoke of four-wheel mechanical brakes, new bullet head lamps and thermostatic cooling. Marie wasn't hearing any of this—all she could see was the black leather seat and cozy rum-

---

"Marie knew she had to have that car..."

---

ble seat in the rear. She knew she *had to* have that car.

It took no time at all to make out the papers, trade in her old Model T and arrange to pay for her brand-new automobile in 8 more months. The total price was $645.

The car was her pride and joy, and she did have it paid for by the end of the year. She held quite a place of respect in the community—a teacher with a brand-new car!

The next year, she began keeping company with a neighbor boy, and within 2 years, they were married. Their wedding date was October 5, 1929—a couple of weeks later, the Great Depression began.

Marie was teaching at a school closer to home. Wes worked as a hired man on a neighbor's farm. Things weren't bad for them.

But in spring, Marie learned that their first child was on the way...I was that child.

Marie would have to quit teaching and stay at home. She told the director of the school she planned to raise chickens instead of teach the next year. On the last day of school, Marie turned the key of the school building for the last time and went home to become a mother of five little girls.

Made to Trade

One night, Wes came home driving a large stake truck. Marie wondered how he was able to buy it. When he happily asked her to sign over the title on her dear little roadster, she couldn't believe her ears. He needed to trade it in on the truck!

Wes tried to explain that he could use the truck to get jobs hauling logs and railroad ties and make the money they so desperately needed. Marie wouldn't listen for a long time, but in the end, she signed the title and watched her dream car drive away.

Her growing family kept her too busy to mourn for her little car and her former career. But once Mom had raised all of us girls, she decided to go back to her first love.

She took classes at night, weekends and during the summer while she taught fourth grade. She earned a master's degree at age 60.

After she retired, she often had dreams about being back in the classroom. It was her favorite dream. That, and the Chevrolet roadster that once kept her in style! ✦

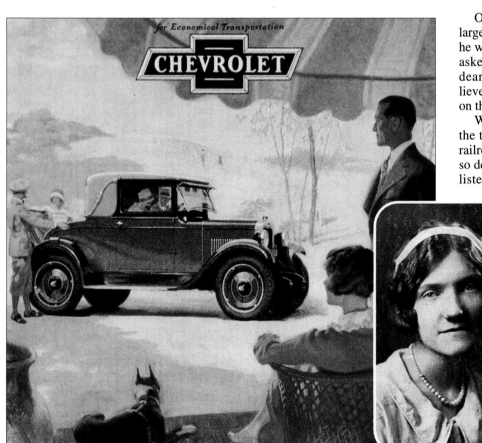

DREAM CAR. When Marie Brower was a young schoolteacher, she fell in love with a snappy Chevrolet roadster. But when she fell in love with the neighbor boy and got married just before the Great Depression, the car had to go.

Mending Mother Put Christmas in the Bag

THREE CENTS doesn't sound like a lot of money, but just after the turn of the century, it went a long way toward our family's holiday happiness.

Every winter, Mother would take in extra work, mending holes in large seed sacks for a local mill. The sound of her treadle sewing machine could be heard far into the night. I helped each morning by folding the sacks into bundles.

Mother turned those few pennies into priceless memories for her 12 children. At 3¢ apiece, those mended flour sacks ensured each of us had a present under the Christmas tree.

—*Arnold Hoerber*
Apple Valley, California

Daughter Recalls Unselfish Mom's Yearning for Education

FAMILY DUTY prevented my mother, Janice Freeman, from earning her high school diploma.

When her father died in 1926, leaving a wife and eight children, Janice was a high school junior. As the oldest, she was forced to quit school and find employment to help her mother.

Her paychecks went toward groceries, doctor bills, house repairs, fuel and taxes. She never spent anything on herself. It wasn't until 13 years later that Janice married and started a life of her own.

Through hard work, she'd developed skills that she carried throughout life.

SACKS OF MEMORIES. *When Christmas came near, his mother made money mending seed sacks, says grateful son Arnold Hoerber.*

She could sew clothing and draperies and upholster furniture. But not graduating was her biggest regret.

I grew up with my mother's values and became a teacher. In memory of her sacrifice, I established a scholarship at our high school. It's my way of carrying on the hope for a better life my mother started in 1926.
—*Brenda Mayer*
Balsam Lake, Wisconsin

Wife's Resources Were Often Put to the Test

WE USED my wife's resources to pay for our first home in 1945. Little did I know how resourceful she would be throughout our 50 years of marriage!

Sylvia's savings as a wartime machinist for IBM paid for our first trailer, which we parked in a friend's yard. We dipped into her savings again when we found out we were expecting our first child.

During the 4 years I was in college on the GI Bill, she made ends meet by selling nylons and Christmas cards door-to-door, and from a job working as a waitress. But we always made it through.

When our "lean" years were over, she focused her energy on helping the community, as a Cub Scout den mother and Welcome Wagon hostess.

Even today, Sylvia buys unwanted carnations from a florist to make bouquets for shut-ins. Now that we are "retired", she's never been busier!
—*Jim Jackson, Prunedale, California*

SISTERS IN SERVICE. Mildred Jordan Etheridge (above left with sisters Sue and Dorothy) served in World War II, reaching the rank of lieutenant, junior grade as a Navy nurse, says daughter-in-law Judean Etheridge of Pine Hill, Alabama. Not only were Sue (WAC) and Dorothy (WAVES) in the service, but three brothers also served. All came home safely. Judean says Mildred and Aunt Dot continue to be an inspiration to her.

Mom Tackled Tough Times on a Tractor!

By Dawn Wrigley, Cheshire, Oregon

BALING WIRE, bubble gum and Mom's indomitable spirit. That could get us through anything!

On a song, Mom faced tough times on our 960-acre ranch in Washington State in the 1960s. Nearly 40 years later, I have a tough time recalling the difficulties we faced, but the songs remain vivid in my memory.

Moving to the ranch had always been Dad's dream, but Mom had been raised a city girl. Moving to that secluded area must have been quite a shock to her—the nearest neighbor was 3 miles away and the closest town 17 miles!

Dad had a job that kept him on the road most of the week, so that left Mom and her two daughters at home with no car. We fended for ourselves much of the time, thanks to Mom's positive outlook.

For instance, if a door fell off its hinges, she made such fun of it that my sister and I would have to recuperate from laughter before we could begin repairs.

When the chimney fell off the roof, she turned the chore into a picnic on the roof!

Nothing daunted my mom. She was chased by bears, cornered on the porch by coyotes and lost a finger in the baler one summer. Still, to hear her tell it will bring peals of laughter and tears of mirth to your eyes.

Arrived in Style

In 1972, my sister was elected prom queen. Mom bought her the most beautiful gown by selling fruit from our few apricot trees and eggs from her hens.

But we had no car…how would my sister get to the dance? Not even that was a problem for Mom. She bundled us up and drove us into town on the tractor. She was unstoppable!

Years later, when I was in college, Mom came for a visit and it finally sunk in—I never saw her get a new winter coat. She had never gone anywhere or done anything that didn't revolve around us girls.

Today when I look back, I realize my sister and I had lots of things, and I realize that was possible only because Mom constantly did without.

Mom went from being a sophisticated city girl from the Midwest to living on a ranch in the Wild West with such flair and style that my sister and I never knew times were tough.

I'm in my 40s now and have learned an important lesson from Mom: When things are toughest, I sing the silliest songs as loud as I can. No one can resist laughing along. *That's* what made my mom so special…she gave me a song to carry me through! ←

FUTURE ROSIE. Evelyn Ramus (posing with her mother, Eva, in 1921) says her mother worked hard all her life, from cooking for a railroad crew to cleaning 26 rooms in the Roosevelt Hotel in Portland, Oregon. Evelyn, now of Ridgefield, Washington, inherited the work ethic from her mother. She was one of many women who went to work in the shipyards during World War II.

SONG IN HER HEART. No matter the problem, Dawn Wrigley's mom, Dorothy, faced it with a laugh and a song. From tractors to goats, she could handle it all and still bring a smile to the kids. The girls never knew when times were tough. Mom just sang a song and made it fun.

FOOD FOR THOUGHT. Others always came first for Lillian Leipprandt (above, bringing food to a church supper, in 1947) says daughter Peg of Pigeon, Michigan. Lillian was a nurse, midwife, youth leader, as well as loving wife and mother.

Afternoon of Fun Meant Plenty of Work for Grandma

ON WEDNESDAY afternoons during the 1950s, my children looked forward to a visit from Grandma.

She would bring them little goodies from the diner she and my father owned, then whisk us off to the beach or to a park where kiddie rides were half-price on Wednesdays.

She'd treat us to dinner at a hamburger place and entertain the kids back home by playing the piano or a game of hide-and-seek. It was a welcome respite for me—I was exhausted after having four children in 6 years.

Many years later, I realized how much effort that Wednesday fun must have taken. Mom had to get up at 5:30 a.m. to open the diner, work until after the lunch-hour rush and drive 25 miles to our home.

She then played all afternoon with four energetic youngsters who wanted to be entertained. After that, she'd make the 25-mile drive home and get ready for another workday.

Luckily I've realized all she's done for us, and I never miss the opportunity to thank her now! —Rosemary White
Oneida, New York

Aunt Ev Relished The Joy of Giving

AUNT EVELYN had a liveliness about her that matched her fiery red hair. What gave her that spark? Helping others was her greatest joy.

One of the first physical therapists in Colorado, Aunt Ev started her career by working with children who suffered from polio.

Once I asked her if she'd worried about being near an illness so contagious. "Maybe at first," she said. "But then I was only glad to be able to help those brave children."

During World War II, she and her husband moved to London to work in hospitals. She worked as a therapist for many young soldiers who'd been wounded.

When she came back to the United States, she suffered from illnesses that left her half blind and crippled. But her disposition always remained sunny and she never lost her sense of humor.

Aunt Ev lived her life sacrificing for others, and when hardship found her, it never got her down.

She told me that each morning when she awoke, she would say to herself, "Something special is going to happen to me today."

Aunt Ev really was something special.
—Carol Mollenkamp
Apple Valley, California

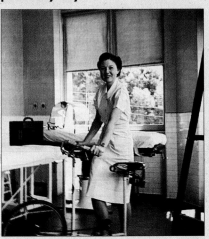

SOMEONE SPECIAL. That was Carol Mollenkamp's aunt, Evelyn May (below, in 1945), a physical therapist who thought first of others and knew something special would happen every day.

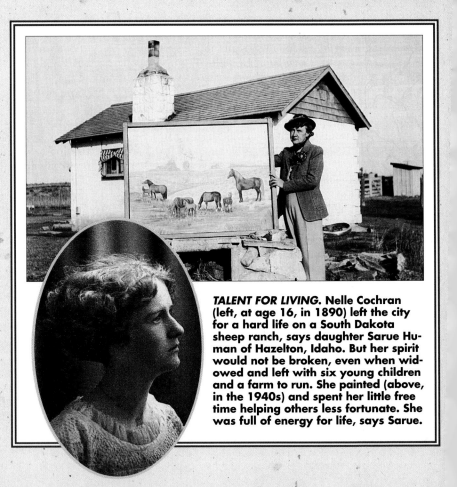

TALENT FOR LIVING. Nelle Cochran (left, at age 16, in 1890) left the city for a hard life on a South Dakota sheep ranch, says daughter Sarue Human of Hazelton, Idaho. But her spirit would not be broken, even when widowed and left with six young children and a farm to run. She painted (above, in the 1940s) and spent her little free time helping others less fortunate. She was full of energy for life, says Sarue.

She Accepted Welfare Aid, But No One Worked Harder

By Betty Butler, Sparks, Nevada

MY MOTHER was a working woman who made sure everything around her "worked" just as hard as she did!

She kept a box labeled "String Too Short To Use" and saved every bit of tinfoil, including the foil wrappers from sticks of gum.

She used to talk about turning glass bottles into canning jars by wrapping paraffin-soaked string around the jar, then

"Mom sacrificed a piece of dignity to keep us together..."

lighting the string. This would score the glass so that the bottle's neck could be snapped off.

My father abandoned Mother and us four children in the early '30s when my youngest sister was 6 months old. I was 2, and my brothers were 5 and 6.

For Mother to raise four children on her own, she had to reluctantly receive Aid to Dependent Children and work in a government-operated sewing center as a way of "earning" this welfare.

Her working day didn't end there—she worked as a cleaning woman and waitress, and she marcelled other women's hair in our home.

Despite Mom's hard work, receiving government aid was a source of shame for her. In a sense, she sacrificed a piece of her dignity to keep us all together.

Kids Felt Her Shame

We kids felt shame, too. My little sister and I would pick up the government-surplus flour, lard and dried fruit in our red wagon. Our embarrassment made us quickly pull the wagon down the alley and scamper across the streets, hoping no one would see us with "poor people's food".

Once that food was home, Mom would stretch it as far as it could go—and then some. By filling out a meal with bread, potatoes and gravy, she could make two cube steaks feed five.

She always made sure we kids had ample food. If there wasn't enough oatmeal to go around, she'd fill our bowls first and then spread a teaspoonful on toast for herself.

My sister and I once met her wrath by being selfish, a vice she detested. We took an empty milk bottle to the store and redeemed it for 10¢, which we spent on penny candy.

When Mom found out, she confiscated the candy and burned it. Not only would she have to pay 10¢ extra the next time she bought milk, we had taken something without her permission.

But Mom had a softer side, and she loved to play, provided the work was done. On Saturday afternoons, when she

PROUD MOTHER. Although she had to accept aid, Vera Covington (above, in 1935) was able to keep the family together. The kids (left to right, Lee, Dwight, Betty and Patty, in 1932) owe their happy lives to her sacrifices.

couldn't afford to send us to the movie house, she'd invent new games with us or entertain us with stories of growing up on the prairie.

Worked for Her Children

During World War II, Mom worked as a bookkeeper for a local dairy in Laramie, Wyoming. That's where she met a mail carrier who became her second husband.

Even after her marriage, she continued to work, even though it wasn't common then. She worked 5 years, until her children were grown.

All four of us are educated and happy with our lives, thanks to Mother. We owe it all to this strong woman, who sacrificed so much to keep the family together and focused on the future. ✦

Seamstress Skills Gave Mother a Whole New Start

By Lorna Trauth
Williamsburg, Virginia

MY MOTHER, Rebeca Stuven Urquhart was born in Santiago, Chile in 1887 and lived to be 103!

What dramatic changes she saw in her long life. Through them all, this petite elegant lady met adversity with courage and grace, inspiring all who knew her.

Mother was born to a distinguished Chilean family. She met and married my father, a young Scotsman, who was traveling through Santiago on business.

They started a family, and after World War I, the couple and their four children moved to London to be near Father's family.

After less than a year, Father grew restless. The adventurer and entrepreneur in him sent him back to South America to find more business worlds to conquer.

Didn't See Dad for Years

Apparently it worked, because he continued to support us in high style in England. We children were too young to question his absence, and in those years, it was common for British men to leave their families for months, or even years, doing business abroad.

In 1926, we joined Father in New York City, where he'd become involved in an import/export business. After 3 happy years, the Wall Street crash changed our lives, leaving us nearly destitute.

Father decided to make a new business start in Mexico. Mother, meanwhile, had to move from a spacious apartment with live-in help to shabby quarters in New Jersey so we kids could attend public school.

For the first time in her life, Mother had no money. What would she do?

She'd made all her own clothes as a young girl. To support us now, she took in sewing, working late every night.

Father's letters became less frequent, and soon his meager financial help dried up entirely. Mother was abandoned, but she never said a negative thing about our father or her situation. "Don't worry," she'd reassure, "we'll manage."

She supported four children to adulthood through her sewing skills. During World War II, while her two sons served in the U.S. Army and Navy overseas, she sewed and knitted for them *and* for charitable organizations like Bundles for Britain.

At the age of 95, she received a commendation from our community for the 45 hand-knitted scarves she donated one Christmas.

Despite having raised her family alone, Mother stayed in good spirits all her life. At her 100th birthday, she remarked, "It's nice to have lived long enough to see so many handsome young men gathered to celebrate my birthday. The only trouble is, I came into this world too early, or they came too late!"

I marvel still at how this tiny lady managed to conquer adversity with such unfailing good spirit, humor and fortitude. ✦

NEVER DOWN. Rebeca Urquhart (above, in 1921, with daughters Luz, left, and Lorna) remained strong even after the Crash in 1929. The family went from well-to-do to destitute, but Rebeca survived and was able to celebrate her 100th birthday in 1987 (top, with great-grandchild and namesake Rebeca).

Her Love Gave Sustenance to Four Generations

By Rodney Sessions, Petal, Mississippi

HARD as a pine knot and gentle as a spring shower, that was my grandma.

I lived on my grandparents' farm in Mississippi, and Grandma spoiled us kids unmercifully.

I grew up a barefoot boy who swam in the creek, hunted squirrels with a dog named "Jack" and had corncob fights with a passel of cousins. Life was good, thanks to Grandma.

Alla Mae Murray was one of the last true pioneers. She and her husband literally took a quilt, an iron skillet, an ax and the clothes on their backs and carved a home out of the forested hills and hollows of east-central Mississippi.

In the early years of their marriage, Grandma and Grandpa only went to the store twice a year, in spring and fall. The rest of the year, they were on their own.

I remember Grandma as the one who rocked us on the front porch on hot summer nights while singing *Rock of Ages* accompanied by the frogs and crickets. She rocked and sang hymns for four generations of children.

Always First to Arise

I remember her as the one who got up first in the morning, when it was so cold there was ice on the inside of the windowpanes. She built the fire so we could dress in front of a warm hearth. It never crossed my mind that she got up and dressed in the icy cold so others wouldn't have to.

I remember her wrapping her head in an old wool scarf and putting on a worn army coat before walking out to milk old "Blacky" so we could have milk

RICH GRANDMA. Alla Mae Murray had riches of the heart money couldn't buy. Grandson Rodney (above, in 1948) was a happy recipient.

for breakfast. I can still hear her feet crunch on the frozen ground and see steam rising from the milk pail.

I remember her herding everyone in the house out to the storm pit when bad weather came up. She reminded me of one of her hens scooping her chicks beneath her wings to shield them from danger.

I remember the breakfasts she'd fix: flowery plates piled high with scratch biscuits, middlin' meat from the smokehouse, red-eye gravy, grits from the gristmill, eggs from the henhouse, homemade cane syrup and hoop cheese from Mr. Sam's or Mr. Bud's store.

Her Garden Was Bountiful

I remember Grandma always working in the soil with her hands. Not only did her garden provide abundant peas, butter beans, corn, tomatoes and other produce, it helped her teach lessons in life.

"Be careful and plow straight rows, for crooked rows are hard to tend," she'd say. When I was older, I tried to stay on the straight path, knowing the crooked path could lead me from life's goals.

Some would say this loving woman was a poor lady, because she left no earthly possessions.

I say she was the richest person I ever knew—as rich as the soil that grows the mighty oak and the fragile wildflower.

Indeed, within her heart, she had the strength of an oak and the beauty of the wildflower—riches she has passed on to all who knew her. ✦

She Gave up Comfort For Husband's Life As a Rancher

MY MOTHER'S storybook upbringing was poor preparation for life as a rancher's wife. But her optimistic spirit sustained her.

Rita Kraus De Rooy (left) was born in 1889 in Luxembourg to a prominent science professor and his wife.

She learned to speak five languages, while a live-in maid cooked, cleaned and even polished shoes for Rita and the other children!

At age 30, Rita sailed to America, met a man and fell in love. They were married on July 1, 1920 in Great Falls, Montana.

Life in the Montana mountains was lonely, money was tight and the work was gruelling.

Even though her days were consumed with cooking for haying crews, raising chickens and rearing children, Mother never lost the gentility of her upbringing. —*Betty Maurer Great Falls, Montana*

STORY TIME. Our mothers and grandmothers taught us so many things, from the time we were small enough to perch in her lap for a story or a reading lesson. But much of what we learned came by example.

Chapter Seven

What Lessons She Taught

The stories that follow are about important lessons in living. They talk of lessons that lasted and shaped a lifetime. You'll find lessons in honesty, in compassion and persistence. And more lessons in coping and surviving and never giving up.

They were taught by strong women who had big hearts and no doubts about the difference between right and wrong. The Golden Rule was pretty much the only rule they needed.

A couple of chapters ago, you read about memorable women who influenced young lives in the classroom. But when children were growing up years ago, at least as much of their learning happened at home, where mothers and grandmothers took the lead.

We tend to forget a lot of what we learn from books. What stick with us forever are lessons learned by watching good lives lived well.

The Lessons Continue

Yesterday, after I'd read the stories in this chapter, I happened to be in the local supermarket. I saw a young woman, not long out of school, doing the family grocery shopping. In the cart was a sleepy toddler halfheartedly gnawing on a bottle of baby formula. Walking alongside was a boy firmly into the Terrible Threes.

What a job that new mother had ahead of her! Fifty years from now, what great lessons learned from her will have shaped those two youngsters?

That little scene got me to thinking about what my own mother taught me about life and living. Besides love and a sense of security, what else had she given me?

Well, for one thing, Mom didn't have much patience with people who were content to sit and complain, rather than get up and *do*. The grade school band can't afford uniforms? No problem. We mothers will make them on our sewing machines.

Ah, but there's no money to buy material. No problem. We'll raise the money with bake sales. Just get up and act!

Mom Taught by Example

Lesson learned: Almost anything can be achieved if you are willing to work hard enough. But Mom didn't sit me down and say, "Son, I have a profound lesson to teach you."

Not at all. She shaped me in a more lasting way. Watching her, it slowly sank into my young brain that it was more rewarding to work than whimper. Everything was possible.

But my wife, Peg, points out the greatest lesson Mom taught by her own example.

"You mother loved you enough to let you go," Peg said. Yes, I thought, that's exactly true. After I left the nest, Mom never again volunteered advice, never told me how to raise my children, never second-guessed my decisions even when they were bad ones.

She'd done her job as best she could, and now I was in charge of my life. She let me go.

Now I had children of my own about to try their wings. They were confidently ready to tackle life on their own. But was I ready to let them? Peg was right. It takes a *lot* of love to truly turn them loose.

For the first time, I realized how much strength and love it took for Mom to let me go. I could do nothing less for my own kids.

Thanks for the lesson, Mom.

—Clancy Strock

Aunt Julia Was Uneducated But Taught Lessons in Life

By Brenda Andrews
Virginia Beach, Virginia

"JUST BECAUSE you are poor, that is no excuse to be filthy," Aunt Julia said, as her hands moved forcefully up and down, scrubbing clothes on the ridges of an old-fashioned washboard.

It was the early 1960s, and my Great-Aunt Julia had taken on the responsibility of raising me. I was a small child then, and Aunt Julia was widowed, childless and 63 years old.

She was immaculate, from her hair always in place to the freshly starched dresses she wore. Every corner of her apartment was spotless. To her, there was no reason to justify leaving a single dirty dish in the sink.

Born the oldest of 14 children to a poor sharecropper in 1900, she spent more time working in the fields than in a classroom. Just a few generations before, it had been illegal for any black person to be educated.

Carried Herself with Pride

A "field trip" to Aunt Julia wasn't an outing to a museum. Her plain brown hands, adorned only with a silver wedding band, had hoed and picked almost every Georgia crop.

As the years passed, she hewed out a life for herself, working as a maid. Aunt Julia wore her crisp white uniform dresses with the pride of a professional.

"Whatever you do, always do it the best you can," she often told me. "And

"It will go hard for you if you don't get an education..."

---

do it right the first time, so you won't have to waste time doing it over."

She routinely walked 5 miles or more to buy cheaper groceries and to pay bills. Not having a car never hindered her from taking care of business.

"A good name is everything. It's worth more than silver or gold," she instructed time and time again.

One afternoon when I was still in elementary school, Aunt Julia galvanized my opinion of education.

"Don't be like me," she sighed heavily.

We were in a store together, and she was awkwardly bent over the counter, struggling with a pencil. She labored to form a squiggly looking "x" mark on her check for endorsement. Her normally bright and confident face was now dark and humiliated. It shocked me.

What Was the Problem?

"I can't write my own name," she admitted, pointing to the ragged "x". "I have to pay some-

one from the little money I make to read and write my letters. And I don't like everybody knowing my business."

She sighed again, looked me straight in the eye and added, "It will go hard for you if you don't get a good education." Mr. Riley, the white store owner, nodded in agreement.

Once I learned to write, she sat eagerly beside me, forcing her tired work-worn hands to form the letters of her name. I tried to guide the rough strokes she made by putting my tiny hands on hers.

Glancing at her face, I saw determination. I knew then that there was no one I wanted to be more like than my Aunt Julia.

Her encouragement carried me into college, and it was there, while I was completing my final year, that Aunt Julia died of a heart attack. She was 77.

I never got a chance to say thank you to my wonderful Aunt Julia. But I've done so countless times in my heart. ↤

LESSON IN LEARNING. If there was one thing Aunt Julia (left and below with niece Brenda) emphasized, it was getting a good education. Brenda did, and graduated from college.

A B C D E F G H I J K L M N O P Q R S T U V W X Y Z

THINK FOR YOURSELF. That was the advice Ruth Pemberton's mother gave her children.

Eight Children Grateful for Wise Mother's Lessons

MY SEVEN SIBLINGS and I recall with gratitude how our mother raised us during the 1930s. She taught us to love one another, to never be jealous of anyone and to be grateful for whatever we had.

She made us self-reliant by not making up our minds for us. Instead, she'd say, "You think of what could happen if you decide this way or that, and then decide what you should do."

She taught us to work and do our tasks as best we could. She often told us, "Whatever you do, do with all your might, for things done by halves are never done right."

My mother was loving and kind to all. I never heard her say bad things about anyone. And she always put us first, before herself. I'll never get over missing her until the day I die.

—*Ruth Pemberton*
Healdsburg, California

Act of Compassion Opened Child's Heart

By Leniegh Schrinar
Riverton, Wyoming

ONE DAY in 1955, when I was 7, I noticed Mom cleaning in an unusual way. Instead of cleaning the kitchen shelves and putting the dishes back, she was putting a lot of things in cardboard boxes. I asked what she was doing. "Just cleaning," she said. I knew better.

Mom took some things from her closet and put them in boxes. When I found her doing the same thing in my closet, I demanded an explanation. She was giving some things away, she said.

"To who?" I asked. "Some people," she answered vaguely.

That was okay, but she couldn't give them any of *my* stuff. I yanked my clothes from the boxes, stuffed them under the bedcovers and threw myself on top of them. "They're mine," I yelled, "and you can't give them away!"

"What are you going to do with those clothes?" Mom asked calmly.

"Wear them!" I screeched. She encouraged me to try them on. I couldn't even button my favorite dress and the hem fell far above my knees. I didn't care. I wanted to keep that dress forever. It was my first store-bought dress, and it was *mine*.

Mom said I could keep my things, on one condition: I had to go along when she delivered the boxes. If I changed my mind, I could quickly nod my head and she'd unload my boxes, too. I had won!

Questions Arose

As we drove through our small Wyoming town, I had lots of questions. Who were these people? Why didn't they buy their own stuff? What difference did it make if we gave them *our* stuff? Why couldn't somebody else do it?

Mom explained that the family couldn't buy things because there was no dad. How could that be? Everyone has a dad! And why doesn't the mom go out and buy what they need?

The mother didn't have a job, Mom said. Well, why didn't she just get one? What was the big deal?

Our 1949 Jeep was only semi-reliable, and it started to slow down as we neared an abandoned house. I figured

CHARITY BEGAN AT HOME. Leniegh Schrinar changed her selfish ways, thanks to Mother Stella (above).

we'd have to start walking now.

But Mom drove around the side of the house like she meant to, and stopped there. She said this was the place.

"Mom, nobody lives here," I said. "There's no car or pickup, just weeds—and no curtains on the windows."

Did Someone Live There?

As Mom got out and lowered the tailgate, a woman with four little kids came out of the house. The children wore nothing but tattered underwear. I had a hole or two in my underwear, but not that many.

Mom didn't say anything as she began unloading boxes. She just acted natural, as if she were delivering the mail. Some of the boxes were pretty heavy—those must have been filled with the food she'd put up in mason jars.

When Mom caught my eye, I gave her a slight nod and she unloaded my boxes, too.

Later, as we drove home, I thought about everything that had happened and felt something I'd never felt before. I kept thinking about those people. What was going to happen to them?

Thank you, Mom, for taking care of the selfish child in me—and for being you. ✦

WORKING MOM. Erla Reynolds (with granddaughter Emma) never worried about getting her hands dirty.

'Tomboy Mom' Showed It's Okay to Be Athletic and Bright

By Anne Reynolds, Arlington, Virginia

MY MOM taught me that it's okay for girls to sweat. As a child during the 1930s, she was one of the few girls to play broomstick hockey with the boys on the frozen ponds around Winnipeg, Manitoba.

In summer, she played basketball, softball and any other sport she could wangle her way into. She rejected traditional "girls' games" because the "boys' games" held more action. She was better than many of the boys.

In college, she was invited to try out for a women's pro softball team. She didn't make it, so she went back to college and became the homecoming queen. She continued playing softball after she was married in the 1940s, and she and my father moved to Florida.

From the time I was small, we spent holidays and weekends working on the family citrus groves. I can still see Mom in her canvas work gloves, yanking vines from the surrounding oak trees or hauling a sack of navel oranges to the truck.

As an adult, I helped her dig a trench about 50 yards long, 2 feet wide and 3 feet deep to lay an electrical cable at one of the groves.

Dirty Hands, Happy Hearts

When we finished, we were covered with sand and sweat, and we were elated. Mom didn't mind getting her hands dirty. She used nail polish only to stop runs in her stockings.

Mom taught me it's okay for girls to be smart and mechanically inclined. She did all the family paperwork, critiqued our homework and drilled us on our spelling.

It was Mom who painted the house and installed new light fixtures. One time, she and I took the dryer apart to replace the belt. She loved figuring out how things worked.

Mom taught me it's okay not to wear makeup. She was a surgical nurse in a children's hospital and had to constantly wash her hands and face. Her only makeup was lipstick, a muted shade of red.

Mom taught me that if I was going to do something, I should do it well. She insisted the house be cleaned from top to bottom every Saturday morning.

Each of us kids was assigned specific rooms to clean. And if we didn't do it right the first time, she made us do it again until it *was* right.

Kids Count

Mom taught me that children are important people. Despite the toll it took on her retirement savings, she gave up her nursing job to stay home with her children. She didn't return to work full-time until the youngest child was out of elementary school.

She was always available to help with homework, bake cookies for a class party or drive us to meetings. Unless there was an emergency surgery she needed to assist with, she never missed

> "*She used nail polish only to stop runs in her stockings...*"

any of our church or school events. She supported us not only with her words, but her presence.

She didn't embarrass me like other parents sometimes seemed to embarrass their children. My friends genuinely thought Mom was fun.

Today, the mother I remember is locked away in a woman with dementia. It's painful to know there's nothing I can do to stop her cognitive decline. The illness is so powerful that when I'm with her now, it's hard to remember what she used to be like.

But when I zoom through the past 10 years to sunnier days, I recall the woman I admire most, a woman whose life gave me life, whose love taught me to love, whose strength gave me strength, whose very essence will never die—my mother, Erla Jean Reynolds. ✦

Mother's Buoyant Spirit Reached for the Stars

By Ruth Lanza, Colorado Springs, Colorado

MY MOTHER, Ruth Willett, taught me how to live and how to die. But she didn't teach me to grow old. Instead, she gave me the courage to dream.

In my first memory of Mama, she's sitting in front of an easel on a summer day, her artist's smock rippling in the breeze, a black paint box beside her and brushes standing in a blue mason jar.

Then one day Mama put her brushes and paints away and never took them out again. Was her longing to paint replaced by other joys? She wrapped her hopes around me and my brother and sister, calling us her "jewels". And she adored my father.

Mama wasn't a hugger. She saved hugging for Daddy, for tucking us in at night, for hellos and farewells. When I brought my own children home, I asked why she didn't cuddle and kiss them. How could she keep her hands off my soft, round angels?

"I want them to run free," she explained. "I love to watch them explore their world, to see how they grow and learn."

Mama was propelled by dreams of grand deeds and a longing for beauty. She often called me to the kitchen window to look across the barren Oklahoma prairie at a beautiful sunset.

She Opened Doors

Mama insisted I take lessons in piano, cello, elocution, voice and painting. She called it "opening the door". I'm sure she hoped stepping through one of those doors would send me soaring into the artistic world of her dreams.

Eyes shining, she often reminded me of the inspiring moment when she saw John Philip Sousa conduct his band in *The Stars and Stripes Forever*. And she enthused about hearing pianist Ignace Paderewski in concert.

As a prominent club woman in our small town of Perry, Oklahoma, Mama often had entertained celebrities before taking them to their speaking engagements. It wasn't unusual for me to come home from school to find poets like Anna Bird Stewart or Edwin Markham sipping tea in the living room.

On March 11, 1937, the principal called me out of class at Mama's request. When I got in the car, she headed for the train station.

"I'm meeting Eleanor Roosevelt," she said. "I want you to meet her, too."

Joined the Crowd

The station platform swarmed with Democrats, adoring women and reporters, but Mama was the one who greeted the First Lady when she stepped off the train. She was an angular woman, wearing a gray coat with a fox collar and veiled hat. Mama escorted her to our Buick and helped her into the front seat.

I remember little of the ride home, except that Mrs. Roosevelt had a high, gravelly voice. She turned to ask me where I went to school and what subjects I liked best. I hope I was as charming as she.

When my father died at age 45, Mama's spirit crumbled. After many weeks, she found the courage to begin life without him.

She bought a flamboyant hat, which she wore backward—she liked it better that way—and took a job implementing the new school lunch program. Five years later, she died of cancer and, we suspected, a broken heart.

When her illness was diagnosed, Mama refused to call my

MODEL MOTHER. Ruth Willett (left, in 1930) taught her children (above, author's on the left) the right way to live.

sister, who was studying acting, or my brother, a law student. "They must be allowed to pursue their dreams," she said.

Mama refused to give in until both had completed their studies, and I'd given birth to my fourth child.

In Mama's last months, I came home with my three children to care for her. I was pregnant, and the days and nights were long for both of us. Several times each night, she'd call me to tighten her sheets. The tiniest wrinkle hurt her back.

"I'm like the princess with the pea under her mattress," she said, laughing at herself. I wept as I returned to my own bed.

After a few weeks, I went home to have my child. The day after Mama heard I'd delivered a healthy baby, she quietly closed the door on this life. I'm sure she rushed joyously into the waiting arms of my father.

I like to imagine that she took out her easel and brushes again, to paint the glories of Heaven. And I wouldn't be surprised if she invited St. Peter to tea.

I've never stopped missing her. And I'll always see her as young, with gentle, smiling eyes looking toward the stars.

She Refused to Let Son Duck the Truth

By Bill Sadler, Brownsville, Texas

FOR MY MOTHER, Bess Sadler, honesty wasn't the best policy. It was the only policy.

My friend Henry lived just behind our house in Edinburg, Texas, and we often played together near our homes. One day in 1932, we discovered a mother duck nesting nearby.

Two 12-year-old boys can be mighty inquisitive—so much so that when the duck left her nest, we went to investigate. There we found six beautiful eggs, so Henry and I decided to liberate two of them.

We reasoned that the mother duck would never miss them—after all, she couldn't count. We'd take them to the chicken yard at Henry's house and put

> "We stammered our apologies, our heads hanging low..."

them under a setting hen. The eggs would hatch, and each of us would have his own duck.

With stealth and cunning, we removed the eggs and made straight for Henry's chicken yard. The plan worked beautifully, except for one thing. My mother was clairvoyant.

She always seemed to know when I'd been up to some mischief, and this time was no exception. Before long, I'd spilled the whole story.

He Was a Robber

Mother looked me straight in the eye. "Son, you and Henry have stolen two of that mother duck's babies," she said.

"But, Mother, they were just eggs. They weren't babies yet."

"*Yet*," Mother said. "That mother duck was expecting to see her babies hatch from those eggs. You boys have stolen two of her babies."

I lamely insisted we didn't mean to steal them.

"Were they your eggs?" Mother replied. "Did you ask the mother duck if you could have two of her babies? Did she give you permission to take them?

"Son, I'm glad that you didn't try to lie. There is only one thing we can do to set things right. You and Henry and I are going to take those two eggs back to the mother duck.

"You are also going to the house of the lady who owns those ducks and tell what you've done and apologize."

My heart sank. I tried to talk Mother into letting us just put the eggs back, but she knew the lesson had to be driven home.

What Would She Say?

With fear and trembling, we went to face the duck's owner. Henry and I stammered our apologies, our heads hanging as low as they would go. The lady accepted our apologies, and Mother told us to take the eggs back to the duck's nest.

When we returned, the lady was smiling. "Since you boys were so honest, I'm going to give you two of the eggs," she said. "You may go back and get them."

Although she never admitted it, I believe Mother paid the lady for two eggs. But I learned a lesson about honesty that has stayed with me to this day. You can't compromise on the truth.

By the way…the eggs did hatch under Henry's hen. Those little ducks thought they were chickens and followed the hen around with the rest of the chicks. ←

HONESTY COMES FIRST. That was what Bill Sadler learned from his mother, Bess (here in 1940).

Brown Brothers

Mom Taught Charity Through Action

By Ruth Fox, Baltimore, Maryland

OPEN HOUSE. Their house was often crowded, like the one above left, says Ruth Fox. Her mother, Dora (above), opened her home to those in need and helped many people get back on their feet.

CHARITY WORK was always second nature to my mother.

We lived in Baltimore in the 1920s, and she was treasurer for a girls' orphanage called Daughters of Hannah.

After each weekly meeting, she'd put the money collected into her shoes and ride the streetcar from the beginning of the line to the end. She wasn't afraid—she always felt a higher power was taking care of her.

When the orphanage had its annual strawberry festival, Mom made sure my brothers and I helped serve. She got all her friends to contribute the strawberries and ice cream. I never remember anyone turning her down.

Mom opened our home to many people who needed help. No one was ever turned away.

An elderly man with asthma took care of odd jobs for other senior citizens in the neighborhood. Every morning, Mom gave him a hot breakfast and packed him a good lunch.

Daughter Learned Lesson

I felt so sorry for him, but his wheezing bothered me. I asked Mom, "Please, can't you feed Mr. Jerry when I leave for school?"

Mom answered, "He has no mother. You do. If you wish to, eat in another room." I understood, and nothing more was said.

There was a poor woman who sold pins, washcloths and odds and ends door-to-door in all kinds of weather. Mom invited her in, gave her food and bought what she could. She never sent the woman away empty-handed.

When the woman's daughter needed a graduation dress, Mom got her one. When the same girl was ready to marry, Mom took up a collection among her friends to pay for the wedding.

A fellow who worked in the garage behind our house was an orphan. Mom

> *"Bring them over— we'll find room..."*

got him to stop drinking, opened a bank account in his name and prodded him to save part of his salary each week. By the end of the year, he'd saved enough money to buy a car. She kept an eye on him, and he called her "Mom".

During the Depression, Mom got a call from someone she'd worked with on charity drives. A family of four had been evicted from their apartment. They

had no money, and it was bitter cold. Mom didn't hesitate. "Bring them over," she said. "We'll find room."

I slept on the sofa and Dad had quite a surprise when he came home from work. I must say, he really was a great guy. He trusted Mom's sincere judgment and let her do whatever she wanted to help others.

Family Grew by Four

It was difficult to manage with four extra people, but Mom did. She went to the gas and electric company to get recipes that were substantial and inexpensive. After 3 weeks, she got her father to provide the family with a rent-free apartment, and Dad found the man a job.

Mom had a burning desire for her children to be well-educated. She surrounded us with books of classical literature (bought on sale) and encyclopedias. She often told us that what you gain in knowledge, no one can take away. My brothers and I all went on to college.

During World War II, my three brothers were in the military. It was a trying period for Mom, but she still mustered the strength to help others.

My mother was an unforgettable human being who left a strong imprint on everyone who met her. She turned people's lives around with love, faith and a sense of justice. She had life dancing to her tune. ←

COUNTRY GIRL. Mary Spinner's mother, Catherine (above), taught her children a love for the land.

Mother Showed Kids How to Appreciate Nature's Beauty

MY MOM lived in town after marrying Dad, but her heart was always in the country. She'd been raised on a ranch and took us kids into the hills of Wyoming every chance she got.

We hiked up windswept hills to admire the vistas and the valleys. We sat on hay bales to watch the magnificent changing colors of a sunset and took walks so we could smell the sweet bitterbrush after a spring rain.

Whether we were out in the country or just in our own backyard, Mom was always telling us, "Now look, listen, feel, smell." She taught us to be aware and to appreciate the blessings of the land.

Now 76, Mom is still an inspiration for our family. I've been blessed to have such a strong and special woman in my life. —*Mary Spinner*
McCammon, Idaho

This Grandmother Had Keen Insight

MY THREE SIBLINGS and I lost our mother in 1951, when I was 7. Gramma cared for Mom until the very end ...then she cared for us.

She was a widow and raised us in her home in northern Michigan with little more than her "old-age pension". Although we were very poor, I never remember being hungry or cold. And Gramma never complained.

At night, I sometimes slept in Gramma's big bed, which was piled high with blankets. Sometimes I got so hot that I'd sneak a leg out, but Gramma always knew. She'd walk all the way around the bed to tuck me back in.

Every Sunday morning, Gramma woke us for church. We had no car, so we had to walk about a mile, and Gramma's arthritis made it slow going. We held her arm as we marched down the street. I only wish I'd held it just a little higher, because she was my hero.

You see, Gramma was blind. But it wasn't a handicap. She saw more than some people with 20-20 eyesight. I learned from her that you can have physical limitations—but they don't limit what your love for others can do.
—*Marge Johnson*
Muskegon, Michigan

MORE PUDDING, PLEASE! Diane Arnold learned to control her sweet tooth, thanks to Nana Ada (above, with Diane's mother, Margaret, in 1910).

Wise Grandma Put a Stop To Pudding Pilfering

EVERYTHING that my grandmother cooked was great, especially the chocolate pudding she made from scratch. I loved that stuff and used to sneak it out of the refrigerator when she wasn't looking.

When it was time for dessert after dinner, there'd be only five little pudding dishes instead of six. Nana always went without—but as a kid, I didn't notice that.

One day when I had a friend over, Nana made a huge bowl of pudding and told us that we could eat the whole thing. Armed with grins and big spoons, we dug in.

Before long, each of us was trying to push the pudding to the other's side of the bowl. We both got tired of that pudding real quick.

I was used to just a little pudding in a dish. Now I had it coming out of my ears! After that day, I never sneaked pudding again. —*Diane Arnold*
Long Beach, California

"Picky Eaters" Learned to Enjoy Variety of Foods

A WISE WOMAN, that was my mom. There was always food on the table for our large family, but it often was ordinary, inexpensive food.

On occasion, one of us kids would complain, "I don't like that. I don't want any."

Mom would reply, "You don't have to eat any. But if you get hungry later on, come back. There'll probably be some left."

There was no offer to fix anything else.

We got hungry and learned to eat and enjoy all kinds of food.
—*Larry Stine*
Brookings, South Dakota

YOU CAN'T FUDGE HONESTY.
Jean Grippin (as a baby, in 1931,
center, and at top right, in 1938)
learned a valuable lesson from her
mother, Ella (above, in 1925).

Conscience Became Her Guide

IN 1944, when I was in seventh grade, rationing was in effect because of the war. My parents were going out to a church meeting one evening, and I asked if a friend could stay with me.

The last thing Mother said on the way out the door was: "Don't make fudge tonight. I need the sugar for canning the peaches."

We made fudge anyway.

As I took the fudge out to the porch to cool, I spilled it down the side of the house. Imagine my fear as I scrubbed the side of the house while my friend held the flashlight.

Many years later, I revealed my deed on that long-past summer night. Of course, Mother knew all along. The clean white stripe down the siding and the missing sugar told the tale.

She knew I would punish myself enough without her saying anything, and she was right. I've developed quite a conscience that helped me during my teen years and beyond.

Today, I'm my best cheerleader and my biggest critic. Thank you, Mother.
—*Jean Grippin*
Honolulu, Hawaii

Mom Taught Child to Look Beyond Hostile Behavior

THE FIRST and greatest teacher I ever had was my mom. Though the "three R's" weren't her greatest accomplishment, she was a genius at interpersonal relationships.

When I came home complaining that Sally Anne was picking on me, she'd say, "Sally may be coming down with something. She probably isn't feeling well. There are a lot of colds going around."

I grew up believing that a good percentage of the population was on the verge of the flu! Now I realize the wisdom of Mom's judgment.

Mom has been called to Heaven, but her philosophy remains intact. I've been a Catholic schoolteacher for 37 years, and when my Sally Annes come to school out of sorts, I generally conclude they're "coming down with something".

Nine times out of 10, I'm right on the mark. Thanks, Mom!
—*Sister Marianne Perrone*
Erie, Pennsylvania

ROOSTER BOOSTER. Patricia Beecher's mom was no chicken...see story at right.

Unusual Photo Revealed Insights to Daughter

TAKEN in the 1930s, this photo (at left) was my mom's favorite picture of herself. She has a proud smile on her face and is cradling a rooster.

When Mom gave me that picture, I asked why it meant so much to her. She explained no one else had ever been able to get near that rooster. He had a terrible reputation and chased anyone who tried to come close. But for some reason, Mom was able to touch him, pet him and even hold him.

This is now my favorite photograph of Mom, too. She taught me that we all have a "rooster" of some sort to hold—abilities that allow us to be or do something absolutely unique.

Some people never even try to hold on to their "rooster". They don't pursue that special ability or give it a second thought.

But those who go after their dreams and grasp them can stand tall, holding their "rooster" proudly—just like Mom.
—*Patricia Beecher*
Horseheads, New York

Caring Mom Kept Families Fed, Clothed, Informed

By Cecile Chmelik
Watersmeet, Michigan

FROM 1946 to 1948, my mother, twin sister and I lived on a large farm in eastern Tennessee. Five other families lived in homes on the farm and worked for Mother, raising tobacco, dairy cattle and chickens.

The families were large, some with as many as 10 children, and it was hard to make a living. Mother made sure each family had clothes, shoes, food, a cow to milk, a large garden and plenty of feed sacks for making clothes. She used those sacks to make clothes for my sister and me, too.

All of the children walked 2 miles to school—some without coats. Mother found coats for them.

Many of the children didn't bring lunches to school, so Mother started a hot lunch program, enlisting neighbors to provide food. The children were shy at first, but the aroma of soup beans and hot corn bread soon overcame their shyness and encouraged them to eat.

Some of those children, now grown, tell me they've never forgotten those hot lunches, and the way Mom cared about each family and its needs.

Helped at the Holidays

Christmas of 1947 was particularly hard. Mother gave each family fresh chickens, bags of beans and oranges and nuts for the children.

My sister and I were taught to give the children any toys we didn't use, and Mother made bean-stuffed dolls for them. I'll never forget their faces when they received those gifts. What joy!

Mother also wrote for the local paper, sharing recipes, news of what was happening in Washington, D.C., or things she read about in books and magazines.

She would invite the neighbors in for coffee and cake, and they'd share ideas on farm programs and local government.

Although our mother died in 1948, she taught us to share what we had and to love our neighbors as we love ourselves. To this day, my sister and I seek out those in need, and I'm proud that my daughter does the same. ↵

SHARE THE BOUNTY. Like this woman, Cecile Chmelik's mother raised chickens. Then she shared with needy neighbors.

A.M. Wettach/RP

LITTLE HELPERS. Cecile (left) and Celeste with Mom Jo.

TAUGHT LIFE'S LESSONS. Crela Sawyer taught her children the "three R's of living", says daughter Bonnie Baumgardner of Sylva, North Carolina. "They were reverence for God, respect for authority and rights for all."

Widow's Iron Will Kept Family Together

By Archie Watson, Sebastian, Florida

NOT ALL good things come in small packages, but my mother certainly did. All 4 feet, 11 inches of her were pure gold—except for her will. That was iron.

My father died in 1926 at age 48, leaving Mama alone to raise six boys. She returned from her sad vigil at the hospital to find the four youngest children in the bed she'd shared with Papa.

She pulled a single bed alongside the big one and began singing them to sleep. I'll never forget the song—*Tell Me the Old, Old Story*, a hymn she and Papa had loved so much. She didn't cry then, but late that night, I felt the bed shake with her suppressed sobs.

Kind friends and neighbors offered assistance, but Mama refused to let any of her sons live in others' homes. She was determined to keep the family together.

Papa had earned extra money by typing news for the county paper. The day after his funeral, the news again began flowing to the editor's desk.

Worked Like a Pro

Though amateurish at first, Mama's efforts soon turned professional, and she began writing for two other papers as well.

Her life became one of feverish activity. The telephone was busy all day as she gathered news. Her afternoons were filled with covering meetings, musicals, flower shows and social teas.

The bus drivers in Tenafly, New Jersey knew her by name—Mrs. Watson. None but a few of Mama's most intimate friends called her Beulah. Though friendly and loving, she had an aura of dignity that demanded respect.

Mama's work kept us together, but food and money were scarce. Many times, we ate cornmeal mush three meals a day. There was usually tea, sometimes with milk. No matter how frugal the fare, we began every meal by thanking God for it.

Mama had a mind of her own and never hesitated to voice her opinion. As an example, one hot day, she saw a peddler whipping his horse and lectured him about cruelty to animals. The rebuke was so mildly worded that the man vowed not to repeat the offense.

And he didn't, either. Mama watched him until she was satisfied of his sincerity.

Helped the Poor

On another occasion, a pitiful-looking beggar was passing through the crowd at a bus stop. No one gave him money, and several people insulted him.

Mama spoke to him quietly about the benefit of earning one's own living. Then she placed her only dollar in his hand, picked up her shopping bag and wearily trudged the mile home without complaint.

One evening, Mama covered a speech by the governor. It was a big occasion, with lots of photographers. After the speech, she edged her way toward the podium.

She told the governor that his speech was good, but she was disturbed to see him posing for pictures holding a glass of liquor. So many young people would see those pictures. Would this have a good effect on them?

Governor Sent Thanks

Several days later, she received a note of thanks. The governor said he hadn't thought of the matter in that light and promised to never again pose with a glass in his hand.

Mama lived for her children, even after we were grown and gone. She stayed in close touch with everyone and showered her grandchildren with warmth and affection.

One day, she told one of her sons, "I've lived a good life—not an easy one, but a rich and full one. I've done all the things I've wanted to do, and I've seen all you boys grow up into fine Christian men. Now my time is in God's hands."

Two days later, she quietly slipped away. People from all walks of life came to pay homage to this quiet, determined little champion. Important people wept unashamedly at her casket.

That was 38 years ago. Yet I still remember with tears and thanksgiving the little lady who made such an indelible impression on my life—and on the lives of everyone who knew her. ⬸

> *"Mama never hesitated to voice her opinion..."*

GOOD LIFE. Beulah Watson (top, with husband John, in 1906) enjoyed a full life with her children (oldest son John, in 1909, above) and friends, like Louisa Springer (below left).

Girl Enjoyed Solitude, Thanks to a Gentle Prod

WHEN I WAS in junior high school, I wanted to go see *Young Tom Edison,* starring Mickey Rooney. No one was interested in going with me.

"I guess I won't go," I told Mother. Her response was, "Can't you enjoy your own company?"

I often think about that afternoon. I sat in the darkened theater, eating a cream cheese and pepper sandwich Mother had made, and learned to enjoy my own company.   —*Rosina Mason*
Silver Spring, Maryland

Grandmother Helped Child Appreciate Her Talents

SEVERAL WOMEN in my life were strong, smart and loving, but Grandma Eva gave me the greatest gift of all. She taught me to love myself.

When I was 6, I was helping her dust, singing Irish lullabies I'd learned from my teacher. Grandma stopped dusting and said my singing was so beautiful that I should make a record.

She opened a cabinet and showed me her record-making machine. By singing into a big microphone, she explained, a blank record would record my voice. Then we could listen to the record over and over.

I'll never forget the pride that welled up in me as I listened to my recording of *That's an Irish Lullaby.* Grandma's face was glowing. She thought I was wonderful—and she wanted *me* to experience *me,* too.   —*Mary Iddings*
Aurora, Colorado

Love of Reading Expanded Rural Family's Horizons

MY GRANDMOTHER passed on a great gift to many of her descendants— the love of reading. I treasure the memory of her singing, rocking a cradle and reading at the same time.

Married in 1891 at 16, she read *Youth Companion* to her children around the kitchen table by lamplight. During World War I, she challenged her daugh-

WHY PIE? Grandma (fourth from left) didn't need a reason to feed the poor.

Grandma Fed the Hungry in Her Own Way

MY GRANDMOTHER lived with us through most of the 1950s. She was a woman of few words, but she taught me much about caring for those who were less fortunate.

Once a week, she'd bake lemon meringue, banana cream and chocolate pies and set them on the kitchen windowsill to cool. The pies would disappear over the course of the afternoon. Later, we'd find empty pie plates on the sill.

The first time I spotted a tattered, unshaven man returning an empty plate, I asked Grandma why she let those "bums" eat her pies. "Because they're hungry," she replied. Case closed.   —*Gary Severson, Everson, Washington*

ters to see beyond homemaking, which was the norm for a rural Nebraska family.

She cajoled her husband into taking the girls 20 miles on the train to go to college. One of her children was a dietitian, another a nurse and another a teacher. A son has a doctorate in agronomy, and one of her great-granddaughters is a librarian.

In every generation of our family, they keep popping up—people who love to read, oblivious to everything else. My grandmother's legacy lives on.
—*Mildred Von Seggern*
Scribner, Nebraska

Making Light of Storms Eased Children's Fears

SEVERE thunderstorms often hit our Kansas farm in the middle of the night. We didn't have a basement, so Dad would tell us to head for the cellar. This was frightening, because we had to go outside to get there, and by then, the storm was usually raging.

To Mom, getting up in the middle of the night to hide from a storm was an unnecessary interruption of sleep. "If we're going to blow away, I guess we'll just have to blow away," she'd say.

Looking back, I think she made light of the situation to ease our fears. She usually joined us in the cellar so we'd know she was safe.   —*Jeanette Urbom*
Overland Park, Kansas

LOVE OF WORDS. Being read to at an early age by her grandma, as these children are, created a lifelong love of reading in Mildred Von Seggern.

Mom's Open-Door Policy Taught Love for Others

UNLOCKED DOORS were my mom's trademark. My brother and I never felt like we came from a small family because there were new faces coming through our door every day.

Uncle Bill moved in for months after returning from World War II. Two of my cousins were raised by

my parents. Other cousins spent more time at our house than their own.

All my aunts and uncles brought their friends to our house, and they were always welcome. Though little money was available, there was enough food for anyone who needed a bit. Mom could always find a quarter to buy someone a loaf of bread.

The neighbors' children were at our home daily. They loved Mom's listening ear and her ability to understand whatever growing pains they were experiencing. When I was a teenager, my friends stopped at the house for breakfast on their way to school.

Yes, all through my childhood in the '30s and '40s, the door was always open, and no one was afraid. Small-town life was different then. Who would ever harm anyone who lived in *Mom's* house?

She was loved by everyone. Sometimes I wonder how she found time to be a mom when so many were asking so much of her.

Mom's open-door policy taught my brother and me to care about others. It also provided us with the rich wisdom that helping others enriches your own spirit.

—*Phyllis Shaughnessy*
Livonia, New York

WARM SMILE AND WELCOME. That's what Phyllis Shaughnessy's mother, Elizabeth (at left and above left), offered with her open-door policy. Phyllis is fifth from left above.

Sunny Disposition Helped Mother Overcome Adversity

A CAR ACCIDENT in the 1930s left my mother a paraplegic at age 28. But she had a sunny disposition, and this sad turn of events didn't change that.

She must have felt blue at times, but I don't remember ever seeing her depressed. She laughed a lot and sang silly songs. "Your mother was born smiling," Grandma would say.

We moved in with Grandma after the accident, and she did all the cooking. But Mother was the baker, working from a little table my father built to fit over her wheelchair arms. He built her an ironing board that fit the same way.

She also did beautiful knitting and sold many sweaters, infant bonnets and shawls.

The long Minnesota winters kept Mother in the house from October to May. She got through those months by enjoying simple things—knitting while listening to the radio, visiting with friends, playing cribbage with my father and delighting in the birds that came to our window feeder.

As soon as the snow melted, she'd send me out to pick a few violets and put them in her little glass vase. It was our spring ritual.

When I was growing up, people would tell me how sorry they were that Mother was confined to a wheelchair. I was sorry, too. Now I realize the great treasures she left me by her example.

Whenever I feel down, I think about my mother—and allow myself to stay at my "pity party" for only a little while. Like Mother, I find sweetness in life's simple things. And every spring, I pick violets for her little glass vase.

—*Joan Reesman*
Franklin, Tennessee

NO HANDICAP. Joan Reesman (with parents in 1937) learned much from her mother.

Gentle Words Eased Pain of Parting

By Kate Lundgren, Elk Grove Village, Illinois

THE DAY had finally arrived. It was time to bid farewell to my friends and walk through, for the last time, the only home I'd ever known.

That house in Chicago was empty; all the furniture had been loaded onto the rickety truck parked in the driveway.

I stood in the dining room, looking up and enjoying the colorful dance of crystals hanging from the

> *"She gave the room a last look..."*

chandelier. Mother was in the living room, shutting the windows. She paused for a moment to gaze outside. When she turned away, tears were streaming down her face.

Mother walked slowly to the spot where the piano had once stood, its outline still visible on the wall. She brushed her hand along the breadth of it, then gently toed the claw-shaped indentations the legs had left in the carpet.

She raised her head slowly, drew a deep breath and gave the rest of the room a last look. The faded rug was threadbare around the edges.

Ten children had crawled, walked, raced and roughhoused on that carpet. Four wedding receptions and a quarter-century of Christmas celebrations and Thanksgiving dinners were held in that room.

I closed my eyes, sank to the floor and imagined the family gathered there. I could still hear the meaningless arguments, the whispers, the speeches, and the kids screaming with glee when Mother's parakeet flew the coop and the dog took off after it.

My mouth watered as I recalled the aroma of roast turkey, mincemeat and pecan pies, fresh-baked bread, candied sweet potatoes and corn on the cob. I was so enraptured that I squealed aloud with joy.

Mother gently took my arm and pulled me to my feet.

"This is only a place, Katrina," she whispered, leading me to the front door. "We will take our home with us." ❖

HOME IS WHERE THE HEART IS. Moving can be traumatic for a child. But a mother knows home is where the family is, and that's what counts.

WHATEVER IT TOOK. Sarajane Ficker's mother, Katie (with husband David), was up to any task.

Her Strength Overshadowed Life Filled with Hardships

MY MOTHER was remarkably strong. Her life was full of struggles, but she knew how to cope.

A childhood accident took most of her hearing. As a young woman, she was widowed while pregnant with her third child. Mom moved home, built a room onto the back of her parents' house and did what she could to make a living.

She took in laundry with nothing but a scrub board. When there was farm work available, she did that. Sometimes she was hired to care for the sick. She did all of this with her little girls following behind her.

By the time the Depression began, she'd married my dad and had two more children. Work was scarce, but with a cow and chickens, we always had milk, butter and eggs. Sometimes that's all we had.

Mother taught me some important lessons during those years: You can be poor, but you don't have to be dirty. Your clothes can have patches, but they can be clean and neat. You may not have steak, but you can make your food look and taste as good as possible. Get all the education you can; you're never too old to learn.

—*Sarajane Ficker*
Vernon, Washington

Mom's Chicken Soup Held Warm Lessons in Living

By Linda Martin, Rochester, Pennsylvania

OUR LIVES changed drastically on that May morning in 1969, when my father suffered a stroke at the age of 42. For the rest of his life, our focus was on helping him recover and achieve the goals he set for himself, and for us.

I didn't realize until after he'd died that none of our accomplishments would have been possible without Mom's endless love and dedication.

When Dad finally accepted he could no longer work as a carpenter, he turned to our farm in Slippery Rock, Pennsylvania. It would be our family's means of survival.

Mom had never experienced life on a real working farm before, but she dove into it with determination.

She became an expert canner, freezer, cook, seamstress, gardener, landscaper, butcher and teacher—and she approached each job with joy.

Did Chores Cheerfully

We all had daily chores, but Mom's cheerfulness made the work seem like play. We learned much without knowing we were being taught.

One of my chores was gathering eggs. Little did I know that when some of these "ladies" got too old to lay eggs regularly, they would become chicken soup.

One Saturday in October, Mom sent us all to the barn to catch the designated chickens and put them in pens. We handed them one by one to Dad, who quickly dispatched them.

I wasn't upset to see some of them go, as I'd suffered many pecks on the hand while reaching under them for their eggs.

Mom brought out large kettles of boiling water, and Dad dunked them in the pots. We children plucked feathers. We spent the whole morning working in our little assembly line.

As we worked, Mom engaged our minds by telling us story after story. Some were her own inventions, some were retellings of classic literature and others were anecdotes from the life of her hero, Abraham Lincoln.

Soup's on!

When all the chickens had been plucked, the soup-making process and storytelling moved to the kitchen. Mom washed the chickens and began boiling them, then she organized another assembly line to chop mounds of onions, celery and carrots.

When the chickens were tender, we boned the meat and had a few wishbone-breaking contests. Then Mom put everything back into a big kettle with seasonings. The

TOUGH TIMES WERE COMING for Bob and Janet Steiner's family when they posed in 1965...but, thanks to Janet, they'd prevail. Richard, 11, Sandy, 9, and Linda, 4, learned without knowing they were being taught.

finished soup was ladled into mason jars and pressure-cooked.

The next day, we carried the cooled jars to the basement. How pretty they were on the shelves, with bright orange carrots floating beside the chicken pieces in a pale yellow broth.

I loved eating that soup when winter came. I felt sorry for my school friends who ate only store-bought chicken soup. I didn't realize we couldn't afford to buy all our food from a grocery store, or that we couldn't afford to let anything on the farm go to waste.

I never felt poor, because our parents didn't let us see the hardships they faced. We always had plenty to eat, because we grew and raised it ourselves.

We had nice clothes to wear, because Mom was an expert mender. And we were always entertained, because Mom was an excellent storyteller. As an adult, I now know we *weren't* poor. We were rich in love—a deep, binding love that remains with me to this day.

I learned, and continue to learn, so much from my mother. I learned how to cook and sew, certainly.

But I also learned patience, loyalty, flexibility, a love of learning and, from both parents, a delight for life that hardships can't squelch.

Thank you, Mom, for being a silent strength in our family—and for being my mother, my teacher, my playmate and my friend. ✦

Widowed Grandma Saved Children From Orphanage

By Mrs. Dean Kirsch
Franklin, Kentucky

BACK IN 1929, my three siblings and I went to live with our grandmother. She realized the situation was desperate. Our mother had died the year before, and our father moved to another state to find work. We didn't see him for years at a time.

So Grandma took on the unending task of making a home for us. Imagine a 54-year-old widow taking in four children ages 4 to 10—and providing for them with practically no income. If it hadn't been for her, I'm sure we would have been put in an orphans' home or foster care.

Luckily, Grandma's 80-acre farm in central Oklahoma was paid for. So as long as we could keep the taxes paid, we didn't have to worry about losing our home.

When someone in the community was ill, the families often came to get "Mrs. Sadie" to care for them. This

meant a little extra income, and as we became older, it was easier for Grandma to do.

We planted a large garden every year and raised chickens, hogs and a calf for meat. We canned lots of vegetables and fruits, and we made jam and

GRANDMOTHER'S LOVE. Being raised on a farm, like the one above, by her grandmother, taught one little girl how to cook, clean, sew and survive.

jelly when we could afford to buy sugar.

Grandpa had owned a car that no longer ran, so Grandma traded it for a nice Jersey cow. We had all the milk we wanted, churned the cream to make butter and made wonderful cottage cheese.

Grandma taught me how to clean, sew and cook. I could prepare a complete meal and bake a pie from scratch

> *"She traded Grandpa's car for a nice Jersey cow..."*

by the time I was 10. She also taught me how to be a survivor. I was the only one of my siblings to finish high school, and I held down two jobs, too.

I lost Grandma when I was 20 and still regret not telling her how much influence she had on my life. She didn't show her emotions a lot, but the sacrifices she made for us spoke volumes.

Although I never really had a mother, I believe I'm a better person for having had the love, guidance and direction of my Grandma Rice, a giant of a woman. ✦

"Run, Run as Fast as You Can... All Kids Should Meet the Gingerbread Man"

NOT LONG after I'd started school, I was reading to Grandma Pegram on ironing day. The aprons, dresses and shirts had been starched, dried and sprinkled.

Grandma had just taken a few strokes on the back of one of Grandpa's shirts when I looked up from my book and asked what gingerbread was.

She set down the iron. "You have never eaten gingerbread?" she asked.

I told her I had not, and she immediately grabbed the sprinkling bottle and redampened the part she'd ironed, rerolled the shirt and put it back in the basket. Then she got out a bowl and sifter.

"First things first," she said.

"What are you doing, Grandma?" I asked. "Isn't this ironing day?"

"You'll probably not remember whether the ironing ever gets finished today," Grandma said. "And I'm most certainly not having a grandchild reading *The Gingerbread Man* without knowing what gingerbread is!"

She was right. I don't remember whether or not she finished ironing that day.

—*Margaret Morrison, Wichita, Kansas*

Her Lessons Were in the Cards

MY GRANDMOTHER, Mina Smith Munro, was years ahead of her time—a believer in women's liberation before the term was ever used. Everyone who knew her was better for the experience.

Throughout her 102 years, Grandma was a gambler—both in cards and in life. She knew reality, adversity and how to survive.

She had only a third-grade education but was one of the best-educated people I knew. She had a voracious appetite for knowledge and read three or four books a week.

She was 14 at the turn of the century, so her memories included some amazing history. She recalled the Spanish American War, and she saw a rally to protest the sinking of the *Maine*. Her mother had seen Abraham Lincoln in person.

As a young mother herself, Grandma ran a laundry in Council Bluffs, Iowa—at a time when it wasn't acceptable for women to work.

Her business motto was "Everything back, but the dirt." She took her four small children with her, providing a

By Kathryn Aartman
Manteca, California

fenced-off area where they could play.

My grandparents later relocated to California. When my grandfather was unable to find work, he left the family to make it on his own.

Undaunted, Grandma opened a drugstore lunch counter and turned it into a

> *"Grandma opened a lunch counter..."*

thriving business, in spite of the Depression and World War II. She parlayed that meager start into two restaurants in Los Angeles, which she ran with my father as her partner.

When Grandma retired, she didn't head for the rocking chair. She visited Canada, Hawaii and Europe. Her plane touched down in Paris on her 70th birthday.

She always had time to help others and time for all 16 grandchildren. She

was the "grand dame" of the family, a lady in every sense of the word. She had a commanding presence, yet everyone felt comfortable with her.

Since Grandma was a gambler, cards were a part of every family gathering. All of us learned to play rummy and poker early on. We joked that we teethed on poker chips.

But Grandma never "let" us win. When we won, we did it on our own. She taught us how to play well and how to bluff, but never how to cheat.

No matter how badly she felt, Grandma always fixed her makeup and hair. She was an impeccable dresser with a great deal of style, and she would never let anyone visit her unless she looked perfect.

Grandma found crowds invigorating and loved family gatherings. When she turned 100, we had quite a blowout and she was the belle of the ball.

Grandma instilled in all of us the feeling that nothing is insurmountable—we're limited only by our own imagination. She gave us a love of life and a love for all people. ↰

She Saved for Years to Repay Decades-Old Debts

BEFORE I was born, my parents and both sisters came down with scarlet fever. Dad was ill for a long time, and one sister contracted rheumatic fever.

Dad couldn't work, so Mother found a job. Though now pregnant with me and not feeling well, she worked long hours, then came home to care for an ill child and an incapacitated husband, besides doing the cooking and chores.

She kept up with expenses as well as possible, but the Depression was on, and her small salary was never enough.

Mother kept working nearly all her life, secretly saving a little money year after year.

When she had saved enough, she asked a grandson to take her back to Grand Rapids, Michigan, where we'd spent those difficult years.

She visited the doctor's son, the new owners of the grocery store where she'd shopped and the daughter of a former landlord.

On each visit, she repaid the outstanding debts incurred all those years before. What an example she set for her children and grandchildren!

—*Thelma Denniston*
Frankfort, Indiana

Loving Mom Left Strong Impression on Daughter

MAMA never had the opportunities her 10 children had, so everything we could do seemed miraculous to her. She said many times that she learned so much from helping us with our homework.

Mama always saw to it that others were happily fed before she ate anything herself. Often, when everyone else had left the table, she'd say, "I'll just put these few potatoes into this bit of gravy and eat that."

During the Depression, she washed and ironed shirts for a dentist to pay our bills. When I saw a beautiful dress in a store window, Mama made a pattern from paper bags and sewed that dress for me.

Once I asked Mama why she hadn't married someone rich. She'd been courted by a rich man once. "But he always ate peanuts in front of me, without sharing," she said. "I knew then he wouldn't make a good husband or father." What wisdom!

Mama had common sense, too. She knew the best way to peel peaches, how to save material when cutting out a pattern and how to iron a shirt without wrinkling the sleeves. Although I took home economics in school, it's what I learned at home that I remember.

When I think of Mama's patience,

her quiet attitude, her giving of herself—even when times were hard—I'm encouraged to do the best I can with God's gifts. I often thank Him for my Christian mother and her example.

—*Elinor Harms*
Grand Island, Nebraska

TRADE-IN VALUE. Elaine Taylor's mother, Annie (above), and father sold this car to buy their first kitchen table and chairs.

Mom's Thrift Paid Lifelong Dividends

SOME PEOPLE save stamps, coins or books. My mother saved money.

Mother had two simple rules. The first was: If you can't pay for it now, you don't get it now. And the second: You must save a portion, however small, of any money you earn.

During their 51 years of married life, my parents bought only what they could pay for outright, including houses and cars. They started out small. Dad sold his car to buy the kitchen table and chairs for our first house, and he rode the bus to work until they could afford another car.

We didn't eat out, and we didn't go on vacations. But we spent many a Sunday hiking or having a picnic in the country. What great memories we created!

My parents raised us in a nice suburban house and paid for two college educations. When they retired, they spent winters in Florida and summers traveling in a 28-foot camper. They spent their last days in a luxury retirement village.

My brother and I learned Mother's secret very early. If Dad gave us 20¢ for helping with a job, half went in the bank. It's a habit we continued through baby-sitting and other jobs—and still continue today. —*Elaine Taylor*
Sinking Spring, Pennsylvania

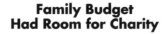

Family Budget Had Room for Charity

WE DIDN'T HAVE a lot of extras during the 1950s, but my mother always managed to give something to charity, especially children's funds.

One day after school, I noticed a brochure showing hungry-looking children waiting to be sponsored. I asked my mother which child she'd chosen.

When she pointed him out, I said, "But, Mom, he's the homeliest one of all." My mother replied, "That's why I picked him. I figured no one else would."

It's been over 40 years, but I've never forgotten those words. —*Kathy Penzotti*
Stratford, Connecticut

WORDS OF WISDOM. It was only a few words, but Kathy Penzotti (with Mom in 1950) never forgot them.

Memoirs Opened Window on a Remarkable Life

By Dan Kidney, West Des Moines, Iowa

FOR YEARS, my naive concept of my grandmother (above) was limited to childhood memories. I never questioned why she was so optimistic—my mother and her sister are named Joy and Gloria.

And I never wondered what her childhood was like. I just thought she was the perfect grandmother, very supportive and always classy.

As a 7-year-old, I was perfectly content to partake of all Grandma offered me. When I visited her, she'd have a bowl of malted milk balls or jelly beans sitting out, easily accessible to young hands. She still does.

She loved to talk to me and come to musicals and plays that I was in. She cooked homemade chocolate pudding, and she hosted holiday dinners with to-die-for dinner rolls.

Innocence is a noble thing to grant a child. I'm glad I had this picturesque image of Grandma for so long.

She Lived History

When I was in high school, Mom said Grandma should write her memoirs. I'd never considered Grandma in a historical context. She seemed ageless.

I was stunned by her story.

Grandma was born in 1918 in a little wooden house in Guthrie County, Iowa. Because of slumping postwar farm prices and then the Great Depression, her family lost their land and had to move more than 20 times.

At one point, all nine children caught whooping cough. Baby twins died of the disease.

The Great Depression wasn't kind to Grandma's family. For dinner, they ate squirrel and rabbit. On at least one occasion, they had only bread, brown sugar and water for supper.

All five of Grandma's brothers, along with her husband, served in World War II. Three of her brothers never came home. She had never let on about any of this to me.

I developed an immeasurable respect for Grandma. This woman, who had gone through so much hardship and loss, was the same woman who'd cooked me chocolate pudding and loved coming to my choir concerts. She was the same Grandma I'd always known but was now beginning to admire.

When she comes to town, we chat amiably at restaurants. When I visit her at the farmhouse, I help mow the ditches. I still never hear a gloomy word from her.

I believe those who deserve praise are those who show grace in extreme circumstances. My grandma is such a person. She has taught me by quiet example. ✦

H. Armstrong Roberts

ON A ROLL. Hands-on learning can leave lifelong impressions. This grandmother passing along kitchen skills to her granddaughter isn't just rolling out pie crust—she's sharing love.

Quilting 'Auntie' Colored Her Niece's Summers

By Chaylene Jewett, Ely, Iowa

I WORK ON quilt tops surrounded by mementos—an old basket, a butter churn, a cuckoo clock. These simple items remind me of my great-aunt, Margaret Hall, who welcomed me to her Iowa home every summer for 10 years.

I never felt homesick for my family back in Utah. It was as if I had two homes. Auntie surrounded me with unconditional love and made me feel needed.

My first summer with her was in 1965, when I was 4 years old. Each morning began with a breakfast of pancakes, bacon and eggs. Then I'd go out to do chores, gathering eggs in a little basket while Auntie milked the cow.

When she finished, we'd pour the milk into a separator, skim the cream and put it in a quart jar with a butterchurn lid so I could make butter. Auntie sold eggs, butter, cream and milk for extra income, and also took in ironing. I

learned at an early age the right way to press almost everything.

Auntie had a big garden, and the activity was nonstop at canning time. I

> "*S*he took time to teach a young girl along the way..."

washed jars until my back hurt. I can only imagine how Auntie's felt.

Her hardworking hands were twisted and crippled with arthritis, but she never complained. She just did what needed to be done, always taking the time to teach a young girl along the way.

Life there was filled with simple pleasures, like quilting. I also admired Auntie's cuckoo clock. Whenever it sounded, I'd drop everything and run to catch a glimpse of that elusive bird—only to find it hidden for another 15 minutes.

Auntie's husband had been paralyzed in a car accident, and she cared for him for 30 years, taking great pains to make sure he was comfortable. Her mother and mother-in-law lived with them, too, and Auntie also cared for them.

Auntie passed on this year, and as I work on her unfinished quilts, my heart fills with warm memories. I could have had carefree summers with my friends, with no responsibilities, but going to Auntie's made me a richer person.

I learned so many lessons from her —standing by your husband through sickness and health, caring for your aging family, the value of hard work. I am the woman I am today because of the example Auntie set.

Now the old egg basket is used for my children's mittens. The cuckoo clock hangs in the dining room, and that wonderful butter churn sits on a shelf. Someday I'll teach my children to make butter the old-fashioned way—with a little cream, lots of cranking and plenty of love. ✦

Heritage Center Museum, Lancaster, Pennsylvania

SEWING LESSONS. The quilts her grandmother made, like the one this woman is working on, created warm memories for Chaylene Jewett.

J.C. Allen and Son

Rushing Through Chore Churned up Trouble

MY SISTER and I detested making butter in our wooden-staved churn, but one afternoon's work produced enough butter to feed our family of nine for a week. It was especially good with the sourdough bread Mama made every Wednesday.

Two clamps held the churn's heavy lid in place. Mama repeatedly warned us never to loosen the lid.

One day during the 1930s, I was playing in the grove when Mama called me inside. I was interested in playing—I simply had no time to make butter! I attached the clamps hurriedly, and halfway through churning, the lid came off.

I heard footsteps approaching and quickly replaced the lid. By the time Mama arrived, she was standing in a greasy mass of half-made butter and watery buttermilk.

The lesson really sunk in the rest of the week, as the family ate Mama's lovely homemade bread *without* butter.
—*Winifred Pommer, Britt, Iowa*

CHURNING MEMORIES. A hard lesson was learned in the 1930s concerning the butter churn. See Winifred Pommer's memory, left.

A.M. Wettach/RP

Decades Later, Mother's Advice Rings True

THE THING I remember most about my mother was her great advice. One of her favorite sayings was, "Love is blind, but marriage is an eye-opener."

I also liked "Fools' names, like their faces, are always seen in public places." I think of that every time I see graffiti on walls.

When Mom thought we were getting too big for our britches, she'd say, "You are never any better than anyone else, but you're just as good." When we talked too much, she'd say, "God gave us two ears and one mouth. He wants us to listen more than we talk."

The one piece of advice Mom felt we should all live by was this: "Remember, honey, this is no dress rehearsal. We only get to live this life once, and you must learn to like yourself just the way you are. If you don't like yourself, it can be a miserable world out there."

We didn't always listen to everything Mom said, but all her wisdom proved to be true—and 65 years later, I remember every word. —*Dorothy Dunkleberger Carlisle, Pennsylvania*

Loving, Patient "Nonnie" Taught Her to Read

IT WOULD TAKE forever to list all my great-grandmother's good qualities, but one example of her patience and kindness was the way she taught me to read.

I was about 4, and we'd sit in the back room and read and read and read: "Nonnie" would explain how to sound out the letters and figure out the words.

After a while, she'd say, "I have to go cook lunch right now. Why don't you look at the pictures.".

While she was gone, I'd try to sound out new words and letters. When she came back, I'd memorize more new words. She worked hard and was so busy, and she still had time for me.

Everyone loved Nonnie because of her outstanding attitude toward others. The neighborhood kids often came to her house to play and have lunch. They treated her like a mom or grandma. When we just had to get out of the house, or we were mad at our parents, we'd go to Nonnie's and talk to her about our problems.

After Nonnie died, I'd sometimes just sit in the back room where she'd taught me to read and remember all the good times we'd had there. Everyone who knew Nonnie was lucky. I will always have a place for her in my heart.
—*Kristin Maves San Jose, California*

GREAT GREAT-GRANDMOTHER. Kristin Maves and her "Nonnie", Virginia Kidwell, share a smile. Now age 12, Kristin wrote the touching tribute that appears on this page.

Hardworking Mom Insisted On Doing Milking Herself

OUR HOME was a happy and caring place, thanks to my mother. She survived the Depression like many other farm women of the era—she cooked, cleaned, washed clothes on a scrub board, baked bread, milked the cows and took care of the chickens.

When my father fell ill, she became the sole breadwinner as well. In summer, she worked long hot days cleaning tourist cabins in northern Minnesota. She traded eggs for groceries, and she sold cut-up fryers to the tourists.

She continued doing the milking herself, telling us, "Never learn how to milk cows, and you will never have to." I think she enjoyed the solitude of the barn while we kids stayed in the house, washing dishes.

—*Vi Lien, Kent, Washington*

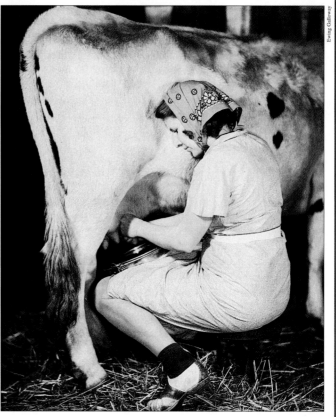

MILKING THE JOB? Lydia Anderson took care of the chickens (top left), and did the milking, like the woman above. Vi Lien suspects her mom milked a bit longer than necessary.

Manners Game Helped Girls Learn Etiquette

MY great-grandmother often took the eldest girl cousins to the best restaurants in Salt Lake City, where we played the "manners game".

When my younger sister was old enough to join us, I explained the rules as if it were some secret initiation. In a way, it was.

The object was to display perfect manners. If you saw someone talking with food in her mouth or reaching for the salt instead of asking for it, you put your forefinger on the edge of the table. The recriminating finger didn't move until the offender begged your pardon or stopped the behavior.

Great-Grandmother taught us when to unfold our napkins and place them in our laps, and when to tear rolls or cut them with a knife. She complimented us when we tried our best and scolded us firmly when we began kicking each other under the table.

I hardly realized it at the time, but she was trying to teach us how to be like her—a lady. To this day, she is still teaching me that.

Through her, I've come to love education and hard work, and to appreciate people not just for who they are, but for how they enrich life.

—*Victoria Stirling*
Salt Lake City, Utah

Struggling Children Found Strength in Mom's Ideals

AS A CHILD of Ukrainian immigrants, I had difficulty in school during the 1930s in Newark Valley, New York. My siblings and I didn't talk "properly", and we observed holy days that other religions didn't have.

When we came home crying because others had been unkind, Mother would remind us that we were Americans, and that the price of citizenship was costly and painful.

She stressed that we were to do the right thing, take responsibility for our choices and always be honest, even when others didn't show the same integrity.

When I married a military man, Mother's teachings helped me during my husband's long tours of duty. We raised our children with my mother's ideals and her work ethic.

I owe my mother for helping me make a happy home. —*Sophie Cox*
Binghamton, New York

PROUD AMERICANS. Sophie Cox's mother, Eva (right), and father, Dmytro (center), taught their children citizenship.

'America the Beautiful' Showed This Child Wisdom

By Jan Joslin, Zephyr Cove, Nevada

IN THE 1930s, people came to Chicago from all over the country looking for work, a better life, the American dream.

Many of them were Southerners, trying to give more to their children than the opportunity in their home states could then provide. One of them came to our house every week to do the laundry.

America was as round as she was tall, and her costume never varied. She wore a white blouse that crisscrossed her ample bosom, a white skirt that hung almost to her ankles and a white apron with pockets as big as grocery bags. Her hair was gathered in a white cotton bandanna knotted at the top.

A Smile on Her Face

Her black face was never without a smile, and her eyes shone when she enfolded me in her arms. "Come on, baby, we got work to do," she'd say, putting me on her hip as she grabbed a full basket of laundry.

America carried me around until I got big enough to help her carry the wicker basket downstairs. We'd push the washing machine to the middle of the basement, then sort the laundry by colors.

Before I put each piece into the sink to soak, I had to tell her what hue it was and then spell the word.

As the washer agitated, America made up songs to match its rhythm. Her rhymes and nonsense lyrics kept us laughing uproariously.

If she wasn't singing, America would talk. She told me about her eight sons, all named for presidents. They were all going to have the education she'd never had. "They're going to be something," she'd say.

America went to school for only 3 years, but she taught herself to read. She carried a book in one apron pocket and often took it out to read a line or two to me. "This is important to your education," she'd say.

If the weather was too cold to hang clothes outside, we cuddled by the big warm furnace and read aloud. Outside, we watched the trees bud and learned about the caterpillars crawling on the basket.

Wherever we were, America always produced something good to eat from an apron pocket—something she'd "baked from the heart".

Dressed Patriotically

Shortly after World War II began, America came to our house wearing a red, white and blue apron. My mother was quiet, watching her. America said nothing as she gathered the clothes. I remember looking at both of them, knowing that something was happening.

LAUNDRY LESSONS. Jan Joslin (left, in 1940, and below, with her mom, in 1939) learned a great deal from the woman who came to do the family laundry.

Finally America turned to my mother. "Mrs. Schwartz, I hate to tell you this, but I've got to help my country. Two of my boys have enlisted and gone to war, and I've got to help them. I'm going to make airplanes or guns or tanks or whatever will help them."

My mother threw her arms around America and they hugged, patting each other consolingly. I burst into tears and ran to my room. America came after me, took me by the hand and said, "We all got jobs to do. Let's get to work."

I never saw her after that day, but I still recall her loving embrace and lilting voice. I'm sure her sons became successful—she wouldn't have had it any other way.

She touched the heart of every person she met. She gave me priceless gifts, this uneducated woman so full of wisdom. She had the willingness to question, a love of books and an unending yearning for knowledge.

Most of all, she had a gift for knowing when to move on and get to work. God bless America. ✦

WOMANPOWER. When most of America's working-age men went off to World War II, America's women stepped forward and proved they could handle most of the jobs the men left behind. But the women did much more. They helped out on the home front and went into military service themselves, doing their share to ensure victory.

Chapter Eight

Rosies One and All

No one realized it at the time, but World War II created a major and permanent change in career opportunities available to women.

Before the war, the traditional jobs were mostly as librarians, schoolteachers, nurses, secretaries and switchboard operators. Everything else was regarded as "man's work". A woman's place was in the home.

Then along came Pearl Harbor and before long, over 10 million men left their jobs as carpenters, mechanics and assembly line workers to join the Armed Forces.

But the free world looked to the U.S. as "The Arsenal of Democracy", counting on it to turn out the armaments, clothing, food and medical supplies needed to win the conflict. Who would take over those jobs?

In the first few months after Pearl Harbor, 750,000 women turned up at the gates of defense plants to volunteer for work—and they didn't just handle rivet guns. By 1944, nearly 3.5 million women were doing everything from building ships and bombers to loading artillery shells.

Could She Cut It?

At first, the men running the factories were skeptical. How could a 120-pound woman possibly hold her own in a shipyard? What did she know about welding or handling a cutting torch? That was work for brawny males.

But the old prejudices and stereotypes came tumbling down in a hurry as women quickly learned their new jobs and proved what they could do.

Their achievements were astounding: By V-J Day, the U.S. had produced almost 300,000 aircraft, 71,000 naval ships, 5,400 cargo ships, 2.5 million trucks, 41.5 *billion* rounds of ammunition and more than 100,000 tanks and self-propelled guns.

Women working alongside men were turning out cargo ships in just 17 days and a B-24 bomber every hour of each work shift!

But that wasn't the half of it. My mom was one of the tens of thousands of women who volunteered to assist the American Red Cross.

She rolled bandages, helped young brides of servicemen cope with the mysteries of military red tape and the problems of being a single mother, and did her best to comfort those whose husbands had been wounded or killed.

Freed Men for Combat

Perhaps the housekeeping suffered and meals were often late, but Mom was determined to make her contribution to the war effort.

Hundreds of thousands of other women enlisted in the military, where they served as nurses, drove supply trucks, worked as mechanics, ferried fighters and bombers overseas and handled scores of other jobs that freed up men for combat duties.

They were greeted at basic training and boot camp with derisive hoots from the men, who chanted, "You'll be sorr-eee." But it didn't take long before they were a welcome part of the military, as they sought no special treatment and went about their work with calm competence.

Rosie the Riveter, celebrated in song and on wartime posters, changed the American work force and the military forever. Indeed, industry learned to its surprise that there were many jobs women could handle better than men.

It's scarcely an exaggeration to say that every woman working today owes a small bit of her job to those valiant millions who knocked down the gates of American industry a half century ago.

How did that song go? Oh, yes: "Anything you can do, I can do better…"

—*Clancy Strock*

Reluctant Rosie Was 'Darn Good Riveter'

By Margaret Nemecek
Whittier, California

WHEN World War II broke out, I was working in a beauty shop in Los Angeles, California. Convoys of trucks loaded with soldiers passed the shop almost daily, heading to the harbor. The men waved, shouted and whistled. I couldn't help but wonder how many would return.

In the evenings, I went to the USO to play games and cards, dance or just talk to the young soldiers. Most of them were away from home for the first time.

When the appeal went out for women to help in the war plants, I left my job and applied at Douglas Aircraft. We were sent to training school for 2 weeks to learn riveting. We practiced on two 6-inch sheets of aluminum that had been clamped together, with holes drilled every square inch.

I put the rivet in the hole and applied pressure with the rivet gun. Meanwhile, my partner applied pressure with the bucking bar (a steel bar) on the backside. This flattened the rivet so it would fill the hole and stay put. The rivet head on one side, and the flattened shank on the other, held the aluminum panels together.

When our training was complete, we were introduced to the big aircraft plant. The building where we'd be working was huge, with no windows. Large doors slid back so planes and trucks could come in and out.

They Built Bombers

One group was led to the area housing the 3-4 section of a B-17. It was a skeleton of a plane—the part in between the tail and the nose. There were no wings—they came later down the line.

The section was in a huge jig, and people were riveting pieces of aluminum onto the ribs. The boss looked at us and told his leadman, "Teach them how to rivet. Make them work. We have a war to win."

Imagine our panic and consternation! The noise was so loud we had to yell to be heard.

How I longed to be back in the one-room Nebraska school where I used to teach, or in the beauty shop. This place was horrible—a man's world. How would I survive? I felt like a sheep led to slaughter!

Dora and I were assigned to work as a team. I worked on the outside with the rivet gun, while she bucked rivets

> *"Someone's husband or brother would fly that plane..."*

inside. This was a great deal different than working on a 6-inch panel. This was for real, on a real plane.

Our leadman did his best to acquaint us with the environment and emphasized the need to do the job right.

I made it through that long, long day, went home and cried. I was determined I wouldn't go back…but then I thought of my brothers overseas and the thousands of young men going into strange places.

Made a Good Team

Well, I went back and I learned to be a darn good riveter. Our leadman taught Dora and me how to improve our speed and rhythm. We made a good team, and we did good work, knowing someone's brother or husband would be flying that plane.

We soon got acquainted with other workers—mostly women—and ate our sack lunches together. Sometimes Hollywood stars entertained us at lunchtime; Red Skelton was my favorite.

Since gas was rationed, six of us carpooled to work, commuting 30 miles round-trip 6 days a week. We settled into a routine that was to last for years.

It seemed like a long time before we heard any good news from the front. But gradually, as our production increased, so did the good news.

It was such a thrill to see one of those huge B-17s roll out of the building. We just knew they and their crews would win the war for us!

I've always been thankful that I worked in the aircraft industry. It helped me to understand what my husband went through, day in and day out.

By the way, I married my leadman after he returned home from the Navy in the Pacific. ✦

Brown Brothers

HOME FRONT HEROINES. Although Margaret Nemecek (right in 1942) hated her job at first, she learned to shoot and buck rivets, like "Rosies" above.

Willow Run Wages Helped Her Pay for College

By Marilyn Steele, Flint, Michigan

AFTER Pearl Harbor, I so wanted to do some hands-on "war work", but I still had 1-1/2 years of high school to complete. Doing my part for the war effort would have to wait.

After graduation, a friend and I applied at Ford Motor Co.'s Willow Run bomber plant near Ypsilanti, Michigan, where the B-24 Liberators were made. We could make big wages—enough to cover our college costs—and help the war effort at the same time.

First we attended a rivet-theory class on a balcony above the final assembly area for completed "ships". We learned to use air motors (drills), rivet guns, countersinks, ratchets and tap wrenches. We learned how to read blue prints and buck rivets.

I was introduced to my partner, Peggy, and our first assignment was in the center wing section, the noisiest part of the plant. We had to wear earplugs and write notes to communicate.

Right away, some joker decided to initiate me and stole my air motor. I wrote a note to the foreman informing him. He wrote back, "Well, steal another!" So, I did.

They Worked Rapidly

After a day there, Peggy and I were taken to the wheel well section to install brackets that held the emergency landing gear cable. We worked quickly and accurately, doing our bit to win the war.

Peggy and I worked so fast that we completed all the work assigned for

> "*W*e learned to use air motors, rivet guns, tap wrenches..."

our shift. So we were given the *next* shift's allotment, too! We were never scolded for our enthusiasm.

One day, told that some famous people were touring the plant, we spotted Charles Lindbergh, Henry Ford and Eddie Rickenbacker. They were all dressed

SCHOOL OF HARD KNOCKS. When Marilyn Steele (above in 1944, and today, top) needed money for college, she helped build the famous B-24 Liberators (left) at a Ford plant.

in dark suits, pointing to the planes and conversing. What a thrill!

Many of the employees had been autoworkers for Ford, and the transition was hard. Production was slow at first. A Senate committee headed by Harry Truman began investigating why it was taking so long to get bombers built.

Things improved, however, and eventually we were putting out one ship an hour. When our production improved, we saw Mr. Truman take a tour of the plant. Katharine Hepburn and Claude Rains visited, too.

The work was very hard, with a lot of standing and reaching. Sometimes we worked 10-hour days. But our hard work paid off, because the B-24 was flown in all theaters of the war and could carry bombs farther and faster than the famous B-17.

After a year, I'd saved enough money to cover a whole year at Michigan State. Then I returned to Willow Run to work and save again. ✦

Ewing Galloway

'Wendy' Contributed To War Effort, Too

By Mary Manroe, Shell Beach, California

EVERYBODY remembers Rosie the Riveter, but not much is said about "Wendy the Welder". I was one of them.

It took a long time for women to be accepted as welders. The work was thought to be too heavy for us. But in early 1943, Cal Ship, near Long Beach, California, decided to sponsor a welding class for women.

I applied and later helped build Liberty ships that carried cargo to our fighting forces all over the world.

About five of us learned to arc-weld and became good friends. We completed the course in a couple of months,

WENDY THE WELDER. Not every woman was a Rosie, says Mary Manroe (above, at Cal Ship). Like the welder at left, Mary did her part.

then took a maritime welding test. We had to show we could do flat, vertical and overhead welds. All of us passed.

The next part was a little harder—walking into the shipyard and facing all the welders with so much experience. But they treated us well.

Put to Work

Someone from the office took each of us to our workplace and introduced us to our leadman, who put us to work. Later on, after they found that women could do the job, the women were marched down walkways in a group, getting whistles and catcalls.

I was grateful that my job was in the plate shop, where we worked on the ribs. We worked outside, rather than in the double-bottom of the ships, which was hard, dirty work. No welding job was very clean, though.

Our attire consisted of leather pants, leather jacket, a black welder's cap, leather gloves and a welding helmet with a dark glass to look through while welding. You didn't look at your own welding, or anyone else's, without eye protection.

When I later moved to western New York State, I applied for a welder's job at a shipyard. They almost laughed. Women were working there as machinists and drill press operators, but they didn't think a woman could weld.

When I got a chance to show them what I could do, I was hired as their first woman welder. I only had to pass a Navy flat test, which I easily did.

This turned out to be a great place to work, too. Before long, they'd taught another woman to weld.

I enjoyed the work so much that I could have made it a career. But when the war was over and the men coming home needed jobs, we were glad to have them take over. ◄

Riveter Worked 10-Hour Shifts

I WAS HIRED by Republic Aviation in Farmingdale, Long Island in August 1943 and assigned a partner who taught me how to drill holes in airplane parts and shoot and buck rivets.

I was 20 years old, and it was the noisiest place I'd ever been.

We worked 10-hour shifts, with every fourth Saturday off. On those days, some of us young ladies dressed up and went to New York City to see the shows and hear the Big Bands.

We were all dedicated to the war effort, producing one P-47 Thunderbolt after another. When the War Production Board approved monthly incentive bonuses, we made even more planes.

I can still see the huge sign over the door that said, "Keep That Line Rolling". What a sight to see so many P-47s on the airfield!

My starting salary was 60¢ an hour. At war's end in 1945, it was 90¢. That was good money then, com-

pared to non-defense jobs.

We lived near the plant runways, where they tested the P-47s. Mom was always worried one would crash on our house. What a roar those engines made.

Being a "Rosie" left me with a lot of memories. I'm proud to have helped my country.

—Josephine Rachiele West Babylon, New York

IN HER WORK TOGS. Josephine Rachiele (right) wore bandanna and heavy coveralls to build P-47s in 1943.

Mother-Daughter Team Became Expert Riveters

By Irene Codding, Kingman, Arizona

IN 1942, my mother and I answered the call for more defense workers, moving from New Mexico to California. We applied as riveter trainees with a company producing C-47 body panels for Douglas Aircraft.

Mother had never held any job except as a bookkeeper-cashier in a business office. I was a college sophomore. Though an unlikely pair, we became specialists in the flush riveting used around cargo doorways and windows.

The factory was so noisy that verbal communication was impossible. Mother and I worked out a system of taps to signal "ready?", "not yet" and "now". Once a steady rhythm developed, we

> *"We were pressed to work faster and longer and on Sundays..."*

became the fastest and best flush riveters in the plant.

Standing on a concrete floor for 9 hours a day was exhausting. Then we were suddenly pressed to work faster, put in longer hours and report on Sundays.

Though we weren't told the reason, we did our best, working at an even faster pace. The contract was completed early, and we began working on wing panels for A-26B planes.

Why the Rush?

One morning as we were getting ready for work, we heard startling news.

"Good morning, Mr. and Mrs. North and South America, and all the ships at sea," the radio announcer said. "Today the Allied invasion of France began. Huge fleets of C-47s augmented the naval armada for the landings."

That was why our C-47 schedule had been sped up!

Later that summer, we were invited to an open house at Douglas' main plant in Santa Monica. We attended attired as ladies should be, in dresses, high heels, hats and gloves. That was a far cry from the denim slacks, navy peajackets, heavy work oxfords and bandannas we had been wearing.

When Mother and I stopped to watch

Ewing Galloway

a demonstration of flush riveting, the tired demonstrators looked at us and asked if we'd like to try it. We stepped up to the panel, picked up the rivet gun and bucking bar, then tapped a "ready" signal to each other.

Mother and I quickly completed a perfect row of flush rivets, handed the

ROSIES IN PAIRS. Like these women above, Irene Codding and her mother made a great pair when it came to riveting aircraft together.

tools back to the men and walked away chuckling at their astonished faces.

Some ladies made very good riveters! ◄

Feisty Crane Operator Won Co-Workers' Respect

MY MOM was raising four children alone, and times weren't easy for us. When World War II came, she went to work at Taylor Wharton, a foundry in High Bridge, New Jersey.

Other women were hired, but Mom was the only one who learned to pour molten metal. She operated a crane, working with men who found it difficult, if not impossible, to accept a woman in such a job.

One crane operator would hightail it down the track whenever someone called for Mom's crane. She'd stop her crane rather than collide with his, and let him do the job.

Then the old-timer complained to the bosses that Mom wasn't carrying her share of the workload, and she was called on the carpet for it.

Mom wasn't a redhead for nothing. The next time her crane was called and the old-timer started racing down the track, she didn't stop. The collision almost knocked him out of his crane.

Eventually she earned the other men's respect and worked at the foundry until the war ended.
                                    —*Eleanor Reading, Flemington, New Jersey*

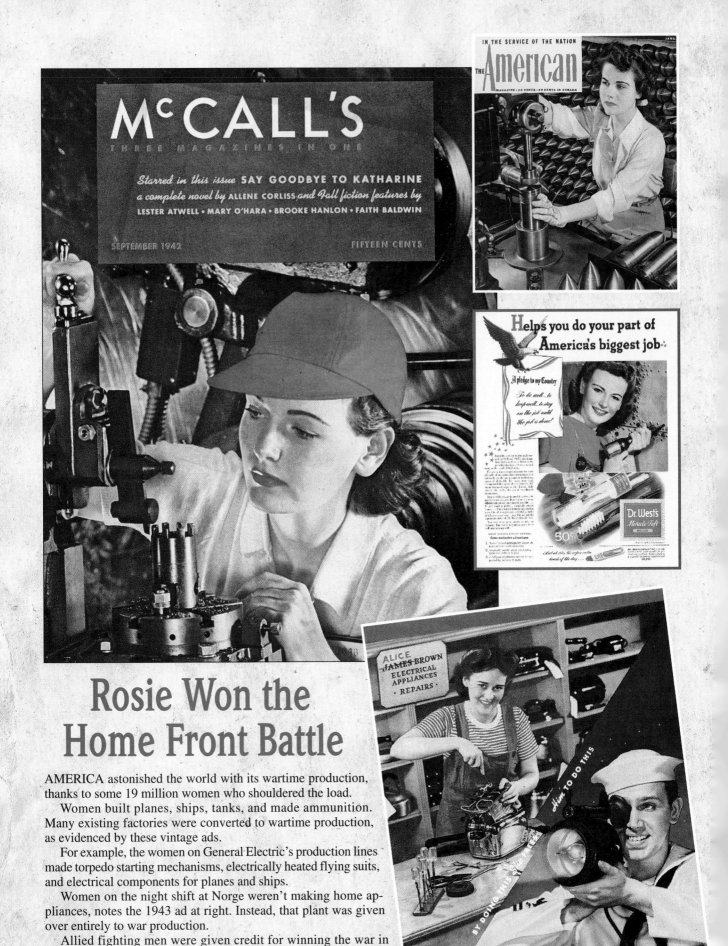

Rosie Won the Home Front Battle

AMERICA astonished the world with its wartime production, thanks to some 19 million women who shouldered the load.

Women built planes, ships, tanks, and made ammunition. Many existing factories were converted to wartime production, as evidenced by these vintage ads.

For example, the women on General Electric's production lines made torpedo starting mechanisms, electrically heated flying suits, and electrical components for planes and ships.

Women on the night shift at Norge weren't making home appliances, notes the 1943 ad at right. Instead, that plant was given over entirely to war production.

Allied fighting men were given credit for winning the war in the field. But equally important were those tireless women who helped win it on the home front. ✦

General Electric Women At War

NIGHT SHIFT

There's a "night shift" in your kitchen, too—if yours is one of the later model Norge refrigerators. The exclusive NIGHT WATCH feature automatically defrosts during the night. After the war, look again to Norge for advanced refrigeration.

Norge distributors and dealers carry on. If you need Norge service, see your nearest Norge dealer. He can help you get first-class service from your Norge appliances "for the duration."

"For outstanding production of war materials" reads the citation accompanying the award of the coveted Army and Navy "E" flag and individual "E" pins to the men and women of Norge.

Wherever American women are working at mechanical jobs in the nation's war plants, they are doing their work well and proudly, for they are serving America. Many of them have never done this type of work before, yet they now are competently performing tasks formerly done by men. In many plants one out of every five women employed is on the night shift! But wherever they are, and whatever these women are doing, they are releasing thousands of men for the armed services, and helping to make the very weapons our men are using. We at Norge, completely in war work, pay tribute to the factory-working women of America and to all other women who valiantly serve both home and country.

NORGE DIVISION, BORG-WARNER CORPORATION, DETROIT 26, MICH.

NORGE HOUSEHOLD APPLIANCES

A BORG-WARNER INDUSTRY

NORGE—only pre-war producer of a complete line of ROLLATOR REFRIGERATORS . . . ELECTRIC RANGES WASHERS . . . GAS RANGES . . . HOME HEATERS COMMERCIAL REFRIGERATION

WHEN IT'S OVER—SEE NORGE BEFORE YOU BUY IN THE MEANTIME BUY MORE WAR BONDS

October 1943 Good Housekeeping

"Thank God for Americans with FIGHTING BLOOD"

Steadfast Through The Years—
Heinz Quality Tradition Will Never Change

5 Only a few years after the close of the Civil War, H. J. Heinz Company was founded by a young American who believed in doing a "common thing uncommonly well." He began by preparing a distinctly superior brand of horseradish—eagerly welcomed by his neighbors . . . Through wars, panics, booms and depressions, the wholesome goodness of Heinz delicious home-like foods has never altered. Back of Heinz 57 keystone label is a 73-year-old pledge of quality—a promise that has been faithfully kept in the past and will be in the future.

The Little House Where We Began In 1869

HEINZ 57 Varieties

SOME OF THE 57: TOMATO KETCHUP, CHILI SAUCE, TOMATO JUICE, BAKED BEANS, SOUPS, PICKLES, VINEGARS, PEANUT BUTTER, BABY FOODS, MUSTARDS

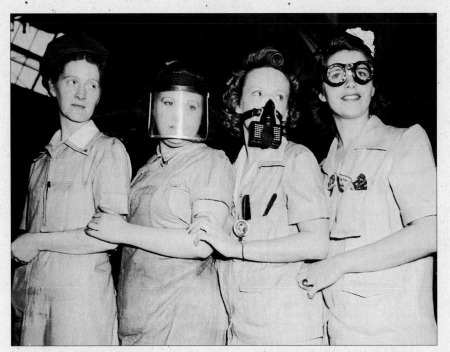

FASHIONS FROM THE '40s. Women who worked in defense plants during World War II, like the four above at the Curtiss-Wright Corporation in New Jersey, had to dress according to their jobs, not the dictates of some fashion designer. In style were caps, face shields, masks and goggles. What those women did for their country!

Work on Airplanes Led To High-Flying Hobby

DURING the war, my husband and I moved to Arizona. I'd worked as a printer in Chicago but couldn't find that kind of work. So I applied for training at Douglas Aircraft in Phoenix. Working there was the most exciting experience of my life.

First I marked blueprints for Navy planes. Then the company needed someone small enough to climb into the planes' floats to do riveting. I was less than 5 feet tall and under 100 pounds, so I qualified. The work was tiring, but exhilarating.

After that experience, I was so enthused about planes that I took flying lessons and managed well in several planes. I never worried about safety. We'd learned at Douglas that all the parts that go into a plane had to be perfect. —*Helen Tackett, Macon, Illinois*

Inspector Made Sure Workers Got It Right

WHEN I BEGAN working at Briggs Manufacturing Co. in Detroit, Michigan, I was sent to school to learn riveting. What a mess!

I'd never held a heavy tool in my life, much less a drill or rivet gun. My poor instructor tried to help me as much as he could, but many evenings I went home crying, my hands covered with blisters.

Later, I was sent to school to become an inspector—possibly because I'd been such a poor riveter. After graduating, I was sent on to the manufacturing line. It wasn't easy.

Many of the men were much older and more experienced on machines than I'd ever be. I often suspected they resented me, especially when I sent a piece of work back. Sometimes I had to send a piece back three times.

But that part of the B-17 wing might be on the very airplane my husband was flying. I wanted it to be the best.

—*Alline Buck, Cerritos, California*

Heat in "Dope Shop" Set Off Sprinklers

I WORKED at Goodyear Aircraft in Akron, Ohio, making parts for the small Hellcat airplanes the Navy used in the war. I worked on ailerons (wing parts) and elevators (tail parts) in the "dope shop", a large room blocked off from the rest of the building.

There were seven ribs on an aileron. The ribs were covered with cloth that was stretched taut. The cloth was painted with the thick "dope", which smelled like ether. Then the ailerons were spray-painted green and hung on a conveyor that went around overhead until the paint dried.

The room had to be kept at a high temperature, even when it was oppressively hot outdoors. And it was a miserable job. The heat and fumes were stifling. The strong odor went home with us on our clothes.

One day the temperature got too high and the overhead sprinkler system went off. We got soaked and had to wade through ankle-deep water.

One day we went to the factory as usual, but our work was done. We received 3 hours' pay for reporting for work.

A lot of the girls wore old shoes to work, and on that day, they simply left them there. At the gate house, where we waited for our bus, a row of old shoes hung over the railing with a sign that said, "We are going back to West Virginia."
—*Evelyn Rhodes*
Uniontown, Pennsylvania

Patient Partner Helped "Rosie" Learn the Ropes

I WAS AMONG the many "Rosies" during World War II, building A-26 bombers at Douglas Aircraft outside Tulsa, Oklahoma. These were the fastest American bombers of the war.

When the supervisor took me to my work station, it was the first time I'd ever been inside *any* factory. The airplanes looked gigantic, and I was apprehensive about climbing the ladder to the wing section.

That's where I met my partner, a man named Fred. I estimated he was about 50 years old. I was 21.

My job was to buck rivets as Fred shot them with the rivet gun. It took a while to learn when to release the bucking bar, and we had to drill out several rivets. But Fred was very patient and never seemed angry or upset with me.

"This is a man's job, and you can refuse to do it," he said. I looked at Fred, who was much smaller than me, and told him, "If you can do this, so can I."

We worked together for the rest of the war and made a good team.

—*Odean Blume, Aurora, Colorado*

Navy Mothers Provided Service on Home Front

WHEN World War II began, Mom said going to work was her patriotic duty and would help shorten the war. It couldn't have been easy. She still had four children at home to care for—and three sons serving with the Navy overseas.

She worked as a sweeper on the line at Post Cereals in Kalamazoo, Michigan. Post produced C-rations for the government.

At the same time, Mom became a charter member of the Navy Mothers' Club of America. This group sent gifts and remembrances to servicemen and provided support for women whose sons were killed or wounded.

The Navy Mothers prayed, provided a shoulder to cry on and attended the funerals—the hardest part of all.

Group members also invited soldiers stationed at Fort Custer to their homes for meals. We had two soldiers with us at almost every Sunday dinner.

On Thanksgiving Day 1942, we were just beginning to eat dinner when the phone rang. It was another Navy Mother, asking if Mom could take dinner to a local man on leave. He was in jail.

Without a word, Mom prepared a basket of food and asked Dad to drive her downtown, leaving her own meal untouched.

My brothers came through the war safely. I like to think that Mom—and all the other mothers working in defense plants and service organizations—did indeed help shorten the war.

—*Barbara Campbell, Battle Creek, Michigan*

NAVY MOTHER. When her sons went overseas to war, Nellie Price (above) worked hard on the home front.

61-Year-Old Widow Joined Assembly Line

MY GRANDMOTHER had been widowed just over a year when Pearl Harbor was attacked. At 61, she'd never worked outside her own home and really hadn't been out at night by herself.

Grandma couldn't drive, so her neighbor, Mrs. Dutro, drove Grandpa's car to Lockheed Aircraft in Burbank, California. They got jobs on the assembly line—working the graveyard shift.

My precious grandmother was a real homebody and very fastidious. She *never* wore slacks. Yet there she was, leaving for work in the middle of the night, wearing slacks and carrying a lunch box. She and Mrs. Dutro both worked at Lockheed until the war was over.

Grandma did what needed to be

GRANDMA ROSIE. Pauline Leedom (right, wearing hairnet, with Mrs. Dutro) became a Rosie at 61!

done, and she did it with pride. What an inspiration! —*Carla Flynn, Sutter Creek, California*

Working in Defense Plant Forged Strong Work Ethic

I BEGAN WORK at a defense plant at age 18 in 1942. Over the next 6 years, I operated a drill press, milling machine, screw machine and lathe, among other equipment.

I also sang in the plant's glee club, which rehearsed once a week. We performed a Gay '90s show and Christmas concerts and entertained the other employees during lunch. The singing was therapeutic for everyone.

That early work experience forged me into a stronger person. At age 71, I'm proud to say I still work full-time as a utility switchboard operator. Working in a defense plant was enriching and taught me to roll with the punches.

—*Velia Costantino, North Kingstown, Rhode Island*

Shipyard Pipe Fitter Found Ways to Fit in

By Thelma Wyman, Fresno, California

MY HUSBAND, Claude, and one of his friends, Fats Reeves, were earning 55¢ an hour as machinist trainees in Tulsa, Oklahoma in 1942.

When they heard workers were needed in California, at starting pay of 90¢ an hour, they jumped in Fats' 1938 Dodge sedan and headed west.

They were immediately hired at Kaiser Shipyards in Richmond, California, where the Liberty ships were being built. Pregnant with our second daughter, I traveled west on the Santa Fe *Chief* to join Claude.

Many months after the baby was born, a neighbor encouraged me to visit Kaiser's hiring hall. She'd just been hired as a welder and was sure I could hook on there, too.

I was 21 years old and had never worked outside the home. But they were hiring laborers to push a broom, and I'd done lots of that.

Put on a Hard Hat

I was one of 20 women hired for an experiment in the pipe-fitting department. I'd be a material expediter, making 90¢ an hour. I had to wear sensible shoes and long pants and keep my hair tied up under a hard hat.

My superintendent, Bill Walsh, showed me how to keep the time cards and requisition slips, and where to check out tools and safety equipment for our 30-man crew.

WORKING COUPLE. Thelma Wyman followed Claude west and found work.

Our crew ran copper tubing to the galley, piped air to the ship's whistle and installed all the hand rails.

And the job went well. I soon made friends with the rigger, who used a fork-lift to load pipe for many crews. Seldom did the men in my crew have to stand around waiting for pipe.

Waited for Welders

Then one Friday morning, several expediters gathered in the bathroom to share some bad news. Each woman held a layoff slip.

They asked if I'd received mine yet. I hadn't. "Well, you will," they said. "They closed down the whole department." It was experimental, after all.

Later that morning, Bill Walsh stopped me on the dock. Did I still like my job? Had I been thinking of quitting? "No," I said. "I want to work."

Bill had my layoff slip—but he'd hung onto it until his boss returned from an out-of-town trip. Then he asked to have me transferred to his regular crew.

I joined the union, became a card-carrying pipe fitter, and soon was making $1.20 an hour. ←

Riveter and Bucker Left Notes for Planes' Pilots

I WAS a riveter on B-24s in 1942 and '43 in San Diego, California. When my partner and I first started, we never believed we could do it. Our boss just kept telling us, "Oh yes, you can." He was so patient.

We trained on old, unused planes until we were good enough to work on the assembly line. My partner and I became very good at our jobs, and our boss was proud of us.

My partner and I wrote notes to the men who'd be flying the planes, wishing them luck. We all took our jobs very seriously.

Our "uniform" was jeans, long-sleeved shirts and steel-toed shoes, with hair either cut short or worn under a net. I wore mine in pigtails. We looked like some kind of a gang! —*Mary Fitzpatrick, Sun City, California*

Teen Spent Summer Working as Riveter

AFTER the war began, we moved from Texas to California, and Dad went to work at Cal Ship in Long Beach. Still in high school and too young to work, I started writing to people in the service—an uncle, cousins, boys from home, boys I'd met in California.

Every day when I got off the school bus at the post office there were at least two letters waiting for me. I was writing to 32 people. Mom once said that every time she needed me to do something, I was writing letters.

The summer after my junior year, when I was 16, I finally got a defense job. My friend Donna and I were hired at the Douglas plant in Anaheim. We worked from 4 to 10 p.m., earning 60¢ an hour plus a 6¢ bonus for working nights.

I became a riveter, and Donna was my bucker. Whenever we began working on a bulkhead, we thought of all the people we knew in the service. We knew we had to make it perfect.

When summer ended, we quit to go back to school. By the time we graduated, the servicemen and women were coming home. But I got to do my part for 3 months. Maybe my letters helped a little, too. —*Audrey Garrett Anaheim, California*

WRITING RIVETER. Audrey Garrett did her part for the war with a pen and a rivet gun.

Twins Did It All—Through Two Wars

By Vera Kringle
Birchwood, Wisconsin

WHEN World War II began, my twin sister and I were in high school in St. Louis, Missouri. When Helen and I turned 18, we trained as riveters at Curtiss-Wright.

The company was building A-25 Navy attack planes then, but production was shifted to C-46 transports, the big planes that flew supplies "over the hump" in the China-Burma-India Theater. The factory had to re-tool, so Helen and I were laid off.

We found temporary jobs as welders at the local boiler works, making boilers for ships. It was much dirtier work than building airplanes!

When production of the C-46s began at Curtiss-Wright, we were called back as riveters. Helen and I worked 10- and 12-hour days, even on Christmas, but we were never tired. Patriotism kept our energy up.

In 1945, Germany surrendered and we were laid off again, so Helen and I joined the Women Marines. Japan surrendered while we were in boot camp. We remained in the service for a year. I

was a police sergeant in charge of a women's barracks.

When the Korean War broke out in the '50s, Helen returned to the Marines and trained men at Parris Island. I went back to building planes.

Another War, Another Wage

But I didn't get that job without a fight. When I applied, I was flatly told that the plant "didn't hire women".

I replied, "I'm a veteran, I have 3 years' experience building aircraft, and I have a right to fill out an application." I did just that, and the following week, I received a notice to come to work.

I was a riveter again, this time on jet fighters like the Banshee, Voodoo and Demon—and at the lowest starting wage. An inexperienced man who started the same day was paid more than I was. For the first year, I was the only woman in my department.

I carpooled with four men who worked in the experimental division. We thought they were working on the fuselage of a new type of plane. Whenever it was moved through the plant, it was kept completely covered and we began calling it "The Body".

In 1955, all four men were transferred to Houston, Texas for more work on "The Body". It turned out to be the first rocket. ✦

SEMPER FI, SIS. After Vera (above, right) and Helen worked in defense plants, they joined the Marines.

NO JOB TOO TOUGH. Vera (right, in both photos) and Helen could handle rivet guns, welding rods and cutting torches.

Inspector Proud to Leave Her Mark on Engines

By Phyllis Donahoe, Sacramento, California

WHEN THE CALL came for women to work in factories during World War II, Velva Butterworth Davis decided it was time to show her patriotism. Recently, she shared her memories of those heady days with me, at a conversation in her Sacramento, California home.

Velva quit her job at a shirt factory in Kansas City, Missouri and went to work at Pratt & Whitney, where they built R-2800-C aircraft engines.

Clad in plant-issued overalls, shirt, shoes and safety glasses, she operated the giant lathes that shaped gears and propellers. Later, she became a gear inspector, looking for invisible cracks that could cause engine failure.

"At final inspection, the gears were placed in a solution and magnetized, subjecting the parts to a magnetic force in a flux of fine metal particles," she told me. "This caused the particles to align in the tiniest cracks, invisible to the eye.

"This was serious responsibility, because such cracks could cause an engine to fail. We were proud of the job we were doing. We turned out the best aircraft engine of the time."

Stamped with Pride

All Pratt & Whitney workers were assigned identification numbers, which they etched on their work. Velva was proud to mark the parts she inspected with her number.

"So many lives, including my four brothers', depended on my accuracy," she explained. "I was dedicated to precision and minute details."

The plant operated around the clock. For 2 years, Velva worked 7 days a week and changed shifts every 3 months. The 11 p.m.-to-7 a.m. shift was toughest. To get to work, she traveled 30 miles each way, taking two buses and a streetcar.

Though proud of her contribution, Velva admits it was not easy. "The war brought dark, lonely, and frightening and days," she said. "It was hard going to work when the rest of the world was going to bed.

"The younger women were lonesome, with no social life to look forward to at the end of their

FINAL INSPECTOR. With four brothers in the service, Velva Davis was a careful worker.

AIRCRAFT PLANT WORKERS including Inez Whitaker (second from left) saw morale boosted by presidential visit.

Thrilled Workers Saw FDR Tour Omaha Plant

I WAS a "Rosie the Riveter" for 2 years at the Glen L. Martin plant in Omaha, Nebraska. I was 19 years old and proud to do something for my country.

In 1943, President Roosevelt came to the plant, riding up and down the aisles in a convertible. It was a great day. Seeing our President was thrilling, and it helped our morale.

I worked the evening shift, going to work in late afternoon and to bed in early morning. I remember working 2 weeks without a day off to help meet the production schedule.

Once we gals stopped at a coffee shop after work, about 3 a.m. As we were leaving, a couple of soldiers started talking to us. I guess our voices were a little loud—someone from the apartment window above dropped a bucket of water on us! We went home damp, but it's been a wonderful memory all these years.

The plant closed immediately after the war, but some former employees still gather for annual reunions.

—Inez Whitaker, Porterville, California

long shift. We'd gather at my home for potluck. Girl talk helped relieve the boredom."

Helped at Home, Too

At home, Velva used her rationed sugar to bake cookies for the boys who came to the local USO. She also shipped cookies overseas to her four brothers.

She saved bacon grease in an empty tin can on the stove. "One pound of kitchen fat gave enough glycerin for a pound of black gun powder. This meant six artillery shells or 50 .30-caliber bullets."

Finally, it was all over. "When they announced the end of the war, I put down my tools and went home, returning only for my last paycheck," Velva said.

"My brother Bernard made it home from his tour of duty just in time to hold Mama's hand before she died. The cargo plane that carried him home was powered by a Pratt & Whitney engine. I like to think it had my identification number etched on it." ✦

Female Electricians Surged to Their Duty at Navy Yard

By Sylva Mularchyk
Santa Maria, California

I BEGAN work at the Puget Sound Navy Yard at Bremerton, Washington in November 1942. I'd been told to report to the electric shop and expected to be put to work immediately on board ship. Instead, I found myself working as a timekeeper.

Then I graduated to "new construction", where my duties included everything from filing blueprints to braising

>――――――――――――――――――
> *"We discovered muscles we'd never used..."*
>――――――――――――――――――

bulkhead tubes. After that, I was transferred to an aircraft carrier, the *USS Lexington*, and worked in the electrical stockade, checking and receiving material.

Then came the break I'd been waiting for. I was one of 10 girls selected for an electricians' training unit. After 14 weeks of training, we'd be journeymen electricians—provided we could pass the exams.

Old-timers asked us, "Think you can pull cable?" We said, "Sure!" with a good deal more bravado than we felt. We'd seen some of that cable in spools on the docks. It was as big in diameter as our forearms.

But our enthusiasm wasn't dampened. We were issued leather gloves and fully equipped electricians' toolboxes. We were no longer just "helpers". We were trainees.

Charged with Responsibility

Women aboard ship were no novelty in any shipyard during the war, but lady electricians at Puget Sound were unheard-of. We faced scrutiny, disapproval, even laughter. Whether the men said it or not, we knew what they were thinking: Has it come to this?

The first few days aboard ship, our worries were purely physical. We discovered muscles we'd never used.

Our first job was disconnecting and removing two large fire control panels on the battle wagon *USS Maryland*.

To get to the storage compartments, we had to clamor down three successive ladders, each set about 6 inches further inboard. We held our breath as we began the descent, our tool bags over our shoulders.

Most of the work was overhead, and we had to exert every aching muscle. We did the job—we'd always said we could—but oh, our aching backs! They say the first 30 years are the hardest, and each week seemed like 30 years.

Lighted Battleship

Then we drew a lighting job on the *Maryland*. We laid out cable runs, studied our blueprints and ordered fixtures. We connected door switches, shunt switches, E boxes and receptacles, and we pulled cable. Then we cut into the main power supply, threw the switches—and there was light.

Along with on-the-job instruction, we attended classes 4 hours a week. We learned to draw sketches and wiring diagrams, and we studied our manuals feverishly.

We were on a destroyer escort, the *USS Porterfield*, the day an excited officer shouted over the address system: "Now hear this! The war is over! All yard workers leave the ship!" The war was over. This was what we'd been working and praying for.

After V-J Day, we went back to work and classes. Our training was nearly over. We passed our final exams and accepted the compliments of our supervisors. Each of us was recommended for the rating of electrician.

We had qualified. Then we got our pink slips. We were women, and our jobs went back to the men. That's how it was in 1945. ✦

TIMELY PROMOTION. Sylva Mularchyk was marking time as a timekeeper when she got her break and became an electrician at the shipyard.

Rebuffed by Military, She Found Work in Defense Plant

WHEN World War II broke out, my sister-in-law, Ardith Tennis, immediately signed up for the military. At 4-foot-11, she was an inch short of the required height.

The night before her physical, Ardith saw a chiropractor in hopes he could "stretch" her that extra inch. He did, but it didn't last overnight.

Ardith was deeply disappointed when the military turned her down, but she wouldn't be deterred. She found a position at Northrup Aviation in California and rose through the ranks to become an inspector.

Many of her stories about those days involve men who were ticked off at having their work refused. But she'd never okay a wing that wasn't perfect.
—*Ella Tennis, North Muskegon, Michigan*

POW's Wife Was Model of Patriotism

By Jane Woods, El Monte, California

MY HUSBAND was a second lieutenant in the Army Air Forces when we married in May 1943. After a 9-day honeymoon, he left for duty on a B-17 named *Little Jan*, flying bombing missions over Italy and Germany.

Little Jan was eventually shot down and the entire crew survived, only to be taken prisoner.

On the home front, I felt packing parcels for POWs at the Red Cross wasn't enough. My sister agreed—her husband was stationed in France. So we applied for work at Curtiss-Wright Aircraft in St. Louis, Missouri, our hometown.

We passed all the exams at the head of our class and were assigned to work as riveters in the experimental lab. We were very proud, as our department was top secret and off-limits to unauthorized personnel.

Safety uniforms and shoes were being introduced for female employees, and I was asked to model them.

Not Bad, for Uniforms

The pictures (two are on this page) were used on posters and billboards around the complex to encourage ladies to wear their uniforms with pride. The uniforms were presentable enough to wear from work to shopping and recreational activities.

I also volunteered to exercise horses at Jefferson Barracks Cavalry Post in St. Louis County. Many of the cavalrymen were on the fighting front, and those poor horses needed to be exercised regularly. It was great recreation for me and some of the other military wives with whom I rode.

Later, my sister and I answered a call for "government girls" to work in the Pentagon. After a 6-week crash course in typing, we were flown to Arlington, Virginia.

We lived at Arlington Farms, a compound with very small private rooms and communal kitchens and laundries. Government buses took us to and from work.

It was a wonderful experience for two housewives in their 20s, and we were rewarded for our contributions to the war effort. Our husbands were among the lucky ones to come home.

Even Before Pearl Harbor, First Rosies Were on the Job

By Anne Wilde, Corning, New York

IN SEPTEMBER 1941, the United States wasn't yet involved in the Big War, but our plants were turning out P-38s and B-17s to send to England. That's when I was hired at Lockheed-California.

Before two other women and I walked through the plant, it had been an all-male domain. We heard no wolf whistles…instead, we saw dropped jaws signifying surprise and disapproval. We were intruders.

There was a wide noisy aisle through the center of the building and it was humming with activity.

Forklifts carried parts and crates. Young messengers on roller skates dashed hither and yon, delivering communiques to departments. Deafening thuds reverberated from the drop hammers.

Put to Work

Our first assignment was "burring" the rough edges on large pieces of sheet metal. We sat silently on stools as we scraped away, well aware the men were watching us for signs of feminine frivolity—silly chatter or goofing off.

For our next assignment, we were given black rubber aprons, goggles and masks, and trained to operate radial drills on stacks of sheet metal.

Then we progressed to numbering machines, punch presses, power brakes, riveting, production control and other tasks.

My favorite assignment was working as a dispatcher and production control clerk. Chasing down lost parts and job orders was more challenging than burring.

We got 30 minutes for lunch when a piercing whistle signaled the break. We ate sandwiches from home or the lunch cart. By now, the men were less wary of us and even appeared proud we could hold our own in the workplace. Eventually, more female recruits arrived, but we three apparently broke the ice.

"We heard no wolf whistles—we were intruders…"

Then came the shock of December 7, when President Roosevelt announced the attack on Pearl Harbor. We weren't on the sidelines anymore—we were in an all-out war.

Patriotic fervor sparked our lives. As we worked, we sang our favorite song, the rousing *Praise the Lord and Pass the Ammunition*. Little by little, our younger male co-workers began to disappear as Uncle Sam called them to duty.

Sometimes now, when I reflect on those days, I wonder what fate held for those young men I'd worked beside.

Though our hearts were heavy for loved ones far from home, I'll never forget the camaraderie we felt as we worked together to preserve our American way of life. ✦

Cadet Corps Launched Many Nursing Careers

In 1943, the call went out for 10,000 more nurses for the Army and Navy: A bill was introduced creating the Nurse Cadet Corps, which would provide training for qualified young high school graduates.

Our training provided an education in medicine that continued almost around the clock. We took classes during the day, worked hospital floor duty at night, cleaned the hospital on our days off and worked in the kitchen in between.

We were in our teens, and we loved it! The uniform was a great source of pride for us, as many of us came from poor families.

In 1944, 12,000 nursing students became senior cadets, and by 1945, graduates were ready for assignments. Senior nurses went to veterans hospitals overseas and on board ships. The younger nurses carried the load at home.

The program ended with the war, but it contributed to the war effort and has proven a great asset to our nation's health care. Thousands of us who graduated as RNs in 1945 are still in the health care-profession.

Many of us look back on those 3 years with wonderful memories. We're grateful to have been a part of it. —*Jean Likens*
Franklin, North Carolina

STILL WORKING. Jean Likens, who took her first training with the Nurse Cadet Corps, became a registered nurse and still works in health care.

'Real Rosie' Was Good Sport with Male Pranksters

By Margaret Artley, Winter Haven, Florida

I REALLY *was* Rosie the Riveter. During the war, my name was Margaret Rose, and I was a riveter and all-around "handy girl" at an aircraft factory. Everyone called me Rosie.

I often worked inside the small, cramped fuselage of Corsair planes. Only slightly built girls could work there, so sometimes I worked as the bucker, holding the bucking gun on the opposite side of the riveter.

One day I was working in the fuselage when I felt a weird sensation. My foot seemed to be vibrating all by itself. I jerked my foot out of my shoe just in time. A drill was coming up through it! My partner had neglected to check whether anyone was inside.

Aircraft building was noisy work, and sometimes we got cramped from spending so much time stooped over. We felt good, though—we knew each Corsair would be flown by one of our boys, and we really tried to do a good job so the planes would be safe for them.

Vanity Was Unsafe

We girls were required to wear bandannas tied around our heads as a safety measure. Most of us hated it; we still wanted to look good. Sometimes vanity won out, and hair was allowed to curl outside the scarf.

One day I heard a scream and saw my co-worker's hair get caught in the shaft of her drill. That sent a sobering message to the rest of us.

But there were bright spots during the war years, and the job gave me my share of laughs. One day a male supervisor handed me a bucket and asked me to go to the tool crib to get some spots for spot welding.

I traveled all over that plant. At each tool crib, they'd give me a serious look and say, "Sorry, but we're fresh out of them. You'll have to try another tool crib."

I'd worn myself to a frazzle by the time I realized they were having fun at my expense. Being naive, and new at this aircraft business, I was sent on many such silly expeditions, like searching for sky hooks or buckets of prop wash.

I refused to be caught up in the merrymaking when someone asked me to go to the tool crib and get some male and female plugs. I just knew it was another joke and refused to go. The joke was on me. There really were such things!

Many friendships were formed during those years. And while this Rosie wouldn't want the war years to be repeated, I'll always fondly remember the sound of riveting and bucking and the shouts of, "Hey, Rosie, we need some more spots for spot welding." ✦

"GO TO THE TOOL CRIB..." Joking co-workers sent Margaret Artley to fetch buckets of prop wash.

A REAL JUGGLING ACT. That's what parenting can be, as any mother will readily attest. At different times, a parent must be a provider, teacher, caregiver, counselor, disciplinarian, cook and all-around fix-it person. Thank goodness for our parents...and thank goodness if we survive being parents!

Chapter Nine

The Toughest Job in the World

Isn't it astonishing? The most important job on this planet—parenting—is left up to amateurs!

These days, the papers tell us we have children raising children. True enough, but teenage mothers aren't a recent phenomenon…perhaps you knew one yourself. If not, you'd likely find at least one by tracing back a few generations in your family tree.

What's most astonishing is that these young women take on the toughest job in the world and handle it so well. It's on-the-job training taken to the nth degree. They learn as they go, often making crucial decisions without really knowing what's right.

It's ridiculous, when you think of it. They couldn't work as a checkout clerk at the supermarket without *some* training. They need to pass state-sanctioned tests to get a driver's license. It takes considerable training to become a beautician.

But there are no requirements for parenthood, which puts an untrained person in some difficult positions. Each day is nothing but a minute-by-minute series of new problems that must be confronted and coped with on the spot.

Eleven Mouths to Feed

A couple of years ago, I visited with a lady who'd grown up in a home with 11 brothers and sisters. Looking back, she marveled at how her mother kept them neatly clothed and well fed, even though the family income was minimal.

"She baked a *dozen* loaves of bread every other day," the woman marveled. "Our clothes were passed down the line because Mom simply didn't allow them to wear out. They may have been patched and mended, but they always were clean."

Yet what she remembered most was how much love and individual attention her mother lavished on each and every child. "She somehow found time to help us with our homework, listen to our problems and tend us when we were sick."

Job Requires Many Talents

Yes, it's all part of parenting. Doctor Mom. Teacher Mom. Diplomat Mom. Nutritionist Mom. Seamstress and Tailor Mom. Director of the Budget Mom.

And that's just the routine stuff. Sandwiched in between, she's expected to teach rambunctious little savages about things like self-control and discipline, honesty and diligence and right from wrong.

As if learning the ins and outs of the toughest job in the world weren't sufficient challenge, nowadays increasing numbers of young women find it necessary to take income-producing jobs, too. They must be both parent *and* breadwinner.

So it's up in the morning, fix breakfast, pack lunches, get 'em off to school, dress for work, put in your 8- or 9-hour day, then come home to where the day's *really tough* work starts.

I've watched four daughters and daughters-in-law try to juggle this new role and marvel at how well they manage. But I also know they have their guilt-stricken moments when they wish they had more time for parenting.

They remember what a comfort it was to know that Mom was always there, always home whenever you needed her. Thousands of years ago, Pliny the Elder observed that *Home is where the heart is.* As he knew, home was where you found Mom, too.

And Mom was the heart of the home.

—*Clancy Strock*

Elderly 'Auntie' Took on Tough Parental Task

By Edith Simms, Clearwater, Florida

BACK BEFORE 1920, my great-aunt, Alice Mary Brent, must have been past 70 when I was deposited with a battered suitcase on her doorstep. I was 6 years old.

Mother couldn't care for me anymore, and my life with my parents had been hectic and unstable. All I wanted was peace and quiet.

Auntie washed and brushed my long stringy hair, bathed me in a tin tub beside the kitchen stove and tucked me into a cot beside her own bed. Tomorrow, she said, she'd begin to civilize me.

I'd completed first grade but hadn't really learned anything. I couldn't read or do even the most simple sums. Auntie set about to remedy this.

At first, she read to me every day. Then came the McGuffey readers. With great patience, Auntie taught me to read. I devoured those readers that summer, and when I returned to school in fall, I was reading at a third-grade level.

She Was Sum Teacher

Arithmetic was more of a struggle, but eventually Auntie taught me to do simple sums.

My "civilization" included learning the catechism and prayers of the Catholic church. Auntie gave me a small rosary for my own, and at the end of the day, we said our prayers together.

On Sundays when we couldn't walk the 2 miles to town for Mass, Auntie would read the Mass to me. Her thick prayer book was filled with marvelous

LIFETIME LESSON. Starting with *McGuffey's Reader,* Edith Simms learned much from her loving aunt.

pictures, and text in both English and Latin.

The stones of an old foundation nearby became our "Stonehenge", which brought me a lesson in English history. When I went to England and saw the real Stonehenge 60 years later, I knew just how the stones would look and feel.

A walk in the woods provided lessons about hills and valleys, cliffs and canyons. A walk by the creek was good for teaching me about harbors, bays, islands, peninsulas and even an isthmus.

Every night after a simple supper, Auntie told me stories about her youth, when she'd helped slaves escape through Ohio to Canada. As a member of the Underground Railroad, she even knew John Brown, the man we sang about in *John Brown's Body.*

Auntie taught me manners and social graces and how to keep myself and my room neat. I learned how to use a dictionary, and if I mispronounced a word, I had to say it correctly so I'd never forget it.

I later took courses in English and public speaking, but the basics came from this well-educated woman who could speak, read and write three languages.

Auntie provided a haven for me until I was 14, when my mother's fortunes improved and I returned to live with her. I've never forgotten the love and lessons she showered on me. She made me what I am today, and wherever she is in Heaven, I hope she's pleased with me. ↢

Blindness Didn't Hinder Mom as Successful Parent

MY MOTHER lost her sight in infancy, but that didn't stop her from becoming a model parent.

I was born August 8, 1933 in Chicago. Mother took lessons from the Red Cross in maternal care throughout her pregnancy and for 4 years thereafter.

Mom proved so adept at bathing her baby that she was designated a "model mother" by the instructor of the course. There were many sighted mothers in the same class.

Though she couldn't see and enjoy it herself, Mother always had a Christmas tree for me from the time I was born until I married.

She was a wonderful cook and spotless housekeeper. She taught me so much growing up that I'd forget she was blind. She taught me about the Lord, too.

Mom did have some help through those years from Dad. But not as much as she could have used, for he was blind, too.

—*Elsie Garloch*
Paoli, Indiana

MODEL MOTHER. Although mother Norah (left), was blind, she was more than capable as a mother. Daughter Elsie Garloch often forgot her mother couldn't see, because she managed so well.

HOME IN THE RANGE? Nona Cirone and her family didn't just live on the prairie, they sort of lived in it—in a house made of sod. That's Nona above with her mother and brother in 1939. Her father, grandfather and uncle built the the comfortable, thick-walled structure on Birdwood Creek, in the Nebraska Sandhills. Later, the family moved into a wooden frame house.

Living in a "Soddy" Wasn't Shoddy

BEING A PARENT is a tough job, but imagine tackling the job in a sod house. My mother did that back in 1938.

We lived on a small ranch in the Nebraska Sandhills then. Today, my mom would be embarrassed to see this photo published (at left) because it was a poor time for our family. But my husband reminds me I should be proud to have been a "pioneer".

We only lived in our "soddy" for a year. It was warm in winter and cool in summer. Mother had the walls white-washed and made this two-room house into a very clean home.

My parents, brother and I moved to a wooden frame home on the same ranch later on. Mother was always there for us kids and seemed to be able to do anything. My brother and I still think she's the best.   —Nona Cirone
Addison, Maine

'Dairy Maid' Enrolled in Nursing School—at Age 59

By Marianne Wright, Amarillo, Texas

MY GRANDFATHER passed away in the late 1940s, leaving my grandmother to raise me alone on their dairy farm in San Antonio, Texas. I had lived with my grandparents since I was 4. Now I was 13, and Grandmother was 58.

For a year, Grandmother ran the dairy by herself. There were 13 cows to milk twice a day, 7 days a week and a barn and milk house to maintain.

Every day she was up by 5:30 a.m. and in the barn by 6. In the afternoon she returned to the barn from 4 p.m. to at least 6 p.m.—sometimes as late as 7:30 if a milk customer was late. But she never complained.

In addition to running the dairy, Grandmother kept up our home, cooked all the meals and tended the yard with its flower beds and beautiful roses.

Then new zoning brought the property within the San Antonio city limits. Grandmother would no longer be able to sell raw milk. I had no idea there

was a problem. She kept it to herself.

Though my grandparents had lived on the property for over 30 years, they didn't own it. Grandmother began selling the cows and dairy equipment, paid Grandfather's hospital and funeral bills, and bought a house for us.

Then she did the most remarkable thing of all. She put herself through nursing school. In 1950, she became a licensed vocational nurse at age 59.

When I was older and realized what had taken place, I asked Grandmother how in the world she'd done it.

"Well," she said, "I was a dairy maid all my life, so the only other thing I could've done was domestic work. I had you to bring up, and we certainly couldn't have existed on the salary of domestic worker." She worked as a nurse until she was 75.

When I was 55, the company I worked for closed. When I decided to make a career change at that age, every-

WELCOME HOME. Grandma Alta Christensen gave little 4-year-old Marianne a home in 1939.

one was very negative about it.

But Grandmother did it when *she* was in her 50s—and that was 4 decades earlier, when women didn't have the same opportunities. This time by example, Grandmother once again pulled me through. ✦

Farm Mom Taught Others' Children and Her Own

WHEN I WAS a kid, I assumed all mothers could do the things my mom did. She raised six kids during the '30s and '40s on a farm in Iowa.

Besides cooking and sewing almost all of our clothes, she still found time to be a leader in church organizations and 4-H.

She taught many young girls how to sew, cook and refinish furniture. There was little money during the Depression, but Mom's skills helped others get by.

Mom remained active all her life until she died at age 92. I wrote the lines below in tribute to my dear unselfish mother:

Dear Mom,

I remember that even in the worst of years, Santa never missed our house.

I remember going to bed the night before my ninth birthday, sure I'd be embarrassed in school because I didn't bring a treat. The I woke to discover the huge box of fudge you stayed up late to make—with our rationed sugar.

I remember sitting in the car in my slip on the way to a family reunion while you sewed the final trim on my sailor suit dress.

I remember you getting up at 2 a.m. to rescue a drowning kitten from the cistern.

I remember you buying me my first store-bought coat, when you needed one far more.

I remember you getting to the mailbox before Dad, then hiding my love letters under the sheet music on the piano, which you knew I'd play after school.

APPLE OF HER EYE. Lucia LaBonte says her mother, Oliva Krapfl (above, using antique apple peeler), was the most remarkable woman she knew. Oliva's nephew Russ Goerdt likely agrees.

I remember how you accepted hearing loss later on in your life with humor, saying, "Sometimes I still hear more than I want to!"
—Lucia LaBonte
Palatine, Illinois

Mom Found Beauty in Bleak Surroundings

ONE of my first memories is of my mother serving hot bowls of stew to about 100 homeless people who came to my father's church on the south side of Chicago during the Depression.

SHARING SMILES. Evangeline Spence and her mother, Ruth, posed in 1934.

We lived in a couple of made-over school rooms at the church, and Mom was involved with everything concerning the congregation, 24 hours a day, every day of the year.

She conducted cooking classes at the church house, showing women how to use the food they got from relief. She taught English to immigrants, and she started sewing classes.

Once in a while, she'd take a break and we'd walk past the bar rooms and past the people sleeping on park benches. She'd stop and show me a flowering weed coming up through a crack in the sidewalk.

She saw beauty even during the Depression on a stark city street…and took time out to share it with her daughter.
—Evangeline Spence
Chelmsford, Massachusetts

She Cared Enough to Be Disciplinarian

ONE of the tasks my mother performed was discipline. By today's standards, some of her discipline might seem severe. But she raised 11 children during the 1930s and '40s, and every switching we got was well deserved. Later, we appreciated our mother for caring enough to correct us.

Many times she gave no spanking at all. She simply told us how hurt she was by our actions. But the most effective disciplinary measure came when we kids were fighting.

We were put on the front porch steps with our other misbehaving siblings. Every 5 minutes, we were to hug and kiss and tell the other one we loved them.

After a few minutes of glares, we'd begin to giggle and all the hard feelings were gone.
—Patsy Cable
Sugar Grove, North Carolina

Story Time Brought Nodding Approval

IN THE EVENING after the dinner dishes were done, it was story time. Mama would sit on the couch with my baby sister in her lap and my little brother and sister sitting on either side of her. I stood behind the couch looking over her shoulder.

While Mama read to us, I'd brush her glossy brown hair. Daddy, meanwhile, sat in his easy chair and read the newspaper. He was listening to our story just the same.

Sometimes our tired mama would be so relaxed by the hairbrushing that she'd start to fall asleep, then wake with a start and read the same passage over again.

"I think you've already read that, dear," Daddy would smile. Mama would place a marker in the book, then send us upstairs to bed.

We'd give Daddy his kiss and hug, then Mama would follow us up to hear our prayers and tuck us in. Thanks to Mama, I always loved the evenings best.
—Marti Kelly, Springfield, Illinois

STORY TIME. The best times recalled by Marti Kelly were when her mom read to her, as this mother is doing.

Blended Family Doubled Mom's Duties

By Janice Swack
North Caldwell, New Jersey

MY MOTHER-IN-LAW was widowed in 1934, while pregnant with her fifth child. Times were hard, and the three oldest children were sent to live with others. Little did Mom dream that in a short time, her family would not only reunite, but double in size!

In 1935, Mom married Myer Swack, a farmer who owned a scrap iron company in West Salem, Ohio. They brought Mom's three oldest children home to the farm, where they met their "new" siblings—Mr. Swack's five children.

What a huge family for Mom to manage! And she managed the farmhands as well. But she did it all without complaint or a moment of wasted time.

As it turned out, the children were all spaced 2 years apart, which was great. The only strange part was that Mom was only 9 years older than Mr. Swack's eldest son. "Oh, well," Mom shrugged. "I married young."

Long Trip for Groceries

Mom bought everything by the case. Since the family was Orthodox Jewish, the farm was perfectly kosher. Much of the food had to be bought in special stores in Cleveland.

This meant a 120-mile round-trip by bus, and Mom made it once a week. Thank goodness the driver helped her load and unload the provisions.

Mom encouraged the children to do well in school and participate in school activities. When my husband-to-be, Myron, was a high school junior, he declined a part in the school play on the pretense that rehearsals would interfere with his chores.

When Mom heard this, she called the school and made it clear that school activities were far more important than chores.

Her belief in the importance of education led the family into a world of academic achievement. Nine of the 10 children attended college.

Among them, they hold nine bachelor's degrees, seven master's degrees, an educational specialist's degree and two PhDs. The family set a record at Ohio State University by attending a total of 64 years of college.

Slowly, each of the kids got married.

BUBBEE. Lillian Swack managed the farmhands and a big family, making sure her kids were educated.

At every Passover, when the festivities were in full swing, Dad would say a special prayer: "We should multiply by next year." And we did, over and over again, until there were 23 grandchildren. Mom's name quickly changed to "Bubbee", the Yiddish word for "grandma".

At 92, Bubbee still has the same wonderful, loving sense of humor as always. Her progeny now number nearly 100, and she remembers to send cards for every event that each of us celebrates. She's the most unforgettable woman I've ever met. ✦

FOLLOWING MOM. Ollie Hubbard (left, in 1945) made sure her daughters had a good home (right, in 1959), working until the farm they lived on was paid off. Later, Ollie enrolled in nursing classes and became a licensed practical nurse. Her daughters followed Mom's example, says Kathy Manns (third from right below) of Lexington, Indiana.

Widowed Mom Was up To Challenge Of Five Teens

By Joyce Blomquist
Bloomington, Minnesota

FIVE OF A KIND. With five daughters to raise alone, Agnes (above, in 1947) had her hands full, says author (standing center). But Agnes managed and the girls turned out fine.

MY PARENTS met and married in the early 1920s, settled on a small farm in Minnesota and had five daughters in 6 years. Then the Depression hit. But the worst blow of all was yet to come. In 1932, our father died unexpectedly.

"I'm so terribly lonesome for somebody who is gone forever," Mom wrote in her diary. "My heart is so full, I want to say so much, but there is nobody to say it to. Everybody has enough trouble of their own without my complaining, so it helps me a little to put my feelings on paper."

Another entry bears witness to her character: "I sure will be glad when (the girls) are a little older, but then maybe I will have even bigger worries. I shall put my trust in God, and my only wish is that they shall grow to love the Lord.

Oh, that I shall be worthy to have this fulfilled."

Made New Start

After the funeral, relatives moved us into town. There was very little money—a small insurance policy and a meager veteran's pension.

On one occasion, Mom went to the welfare department for a pair of shoes for one of us. The head of the department said, "Agnes, why don't you ask for a pair for you, too?"

We remember Mom chopping wood for the stove in the dining room, baking bread for a new neighbor or someone who needed attention, sewing clothes in the wee hours for the "poor" family with six children. She also took in ironing from time to time.

Once we were all in school, Mom went to work in a department store. She never let on how poor we really were.

As we grew older, we were busy with school events, extracurricular activities and church programs. Mom's prayers were answered; we did grow in knowledge and love for her God.

Turned to Prayer

Once someone asked how Mom kept her sanity, raising five teenagers alone. "If I had worried instead of praying," she replied, "I probably would have lost it."

Mom never discouraged our thoughts of attending college, and we all went, thanks to part-time jobs and the wise management of every penny. Four of us became schoolteachers and one a missionary to Ethiopia.

All of us married within 7 years, and Mom has always been extremely proud of our husbands. When it's time for her funeral, she's told us, we are to laud not her, but her sons-in-law.

Though we were scattered around the country, Mom was there to give each of her 18 grandchildren their first home baths and go on "night duty" so the parents could get some sleep.

Those grandchildren, now parents themselves, often mention her calm nurturing.

After we left the nest, Mom stayed busy visiting hospitals and nursing homes. There were shut-ins to see and people to comfort, and she didn't just come for coffee. She found floors to scrub, meals to make, groceries to buy and baths to give.

Now 92, Mom lives in a building for seniors, still interested in world events and neighborhood happenings.

When she hears of the death of someone younger, she'll say—not morbidly, but with longing for her heavenly home—"Why wasn't it me?" She's satisfied when reminded that perhaps it's because her work here is not yet done. ↤

THANKS, MOM! The daughters paid tribute to Agnes in 1995 (below) with a fun visit. These days, even Agnes' grandchildren have children, and she remains interested in their lives.

Verse of Thanks Stood The Test of Time

I LEFT HOME to join the Navy in 1943, when I was 17 years old. On Mother's Day 1944, I sent this poem to my mother:

From Your Little Kid That Used to Be

Hello, Mom! Remember me?
Your little kid that used to be.

The one you nursed and washed and fed,
The one you tucked right into bed.

Well, Mom, now that I'm older grown,
I send this note for you alone.

I thank you, Dear, for all you've done,
To make my life a pleasant one!

My mother passed away in 1988, and I found this note among her things. I had long forgotten about sending her this verse. Today I'm grateful I sent her this verse of thanks for all the tough tasks of parenthood.
—*Darwin Larson, Pahrump, Nevada*

Loving Mom Adopted Schoolful of Teenagers

WHEN I was a freshman in high school at Uhrichsville, Ohio, I met Leona Blackwell through a classmate. Leona was my classmate's mother, but she became mine, too.

She became "Mom Blackwell" to many in our teenage crowd. Relating easily to teens, she always seemed to enjoy having us around. At the drop of a hat, we'd show up at her house with our 78-rpm Big Band records.

Her living room and dining room would become our dance hall, and several household items, including lamps, were broken during our jitterbugging. That never seemed to faze her.

"Mom" always had an abundant supply of chocolate cake and cookies to feed our hungry group. Any time I had a "teenage problem", she would listen and offer good advice. She even helped with difficult homework assignments.

After graduation, many of us went into the service for World War II. For years, she sent boxes of goodies to us. I received a box of cookies every month when I was overseas.

Mom and her husband, Pat, provided a loving home for their own three daughters as well as a load of "adopted kids". Though this loving couple passed away in the 1970s, we've never forgotten them.

Today, on occasional visits to Uhrichsville, I pass their old home and love to recall the great hours I spent there. And I especially recall Leona Blackwell, the great lady who once became "my mom". —*Lee McCool*
North Olmsted, Ohio

Mom's Discipline Was "Thimbolic" Education

I NEVER considered Mom sneaky, but she had an uncanny knack for suddenly materializing within arm's reach whenever I was doing something that merited admonishment.

If she happened to be mending clothing, I might receive a mild thump on the head with her thimble-armored finger.

That happened back in the 1930s, and after these many years, I recall Mom's "thumps" in the same way as they were administered—with much love.

For the hand that wielded the thimble was the same hand that handled the Mercurochrome dauber and sprinkled raisins on the cinnamon roll dough and gave me a gentle pat on the behind to send me off to school.

Today, a thump with a thimble would probably be cause for arrest. But I'm here to testify that Mom's "impressions" on me worked wonderfully as motivation and through the years have continued to be a blessing.

—*Bob Mitchell*
Midwest City, Oklahoma

Mama Made Sure Her Hungry Brood Was Fed

MAMA AND PAPA married in 1922 and raised six children in Little Chute, Wisconsin. Papa was a storekeeper, and Mama helped him stock shelves.

As far back as I can remember, Papa allotted Mama $40 a week for groceries. As the years passed, she needed more to feed her ever-hungry brood of growing kids, but was too proud to ask Papa for more money.

When he was away from the store, she'd go downstairs and help herself in

WHAT'S FOR DINNER? When you're still a bottle baby, like tyke watching Mom prepare dinner, the menu doesn't change much. But Mom still has plenty of work at mealtimes, preparing bottles of formula.

HEY, MOM, WAKE UP. Even when she was tired, Georgia Jones still had time to read to her children, says daughter Sandra Slaybaugh of Watauga, Texas. Here, brother Arnold was hanging on every word.

the darkness, restocking her larder. Her usual choices were staples, plus a few treats like imported cheeses and canned crabmeat and lobster.

Because Mama was very religious, we kids questioned her about this "stealing". She adamantly informed us she had discussed it with the priest and was told, "What's his is yours!"

Many years later, I asked Papa if he knew about her pilfering. He laughed and said, "Of course, I did! It took a while, but I figured my inventory didn't lie. She was having such a good time I didn't want to spoil her fun!"

I remember many occasions at the dinner table when Papa remarked, "Mama, I don't know how you do it on $40 a week. You're such a good shopper, you get more for your money than anyone I know. And your meals are so good!

Mama would just smile and say, "Thank you, Papa." —*Betty Flanagan*
Kaukauna, Wisconsin

OPEN WIDE! The word "*yuck*" is written all over the face of young Pipp Gillette in this 1951 photo sent by his dad, Guy, of Yonkers, New York. Grandma Lucy Porter was having a little fun with Pipp while potting plants in Lovelady, Texas. Lucy ran a general store there, working 12 hours a day while her husband, Hoyt, ranched.

Chapter Ten

She Was a Character

Laughter keeps the mind from dwelling on misery. Sometimes life takes such bizarre twists and turns that you're left with only two choices—sitting down and having a good cry or a good long laugh.

One of my favorite stories about a strong woman's sense of humor comes from Ernest Webber, an occasional contributor to *Reminisce*. Ernest grew up poor in the Ozarks during the 1930s. But his mother was more than a match for tough times—and sassy kids.

One day when he was barely old enough to attend school, Ernest was supposed to be helping his parents pick cotton. But he paused during the backbreaking toil and began to play with a remarkably large grasshopper he'd captured.

His mother sternly ordered him back to work. Ernest looked at her and defiantly swallowed the live 'hopper in one gulp! Who was Mom to order *him* around? He'd teach her a lesson.

Was She Hoppin' Mad?

Did Mom scream in alarm? Did she scoop him up and run to the doctor for advice? Hardly. With a serene smile, she said, "Ernest, when you swallow them whole like that, you lose a lot of the flavor. Now get back to work."

A sense of humor wasn't one of my own mother's strong assets, but even she saw the humor in a dilemma thrust upon her during World War II.

She was riding on a typically overcrowded passenger train when she saw two young sailors burst through the door at the far end of her car and frantically scramble down the crowded aisle toward her. Not far behind came two MP's in hot pursuit.

As the fleeing sailors reached Mom, one of them handed her a small bottle of whiskey and said, "Quick, hide this!" and hurried on his way.

Now, you must understand that there was nothing in the world Mom detested more than Demon Rum. Absolutely nothing. So what should she do? She had a split second to decide.

"Well, I hid it under my skirt," Mom later confessed with a little smile. "I know I shouldn't have, but...well, they were such nice-looking young men, and they *were* serving their country."

Frustrations Could Be Funny

Surely no one had a funnier outlook on all the frustrations and aggravations of family life than Erma Bombeck. Small wonder she was every woman's favorite writer.

No one ever reduced the problems of child-rearing to its bare fundamentals quite like she did. It really was quite simple. She and her husband had it down to two things: *It's our house, and we're bigger than they are.*

Another mother I admire effectively dealt with the familiar blackmail every kid tries at least once—the threat of running away from home.

"Well, if you think you must," she said with total calm. "But let me pack you a lunch. What sort of sandwich will you need for your trip?" Suddenly leaving home lost a lot of its appeal.

As the stories that follow prove, a lively sense of the preposterous and the ability to laugh in the face of adversity carried many a strong woman through difficult times.

How else can you keep your composure when confronted with a youngster who decides that a grasshopper is a good source of protein?

—*Clancy Strock*

Mom Held The Power In This Dispute

By Nellie Bubbico
Port Charlotte, Florida

SO MANY people touched our lives when the Great Depression settled over our family. But the person I recall most clearly was the man who came to read our electric meter in Harrison, New York in 1929 and '30.

The Meter Man was always neatly dressed in a white shirt and tie. Since he had to come into the house to read the meter in the cellar, he was polite, very businesslike and always allowed in. After several monthly visits, we got to know him.

Mother was a gracious woman, and she'd invite the Meter Man to have a cup of coffee at the kitchen table after he read the meter. Most of the time, a fresh loaf of bread was sliced, too.

Many months passed, and we got behind on our bills. I don't know how long a "grace period" the utility allowed, but we had to be well beyond it.

LIGHTS! ACTION! When Mary Gasparrini (upper right, holding daughter Nellie, in 1923) couldn't talk the meter man out of turning off the lights, she swung into action.

I'll never forget the day when our friend the Meter Man had to come to the house to turn off the electricity.

He had a short chat with Mother, went to the cellar and actually did turn off the power at the meter.

As he was coming up the steps, Mother closed and locked the cellar door right in his face!

He was trapped in that dark cellar, and I can still hear him begging, "Please, Mrs. Gasparrini, *please*!"

"No!" Mother replied. "I have 11 children to take care of and I am not going to unlock the door until you turn the power back on."

"Please, Mrs. Gasparrini!"

"No!"

Then the lights came back on.

Mother opened the door, the Meter Man came back up the stairs, then sat down at the kitchen table for a nice cup of coffee with Mother and a warm loaf of her homemade bread. ←

HOW STRONG WAS SHE? Strong enough to hold her daughter up with one hand! Sandra Zellers of Fort Wayne, Indiana recalls her mother, Esther, amazing people with this feat. Here Esther's holding up 3-year-old Sandra.

Sunday Drive Was a Dusty Disaster

By Claralee Dillinger, Rozet, Wyoming

MY GRANDPA HENRY was a dour German of the old stripe, and he found it hard to see the funny side in things—especially when the joke was on him.

But Grandma Clara could see the lighter side in anything, no matter what the situation. A good example was the day Grandpa taught Grandma how to drive.

It happened around 1923, near our family homestead at Upton, Wyoming. Back then, Grandpa was the proud owner of a new car—one of very few in the area at that time.

Clara was less enthusiastic about the contraption. After all, she was a good horsewoman, an accomplished rider and quite able to handle a team.

One day, the family dressed up to visit Henry's older brother, Charlie. Back then, folks were more formal than they are now, so Grandma, Grandpa and their three children were very nicely dressed, even for this jaunt across the prairie on a two-tracked trail.

Gates Weren't Great

One of the trials of going anywhere then was the cumbersome opening and closing of gates. Grandpa was a cattle rancher and very careful to securely close any gate.

The gentlemanly thing to do was to drive up to a gate and allow the lady to remain seated. The man would open the gate, get back in the car, drive through, get out and close it again. This added a lot of time to any trip.

To save time on this trip, Grandpa suggested that Grandma drive the car through each gate as he opened it. He pulled to a stop at the first gate. She wasn't sure, but she nervously crawled into the driver's seat when Grandpa got out.

He instructed her how to pull the car ahead. She listened dutifully, but fearfully, in the idling car. Then Grandpa walked over and unhooked the wire gate. As he was dragging it aside, Grandma's foot slipped off a pedal, and the car roared forward—right at unsuspecting Grandpa's back!

Down he went, face-first into the powdery white dust. The car merrily straddled his prostrate form, passed over him and chugged on down the road. After a lot of yelling, arm waving and pandemonium, the three children helped Grandma get the car stopped.

> *"Down he went, face-first into the powdery white dust..."*

Was He Hurt?

Feeling like a killer, poor Clara turned around in her seat to look back. Grandpa arose, and the entire front of his Sunday suit was coated with white dust. He was unhurt, but his dignity was considerably flattened. He closed the gate and grimly strode back to the car.

When Clara realized that the only injury he suffered was to his dignity, her tears of fear turned into tears of mirth.

As they bumped down the road, she tried hard to stifle her snickering. The farther they went, the harder it was to control her chuckles.

Soon she burst out in waves of laughter, recalling the preposterous picture of Grandpa well-dusted in flour. No matter how much he harrumphed and huffed, the sight of his dust-covered suit set her off once more.

Clara never drove a car again...and that suited her just fine.

Rainy Day Brought Laughter

GRANNY was a kind person with a wonderful sense of humor. She laughed often and consistently looked at the good side of things. Just thinking of her brings back a memory from 1937 and a special Sunday at "The Cove".

This was a rural Georgia community surrounded by mountains, and most of those who lived there were related. Once a year in summer, they would have an "All Day Singing with Dinner on the Ground"—in other words, a big festive picnic.

Barbershop quartets came from miles around, and the singing was non-stop. People brought food, and oh, my, there was fried chicken on tables as far as you could see, plus butter beans, fried okra, sliced ripe tomatoes, "roast'n ears" and all kinds of pies and cakes.

One year at the height of the celebration, it began to rain, so everyone scampered under shelter. The women were in their Sunday best, which in those days meant crepe dresses. Crepe, of course, shrinks when wet.

The women's dresses began getting shorter and shorter. Soon Granny and my mom were pulling at the bottoms of their dresses trying to stretch them.

Other women joined in, because their dresses were shrinking higher than their petticoats. Oh, the laughter!

As time went on, women got down on their knees stretching their skirts while others were furiously fanning, hoping to dry them out.

I don't remember how that day ended, but I do recall all the wonderful laughter—and the fun had by Granny and Mom.
                                    —Anene Ristow
                                    La Crosse, Wisconsin

Fun-Loving Mom Could Tame Ferocious Beasts

MY MOTHER, Elaine Meissner, was born in 1913 and lived all her life in St. Paul, Minnesota. She was such a fun and funny lady that whenever we kids had nothing to do, we knew she'd find something fun for us.

She patiently taught us how to play jacks, jump rope and make snow angels. She showed us how to make our own fun, and we didn't need the expensive toys of today.

When a neighbor child became ill with polio, it was Mom's idea to have a carnival to help raise money. One special attraction was billed "The Most Ferocious Animals in the World".

People paid 2¢ to peek inside a covered bird cage to see them. They were two sleeping kittens wearing leopard suits Mom sewed.   —Corinne Wilson
                                    St. Cloud, Minnesota

Did She Discover the Fountain of Youth?

GRANDMA and Grandpa were married in the Missouri Ozarks in 1934. Money was scarce, but they got by with a lot of hard work. I think a lifetime of hard work helped Grandma stay in great physical shape. A year before she died, she could swing a pick or an ax alongside men less than half her age.

Grandma's sense of humor also helped her get along. One hot summer day, she placed the lawn sprinkler under my 80-year-old grandfather's chair and waited for him to sit down.

When he did, she turned the water on full force, making him jump as high as the spray!
                                    —Tracy Kile
                                    Branson, Missouri

FULL OF FUN. Lois Vining and her husband, Lester, celebrated their 60th anniversary in 1994 (above). In 1953, Lois was a cave guide at Silver Dollar City in Missouri (top right).

CREATED A CARNIVAL. When a neighbor needed money for a sick child, Elaine Meissner raised it with "ferocious animals". This portrait was taken before her wedding.

Her Cooking and Quips Kept Family's Spirits up

By Ina Hancock, Gilbert, Arizona

WHEN my mother, Mada Petersen, was growing up in Heber, Arizona, *her* mother never turned away anyone who came to the door for food. Their home was a place where everyone was loved, including visitors. I guess that's why Mother was the way she was.

We lived on a ranch in northern Arizona during the 1930s and '40s. Whenever people stopped by our house, the first thing Mother asked was, "Have you had anything to eat?" Regardless of the reply, she'd start for the kitchen, saying, "It won't hurt you to eat once what we have to eat all the time."

That was only one of Mother's memorable sayings. She had a sense of humor and way with words that made every crisis seem small.

"It will feel better when it quits hurting," was the line she used when one of us kids got a scrape and ran to her for sympathy. She was right!

When I was little, I was terribly afraid of the dark, but sometimes Mother would need something from Grandma's house, which was about a city block away. She'd send me on an errand in the dark, though I protested.

WORD OF WISDOM. Even as a little girl, Mada was smiling (below left). It was the same years later (right), just before her marriage.

"Don't worry, honey," she'd say. "If someone catches you, they'll turn you loose when they see you in the morning."

Yawned and Stretched

When Mother woke up in the morning, she'd often yawn and say, "I could stretch a mile if I didn't have to walk back."

And she used to tell us girls that if we sewed anything on Sunday, we would have to take the stitches out with our nose in Heaven.

Mother was a fantastic cook but never used a recipe. She said she never got tired of her own cooking because nothing ever tasted the same twice.

She took meals to those who were sick or had problems. She wrote weekly letters to men and women in the mil-

itary and to those serving church missions.

When Mother was 65, her heart began to wear out. She could barely walk across the room, but she refused to give up. The doctors told us she wouldn't make it through the week. She defied them all, living another 3 years.

The afternoon before she passed away, her daughter-in-law came by. Though Mother could hardly get out of her chair, the first thing she said to her was, "Honey, have you had anything to eat?" ←

HAIR RAZING. Ina Hancock (above with husband) says her mother, Mada, was up for anything, even cutting the local ranger's hair outdoors (below).

Grandma Enjoyed A Fare Fight

MY Sicilian grandmother was very frugal and accounted for every penny she had. If she could ever save a nickel, that was big deal to Grandma. The city bus system in Newark, New Jersey was a good example.

Whenever Grandma had to cover a lot of ground, she'd reluctantly take the bus. One day, she and granddaughter Fran were waiting at the bus stop. Little Fran knew what was about to happen but was powerless to prevent it.

As the bus appeared in the distance, Grandma would say, "Francesca, when the door opens, you jump into my arms and I will carry you on. That way I only hafta pay one nickel."

"But Grandma," Fran would protest, "a child is free only if she's 5 years old or younger. I'm 12."

"It doesn't matter," Grandma sniffed. "Remember, you jump when I say so."

The bus would stop, the door would open, Fran would jump into Grandma's arms and they would board.

The bus driver would always say, "Lady, that kid is over 5 years old. Ten cents."

Grandma would defiantly respond, "Iffa I canna carry her, noah extra nikol."

The driver would look at them, shake his head and say, "Okay, lady, you win. One nickel." —*George Denardo Camarillo, California*

She Drove a Hard Bargain

THE MAIN THING I remember about my mother, Mary Ann Haley, was her ability to dicker. Mother had 10 children, so she needed to stretch every dollar.

Mom dickered with the grocer, the fruit man, in short, with *anyone* who charged money. Dickering was an art to her and she believed her adversaries enjoyed it as much as she did.

One time, our large Belgian shepherd, "Zak", was hit by a car. Mom was always careful not to bring dogs, or people, unnecessarily to doctors. But this time, the necessity was clear even to her.

Walking into a crowded waiting room at the veterinarian's office, she announced in a very loud voice, "If you can fix him for $25 or less, we've got a deal!"

The vet fixed Zak's dislocated hip, and when we picked him up, the bill was, indeed, $25. —*Kathleen Pucher Beacon, New York*

The Race Was on!

MAMA had nine children to care for on our Alabama farm in the 1930s. We'd work hard out in the fields all day, and late in the afternoon, we kids would feel so weary—until we heard Mama yell, "Beat ya to the house!"

Our energy level surged as we broke into a dead run. Mama would wait until we got a good head start, then take off after us. As she caught up to us, she'd pick us up, one by one and set us back down. Then she'd run past us and up the porch steps.

In my mind's eye, I see this wonderful woman pushing her children into a friendly game of competition, after leaning on them all day to do their "work". In truth, she could have done it herself with a lot less worry and trouble. —*Hugh Hood, Petersburg, Texas*

GIDDYAP! Ellen Tomasek (above, with son George, in the early '50s) could make even hoeing weeds fun, says daughter Kathleen Zmitko of Owosso, Michigan. On this day, she "saddled up" a sheep. Ellen knew she could make her children laugh by acting like a kid herself.

This Sense of Humor Ran Hot and Cold

MY MOTHER, Florence Nightingale Arnold Hickerson, was always a fun-loving person in spite of all the hard work she had to do on our Colorado farm.

One hot June Sunday, Mom's sister and her family come to our house for dinner. After feeding us a delicious meal of fried chicken and fresh vegetables from the garden, Mom served homemade ice cream.

It was so good and *so* cold (homemade ice cream is much colder than the kind found in stores today).

Uncle Roy, a short roly-poly jolly guy, took a bite of his and said, "Florence, this is too cold. Can't you warm it up a little?"

Mother calmly walked to the stove and picked up the teakettle. Just as calmly, she walked around the table to Uncle Roy's place and poured boiling water over his ice cream!

The rest of us sat in stunned silence, but Uncle Roy laughed so hard, he almost fell off his chair. —*Mary Ann Kunselman Longmont, Colorado*

FUN FAMILY. Florence Hickerson (front right, next to daughter Mary Ann, in 1940) was always up for a laugh...even if it ruined good ice cream.

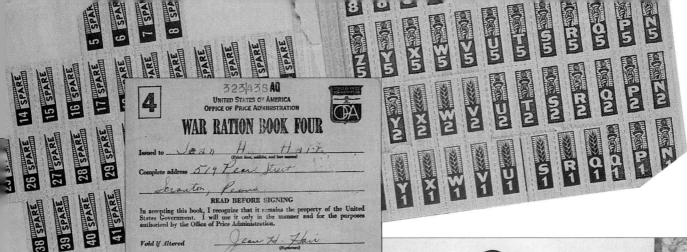

Her Humor Kept Baby In Shoes

By Melvin Buhrkuhl
Stockton, California

WHEN I THINK of my mother, I'm reminded of the old story about two men who were hunting wolves for a large bounty.

The men set up their wilderness camp. At night, as the fire died down, they fell asleep. Later on, one awoke and saw a pack of 30 wolves surrounding the camp, ready to attack. Rushing to wake his friend, he exclaimed, "Look! We're rich!"

This was the way Mother looked at life whenever things were down. She had a great sense of humor and didn't worry about failing at a task. Failure, she said, gave you a second chance to do something right.

During World War II, shoes were a rationed commodity. When my 2-year-old brother, Dale, had outgrown his shoes,

---

> *"The ration board needed a laugh that day..."*

Mother had to fill out a detailed form to justify his receiving another pair.

"Fiddle dee," Mother said, drumming her fingers.

The first question asked, "Where will these shoes be worn?"

"On the feet," Mother wrote. "One on the right and one on the left."

She completed the form with the same kind of joking answers…and subsequently received an extra shoe stamp.

Our neighbor filled out the same form seriously, and in detail, and was rejected.

Mother said the ration board needed a laugh for the day, and that was why she received the shoes for Dale. ←

LAUGHS NOT RATIONED. When Laura Buhrkuhl needed a pair of shoes for Dale (front left), she provided the ration board with a laugh that earned her a stamp. That's son Melvin in the middle.

GRANDMA THE REF. Great-Grandmother Maud Burt knew how to keep little Kenneth and Vernon busy, recalls Francelia Orcutt of Lynden, Washington. The boys were sparring in fun, which their referee was full of.

Volunteer Organist Played A Hot Little Number

MY GRANDMA was born in 1891, and one Sunday around the turn of the century, she accompanied her Aunt Josie to church in Yolo County, California.

The organist wasn't able to play that day, so the pastor asked for a volunteer. Not quite 10 years old then, little Edith had taken some piano and organ lessons, so she stepped forward. Unfortunately, her repertoire was limited.

When the pastor signaled her to begin playing, she ripped into a rousing rendition of *There'll Be a Hot Time in the Old Town Tonight*.

An embarrassed Aunt Josie tried to stop the child, but the kindly pastor told Aunt Josie to let Edith continue.

I would have loved to be there. Grandma's "hymn" selection must have made a merry moment for churchgoers that Sunday. —*Mollie Lee Pryor Woodland, California*

Inquisitive Kid Was Stumped By Mom's Explanation

WHILE I was growing up in the 1930s, I asked my mother, Ella Rush (below), the inevitable question: "Mom, where did I come from?"

She told me a buzzard had dropped me on a tree stump.

I soon had picked out the special stump where I believed I'd been dropped. After that, I could never walk through our barn lot without looking at that old thorn tree stump. I felt so thankful that Mom found me and took me in to care for. —*Anna Clingman Carmel, Indiana*

Not Too Young to Marry

MY MOTHER, Ruth Jewell Martin, was born in 1902 in a small town in Missouri. When she was 15, she hid her lunch box after school and skipped off to marry young Walter Garrett.

She'd never lied before and didn't want to now. So she wrote the number "18" on a piece of paper and slipped it into her shoe.

That way, when the judge asked if she was 18, she could reply, "I'm over 18." —*Jane Martin Fulton, Missouri*

You Can Bet Mom's Spunk Made Dad Chuckle

WHEN this incident happened back in the 1930s, Mom wasn't laughing. But Dad chuckled over it for the rest of his life.

Dad was a road builder, and he hired crews of 20 to 30 men. Mom was the bookkeeper, purchaser of supplies, keeper of the cookshack and commissary, and general manager in Dad's absence.

Dad had strict rules against drinking and gambling in camp. One day he left on a business trip, and two troublemakers in camp alerted some gamblers in a nearby town. The coast was clear!

Two gamblers soon arrived in a fancy touring car. They set up a dice game on the commissary porch.

Mom approached the men and recited the rules against gambling. Both men laughed loudly, saying, "And who's going to stop us?"

Mom went to her trailer and grabbed Dad's big heavy revolver. She returned and never said a word. She took wavering aim at the porch beneath the men.

The heavy gun bucked and roared like a cannon, shattering pieces of the porch and sending the gamblers (and Dad's men) scrambling into the brush.

Dad told this story for years, and his closing line was always the same: "Then she shot the porch right out from under them!"

—*Bill Robinson Bishop, California*

PISTOL-PACKIN' MAMA. When Alma Robinson was put in charge of husband Frank's road-building work camp, the men learned the rules against gambling still applied. That's Alma and Frank at left in 1929 on the Oklahoma panhandle. Son Bill and his little sister, Edna, posed on the running board of the family auto in 1936—roughly the same time Mom proved her prowess with a pistol.

Her Sense of Humor Was 'Thumbs up'

By Dorothy Grable Willess
Vista, California

THE MOST REMARKABLE woman I've ever known was my mom. Her sense of humor was a big reason I feel this way.

In 1982, four of us drove from Vista, California to Sandy, Oregon to visit Mom. I drove there with my daughter, Debra, her friend Julie and my sister-in-law Fefe.

We reached our destination and enjoyed a nice visit. Then we asked Mom to come back to spend some time in Vista with us. She agreed on one condition—that we'd stop in Sacramento so she could see two of her grandchildren.

We got on the road, and four of us shared the driving. It was a hot day, and as the miles passed, we got more tired and irritable.

Debra was taking her turn behind

"Mom said she didn't know I could be so stubborn..."

---

the wheel when I became irritated with her driving. I began to pick at her. I suggested we stop for something cold to drink and offered to take over the driving.

That would have been out of turn, so Debra retorted that if she couldn't finish her turn, she'd get out of the car and hitchhike back to Vista.

Mom Played Peacemaker

My mom tried to make me back down and let Debra finish her turn, saying she didn't know how I could be so stubborn. She found out what stubborn was when she attempted to talk Debra out of hitchhiking!

We stopped and I decided to phone the grandchildren to get directions to their place. Returning to the car, I saw Mom removing her luggage along with Debra's.

"What's going on?" I asked.

Mom informed me that if Debra was going to hitchhike, she would go along with her. Mom didn't want her granddaughter to be on the road alone.

The ridiculous picture of my 73-

MADE IT SAFE AND SOUND. When Debra (left) and Dorothy (center) argued during a trip, Dorothy's mom, Melva Grable (second from right), solved the spat.

year-old mother and 27-year-old daughter hitchhiking made me burst out in gales of laughter. That caused a chain reaction, as Fefe and Julie joined in.

We gave each other hugs and reloaded the luggage, then Julie drove on to our destination.

I guess Mom calmly weighed her options and picked the best one. She never seemed stumped in her wisdom on how to handle tense situations. She so often used humor to help people out of embarrassing predicaments.

Whenever I face a problem today, I ask myself, "How would Mom solve this?"

My brothers often say to me, "Dorothy, you're just like Mom." If they only knew how pleased I am to hear that! ❧

GOT ANOTHER ONE OF THOSE STINKERS! When Rose Marchese's two sons left for Navy duty in 1943, she had to handle many of their farm chores. As her proud grin in this photo attests, she successfully waylaid marauding skunks trying to raid the chicken coops. Today, her boys Roger and James, Oakland, New Jersey, fondly recall their hardworking (and sharp-eyed) mother.

Grandma Hitchhiked 2,500 Miles

By Ruth Root, Everett, Washington

JULIA BRANNOCK wasn't your typical grandmother, but I'm proud she was mine. She was born in the mountains of North Carolina in 1865, and much later, she moved to California.

It was from there Grandma's "great adventure" began in 1930. I have the original pencil-written letter she sent to relatives in Virginia after she hitchhiked from Los Angeles to Boise, then back.

Here, in Grandma's words, is an excerpt from her letter. To give you a better picture of this interesting character, her spelling and grammar have not been corrected.

"I kinder got hungry for air and sunshine and outdoors and tolde Rosearl (youngest daughter) I had been raising babies 41 years and I had the last one up to where she could take care of herself.

"I was going to walk to Idaho and get what I was so hungry for and I started the 3rd day of June the day I was 65 years old.

"It's 2,000 miles but I wanted to go by San Francisco. It made my trip 500 miles further but I should worry—the sun shined up there.

"I bought me a hiking suit and a little pack on my back with big white letters painted on it—From L.A. to Boise. I started with $30 and Rosearl was to send money ahead of me when I wanted money.

"I expected to make the trip in 2 weeks. The children expected me to make it in a month.

"I staid in hotels at night and eat at restaurants and had the nicest trip. I went by San Francisco and Oakland and Portland, Oregon and Pendleton, Oregon. That made the trip 2,500 miles and I got there on the 12 day of June…

"I made it in just 9 days…I got to Payette with $11 of the $30 I started with.

"And I spent the summer up there fishing, hunting, visiting and having a regular vacation like nobody's business. I went one trip 100 miles north of Payette into the mountains on a 9 days trout fishing. I caught over 200 trout. There was six of us and each one caught about the same amount…

"And when I got ready to come home I wanted to see some new territory and I came home the southern route. I came by Salt Lake City, Utah and crossed about 1,000 miles of desert…

"I am quite sure I never walked over 20 miles out of the 2,500. When I struck a city I took a street car and went through to the highway…as soon as I struck the highway I was always picked up. Some days I would make 3 and 4 hundred miles a day…

"Well that gets me back home…"

Yes, that was my grandma. She was a dauntless, determined, plucky person. By her remarkable life, she's shown us that age alone should never be an excuse for not tackling a new challenge. ✦

HIT THE ROAD. Julia Brannock wore a customized backpack (above left) when she hitchhiked to Idaho in 1930. That's Julia above, in 1929, and at left, with granddaughter Anne and daughter Lela (Ruth's sister and mother), in 1920.

She Could Do Anything...
Even Make Fish Vanish

GRAMIE CRAMER was "gramie" to her entire community. She was a loving, kind personality who'd perfected mothering to such a degree that it involved her neighbors.

The old porcelain table in her pantry never had fewer than five or six pies on it, and every Saturday morning, she'd frost several cakes. The neighbors always appreciated Gramie's goodies.

As her only grandchild, I rated highest on her list. Weekends spent with this special character were memorable. For instance, Gramie could make just about any toy out of folded newspaper. She made animals, kites, houses, furniture—even a rocking chair that rocked.

As evening came on, she'd entertain me by making hand shadows on the wall. Why, there wasn't anything Gramie Cramer couldn't do!

Once in a while, I would accompany Gramie Cramer to the stream to do some fishing with Grandpa. Gramie was an avid fisherwoman—but one without a license.

One day when the game warden approached, Gramie cautiously placed her rod nearer Grandpa. Then she slipped the newly caught fish she was holding right inside the bodice of her dress.

The fish flipped and flapped in her dress, and I believe the game warden extended his visit somewhat, but Gramie remained unfazed all the while the commotion occurred.

She wasn't fined or even reprimanded, but I'm sure the game warden had a lot of fun with that story later on.
—*Shirley Jenkins*
Pittsburgh, Pennsylvania

GRAMIE AWARD. Shirley Jenkins felt like a prize as Gramie Cramer's only grandchild.

Mom Relaxed the Rules On Threshing Day

I SQUEALED with delight as I took a flying leap from the stool beside my bed and landed right in the middle of my mattress. My sister leaped onto her own mattress, and we giggled together at the fun of this unusual experience.

We'd never been able to jump on our beds before, but just this once, Mom made an exception.

The Depression was on, and like most folks in our rural neighborhood, we couldn't afford new mattresses for our beds. So Mom purchased a whole bolt of ticking and sewed six ticks for the beds in our home.

At threshing time every fall, she would stuff each tick with as much clean fresh straw as possible, then sew the open end closed.

At first, the ticks looked like fat pillows, but several weeks' use would result in a 4-inch-thick mattress. Now here we were, my sister and I, initiating our new straw ticks. We knew we could only do this once, so we relished every jump.

We were having so much fun, we never even realized the hard work Mom was doing on the farm during threshing day. One of my fondest memories of Mom is the look on her smiling face as she watched us leap, with a scream, into those straw ticks.

Even after an exhausting day, she could find pleasure in watching her children have fun.
—*Annette Oppegard*
St. Paul, Minnesota

Skunked on His Birthday

DURING the late 1940s, Arnold and Lavina Smith were raising their family in Dillon, Montana. Money was tight, but Mother wanted to give Daddy a birthday present.

Hoping to please him with something he really wanted, she asked for his input daily. "Nothing," he'd reply.

On the morning of Dad's birthday, Mom returned from town with lots of boxes and wrapping paper.

After dinner, my sister, Lana, and I watched with delight as Daddy opened a big wrapped gift box...which contained another, which contained another and so on through 12.

Finally, in the smallest box, Daddy found a tiny card decorated with a skunk holding a daisy. On it, Mom had written, "Well, what did you expect?"

Daddy laughed and kissed Mommy. Lana and I giggled, and I enjoy remembering it to this day.
—*Patricia Smith Brewer*
Lakewood, Colorado

Cliff Wirth

Mom Had a Beef with Rationing

Editor's Note: This story was written by Marie Aiken of Seattle, Washington. It was shared by her daughter, Nina Gordon, of Dallas, Texas. Nina says her mom's own words illustrate her gift for humor better than anyone could describe it.

HOW WELL I recall that summer day during World War II. I did my housework with a song in my heart…*God's in His Heaven, and all's right with the world…*

After all, it was the first of the month and we'd just received our new supply of ration stamps.

They were blue, for canned fruits and vegetables, and red, for meat. It took ingenuity for a housewife to make the stamps and days of the month come out even—especially red stamps.

In those war days, I bought a huge beef rump roast the first of the month and parted with a goodly supply of red stamps. In the following days, we had hot roast beef sandwiches, cold roast beef sandwiches, beef stew, stuffed green peppers, hash and on and on. On the last day, we'd enjoy soup, made with the bone I'd carved from the roast on the first day.

No Peanut Meat Loaf

Yes, I was feeling good this Monday morning, for yesterday was the first day of the roast, and with careful planning, there were at least 10 meals left. No substitute like peanut meat loaf for us!

So happy was I, that I generously said yes when my 4-year-old daughter, Nina, came in with a request.

"Mama, there's a dog in our yard and he doesn't belong to anyone. He's hungry. Can I feed him something?"

"Give him the bone in the refrigerator," I magnanimously offered.

I heard the refrigerator door open and close, and then the back door slammed shut. I gave a motherly contented smile and went on with some drudgery cleaning.

Suddenly, God in His Heaven sent a small voice to tell me that all would not be right in my world if I didn't have a look-see in that refrigerator!

It Was Panic Time

Sure enough, there sat the bone, all alone. I looked out the kitchen window, and there sat the dog eating my roast. I panicked. *What to do?*

I couldn't afford to spend any more red stamps this week. And it was too early in the month to sell the family on peanut meat loaf.

This called for fast action! I grabbed the bone, ran out the back door and threw it with all my might toward the farthest corner of the lot.

The dog dropped the roast and ran for the bone. I ran for the roast, tucked it under my arm like a football and headed for the house. Then the dog saw my maneuver, and the chase was on.

By now, the neighbors had formed a cheering section over the back fence. "Go, Aiken, Go!"

I made an end run around the clotheslines. Behind me was the dog, ahead of me were my kids, holding the back door open and shouting, "C'mon, Mom! You can make it!"

I gave it all I had and dove over the goal line into the kitchen. Sweeter words were never heard than those uttered by my son Bruce, who said, "Gee, Mom, could we ever use you on our football team!"

I trimmed the teeth marks from the roast, washed it good and cut off a sufficient amount to make chili for dinner.

The family, especially Nina, thought it best not to tell Father about the excitement of the day. He was sort of finicky about food sometimes.

But he liked his dinner that evening. In fact, he said it was the best doggone chili he'd ever eaten. ←